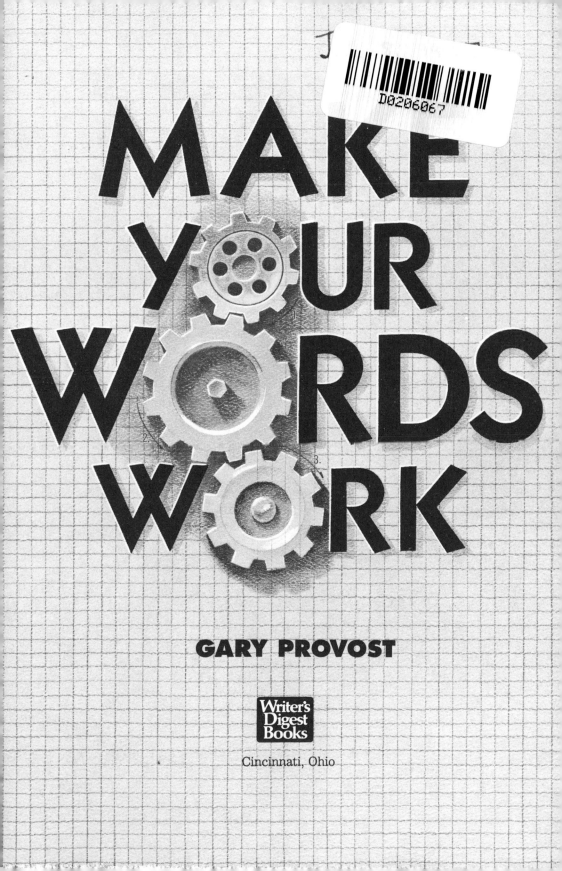

MAKE YOUR WORDS WORK

GARY PROVOST

Writer's
Digest
Books

Cincinnati, Ohio

Permissions

I want to gratefully acknowledge permission to reprint the following material:

Excerpt from *The Great Gatsby* by F. Scott Fitzgerald. Copyright © 1926 Charles Scribner's Sons; copyright © renewed 1953 Frances Scott Fitzgerald Lanahan. Reprinted with permission of Charles Scribner's Sons (Macmillan Company).

Excerpt from *A Catskill Eagle* by Robert B. Parker. Copyright © 1985 by Robert Parker. Reprinted with the permission of Delacorte Press.

Make Your Words Work. Copyright © 1990 by Gary Provost. Printed and bound in the United States of America. All rights reserved. No part of this book may be reproduced in any form or by any electronic or mechanical means including information storage and retrieval systems without permission in writing from the publisher, except by a reviewer, who may quote brief passages in a review. Published by Writer's Digest Books, an imprint of F&W Publications, Inc., 1507 Dana Avenue, Cincinnati, Ohio 45207. 1-800-289-0963. First paperback edition 1994.

98 97 96 95 94   5 4 3 2 1

Library of Congress Cataloging in Publication Data

Provost, Gary
   Make your words work / Gary Provost
      p.   cm.
   Includes index.
   ISBN 0-89879-636-9
   1. Authorship. I. Title
PN145.P75   1990
808'.02 – dc20   90-42331
                                                                          CIP

Dedication

To all those Writers Retreat Workshop writers who have shared their hopes, their work, their jokes, their lives, and occasionally, their dessert, with Gail and me at a gracious Victorian house in Bristol, Connecticut. And to all those yet to come.

Other books by Gary Provost:

The Dorchester Gas Tank
Make Every Word Count
The Freelance Writer's Handbook
The Pork Chop War
100 Ways to Improve Your Writing
Good If It Goes (co-authored with Gail Provost)
Fatal Dosage
Popcorn (co-authored with Gail Provost)
Finder (co-authored with Marilyn Greene)
David & Max (co-authored with Gail Provost)
Across the Border
Without Mercy
Beyond Style

Contents

Acknowledgments

Some of the material in this book appeared in different form in *Writer's Digest* magazine. I want to thank Bill Brohaugh and Tom Clark at *Writer's Digest* for their work on the original articles.

At Writer's Digest Books I want to thank Carol Cartaino, Jean Fredette, Anne Montague, Sharon Rudd, and Howard Wells.

Thanks also to the many writers whose work I have used as examples in this book, and to the writer friends who shared with me some of their time and knowledge:

Woody Allen, Cleveland Amory, Jim Bellarosa, Saul Bellow, Anne Bernays, Michael Blowen, Lou Burnett, William Faulkner, Phyllis Feurstein, William Goldman, Ellen Goodman, Gary Goshgarian, Ted Groff, Christopher Hewitt, Crosby Holden, Bonnie Ireland, Trish Janeshutz, Justin Kaplan, Christopher Keane, Elizabeth Loftus, Steve Lowe, Gregory McDonald, Joe McGinniss, Gabriel Garcia Marquez, Marie Melville, Edwin O'Connor, Robert Parker, Gail Provost, Bob Reiss, Ruth Rosing, Erich Segal, Scott Spencer, Dan Wakefield, Douglass Wallop, and Denise Worrell.

Thanks also to Evan Marshall and Russ Galen.

Introduction

Writing dreams do come true.

For many years I was the person who was always doing what you have just done, picking up books about writing technique, hoping they would help me get closer to that fantasy of being a published writer. I was a dreadful writer, I really was. But in the past fifteen years I have published five novels, five books for writers, a sports book, a thousand magazine articles, short stories and newspaper articles, two poems, and four true crime books, one of which was made into a movie. I have won the National Jewish Book Award without being Jewish, and I came close to being the new Ann Landers, without being female. In my twenties I couldn't even get a word published. Now writing dreams come true for me every day.

They come true because I learned how to write well, and in this book I will tell you what I have learned about good writing. My teachers have been my own mistakes, occasional editors who have been kind enough to set me straight, and my students, several of whom have generously allowed me to publish excerpts from their work.

What you will learn here applies to your fiction and your nonfiction. There is nothing here that should be discarded by the writer who works exclusively in one form or the other. The best fiction writers have influenced the greatest journalists of the present, and they, in turn, have been influencing the new writers of fiction. Increasingly, the difference between nonfiction and fiction is one of content, not of form or technique.

There is only one quality that I ask you to bring to this book. Humility about your writing. You cannot succeed without it. You must have the humility to know that writing that looks clever to you might be boring, that something beautifully written might be unnecessary, that something very personal to you might be meaningless to distant readers. You must accept the fact that a trained editor might see in your work liabilities that you thought were assets. And you must be capable of erasing any sentence you have written, if informed and unprejudiced voices can lead you to the truth about it.

If you can do that, the battle is already won. Read the book. Do the exercises. Read the book again. When we are done you will have a greater understanding of what it is that makes writing work for the reader. Your writing dreams won't come true the next morning. Nor will they come true the following week. But if you take these lessons to heart and keep plugging away, they *will* come true. You will succeed as a writer just as I have succeeded, not because this book will close the gap between you and your writing dreams, but because *you* will have learned how to close it.

Chapter One
Some Questions Answered

Can Writing Be Taught?

No. Throw this book away.

Yes, yes, of course writing can be taught.

I'm not sure why this question keeps coming up, but it does. People ask it of me and of all writers, at parties and bus stops, and I feel like replying, "Geez, I dunno. I didn't use to know how to write good but now I do, so yeah, I s'pose it can be taught."

My friend Frank plays the mandolin, and nobody has ever asked him if mandolin playing can be taught.

Anyhow, yes, writing can be taught. This assumes a certain basic understanding of language, just as the teaching of accounting assumes an ability to add and subtract. It's true that some people will never get the hang of writing well, just as some people never get the hang of riding a bicycle. There are always exceptions. But good writing, writing that works, does contain observable, repeatable phenomena, and the person who has noted them can "impart knowledge or skill; give instruction; provide knowledge of; cause to learn by example or experience." Those are my dictionary's definitions of *teach*.

However, to teach writing one must first make some arbitrary distinctions. A piece of writing is not like a car, for example, where something is either a carburetor or a spark plug, no matter how you hold it or where you view it from. You can't unscrew and yank out one part of writing and drop it in a bag without dragging along chunks of all the other parts, but for the purposes of teaching writing we pretend that you can do just that.

If I wanted to teach you how to make a car, it would not be enough just to march you down to your local Chevrolet dealer and have you stare through the showroom window at a new red Cavalier. I'd have to throw open the hood, rip off the doors, thresh out every screw and wire in that car, and lay the parts across the floor. Then I would have to piece them all back together again so that you could see how the car was made. In fact, I would have to do this several times for you to understand.

So to teach you to write, I'll pretend that it's like a car as I break writing down into parts called *description,* or *dialogue,* or *style.* But because writing is not really like a car, the part that I call *style,* for example, won't look exactly like the part that another author or teacher calls *style.*

As you read this book you will hear many ideas repeated in different ways. That's because writing rules overlap. They dovetail. Tickle one and another giggles. When you follow the style rules *be specific* or *use active voice,* you often eliminate words, so you *avoid wordiness.* When we discuss *dialogue,* you'll see that one purpose of dialogue is to characterize. When we discuss *characterization,* you'll see that one way to create characters is through dialogue. And so forth.

Any collection of words can be many different parts of writing, depending on how you look at it.

Consider this sentence:

> Beneath the lefthand pocket of his corduroy jacket, bulging like a tumor, was the pearl-handled revolver Leo always carried out of fear that Chinese bandits were going to kidnap him.

Think about that pearl-handled revolver for a minute. What element of writing is it? Is it description? Is it style? Is it characterization?

It's all of them, depending, as I say, on how you look at it.

It is description, because the pearl handle gives you a color and a texture to see, and the shape of the revolver creates a memorable bump that will summon to mind the larger picture of Leo. It is style, because I said *revolver* when I could have said *gun,* or *pistol,* or *piece,* all of which would have given you a slightly different sense of the weapon. The pearl-handled revolver is also characterization, since it embodies the raging paranoia that is one of Leo's character traits.

So when you make the right choices, every word will count, and if you've just learned that, then you know for sure that writing can be taught.

What Do You Mean by "Writing That Works"?

By writing that works, I mean writing that does the job it's supposed to do, whether that job is to inform, entertain, anger, or instruct. Writing does not work if it only entertains when it is supposed to instruct. It does not work if it only angers when it is supposed to educate. Whether a piece of writing has been put together to convey factual information or to create images in a story, it should be judged not on good grammar or adherence to the rules of composition (both of which are tools, not goals), but on how well it does its job. Does it work? Does this word reveal my character's feeling? Does this sentence convey the popularity of stock car racing? Does this paragraph communicate the feeling of despair these refugees have?

For any given idea there exists a variety of technically and grammatically correct word combinations that can be used to communicate it. But each word combination alters the idea. It is the form the writer chooses, the words he picks out, that determine's the content of his work, what he really says, and whether or not the writing works. For example, here are two grammatically correct sentences about the same fact:

> The twenty-seven-year-old father of three little boys died last Friday afternoon in an accident at work.
> Twenty-seven-year-old Hubie Humwicker drowned Friday afternoon when he tumbled into a three hundred-gallon vat of chocolate syrup.

Both sentences are accurate and readable, but I controlled your reaction to the information by the facts and words I chose to use, and the writing in either sentence is good only if it is consistent with the effect I wanted. With the first sentence I wanted you to feel sad for three kids. In the second sentence I wanted you to smile. If I had wanted you to feel sad and yet still told you about the vat of chocolate syrup, the writing would not have worked.

Writing that works is also writing that assigns a job to every word in a sentence. Every word, every sentence, every paragraph must be doing some work or it should be fired. You don't need a pink slip. You need a blue pencil or a large wastebasket.

The writing that has worked in the past is an enormous body of evidence we can sift through for clues to good writing. The successful writers of today, the ones who are getting published and cashing checks, are those who recognize what made someone else's writing work. Writing that works is writing that works every day for the average professional writer. With that in mind, my examples will not be extracted exclusively from the works of Nobel Prize winners and dead Russian novelists.

What, No Dostoevski?

If you go into the library and thumb through books about writing (the 808 section in a Dewey decimal system library; the *P* section if it's on the Library of Congress system), you'll find that many authors proffer a bit of advice and then wheel out the excerpts from Fyodor Dostoevski and Henry James to prove the advice is sound. While it's nice to know some great writers have honored some good rules of writing, it's more important to realize that these rules have worked for published writers in general. So, with all due respect to Henry James, his work will not be appearing in this book.

I have a large bookcase containing around three hundred books — paperbacks, mostly. Among them are bestsellers, such as Irving Wallace's *The Plot* and James Michener's *Centennial;* books that were made into movies, such as *Dog Day Afternoon* by Patrick Mann; and books that can't be filmed, such as *Getting Things Done* by Edwin C. Bliss. This motley collection includes fiction, like James Kirkwood's *Some Kind of Hero*, and nonfiction, like Alan Moorehead's *The White Nile*. There are books like *Marilyn* by the famous Norman Mailer and books like *Son of The Great American Novel* by the not-so-famous James Fritzhand. No logic, no pattern shapes this collection. It represents nobody's recommended reading list. It's just a bunch of books, and the only thing they have in common is that I bought them, borrowed them, received them as gifts, or had them bequeathed to me by the previous tenants of some of the crummy apartments I've lived in. These books represent neither the best nor the worst of writing. What they do represent is writing that's being published and bought today, writing that's bringing some money and some fame to its authors, writing that works.

Throughout this book, whenever I need a published example to make a point I will either write it myself, clip it out of a newspaper or magazine, or cull it from one of those three hundred books. If I lead you to believe that something is an important key to good writing, and then I have to go rummaging through the public library for proof because I can't find a single example out of three hundred miscellaneous published books, then I'm wrong. It's not important.

And, incidentally, while we're on the subject of "good writing," what exactly does that mean? Well, for our purposes in this book good writing means "writing that can get published." A hard definition, perhaps, but useful. If you're planning to write stories and hide them in a bureau drawer, you can write any way you want. The techniques in this book are for people who want to publish their work and get paid for it. So every piece of advice that I give you here is my way of saying, "If you do this, it will bring your work closer to being publishable."

Do I Have to Do the Exercises?

Hey, it's your life; you can do whatever you want. But I think your writing will improve faster if you do the exercises. Think of them as games. You don't have to write in the book or make neat columns of numbers. Just grab a pen and some scrap paper and crank up your imagination. Write silly answers if that makes you feel good. (It always makes me feel good.) Don't feel pressured to get "right" answers. There's no score. These exercises are not supposed to produce Pulitzer Prize-winning prose. They are intended merely to tickle your creativity and help you put into action some of the techniques presented in this book.

One Final Question, Gary; Why Is Getting Published So Hard?

It's not. The most important thing I've learned in my career is that getting published is easy. Writing well is what's hard.

And why shouldn't it be? You are, after all, trying to make a reader believe in a dream. With a scattering of black lines on white paper you are trying to convince him that movie stars and professional athletes are in the room with him talking about their work, that a voice is instructing him in the finer points of cooking chicken, that a pirate ship is on the horizon, that two hesitant lovers are finally kissing, that a spaceship from the planet Zo is about to land.

Of course it's hard. You have nothing to work with but words and the unpredictable mind of a reader you have never met.

Just because every bozo you meet in the grocery store tells you, "Yeah, I'm thinking of writing a book myself," doesn't mean that writing is easy. Where is his book? Have you read it? No, because he discovered one rainy night that writing was harder than giving blood, that he had not the vaguest idea of even how to begin.

Maybe you're not getting published as often as you would like. Maybe you're not getting published at all. There's a good reason. It's because writing well is so damned hard that your writing may not yet be good enough. If you can accept that fact, then you will probably succeed as a writer. If you resist it, if you blame your rejections on moronic editors, narrow-minded publishers, and a public that just doesn't understand what you are trying to say, then your failure is as certain as tomorrow's sunrise. You must have humility about your work. It is the only thing that can save you.

I know what I'm talking about. When I was in my twenties I wrote seven wretched books that I thought were destined for bestseller-dom. I sent each to about thirty publishers and collected enough rejection slips to wallpaper a medium-sized garage. And each time a manuscript came back I thought, "My God, this editor is an idiot!" I was astounded at the number of fools who were allowed to sit in editorial offices. Not only that, but I knew that somebody was letting these idiots read my short stories and articles, too, because those were also being rejected.

Now I'm smarter. I know a lot more about good writing and I know that constant rejection means only one thing: The writing isn't good enough. It was true for me then, and it's true for you now.

Why is that so hard for us to accept? One reason is that our writing is so personal. When someone says our writing is not good, they pierce the skin. It feels as if they have come very close to saying *we* are no good. People used to tell me things that were wrong with my stories and I would go cold and stony on them. Of course, when I got home I'd make the changes, but still, I was hurt. That's human nature. The other reason we have trouble accepting the fact that our writing isn't good enough is much simpler. It looks great to us. And hell, we ought to know. We wrote it.

That is at once the cruelest and the kindest thing about writing. The cruelty is that we can write something that's quite atrocious, and if we are new to the craft it will look wonderful to us. We all think our baby is beautiful. No wonder we're shocked when it is spurned. I've written a lot of stories that I thought were fabulous, and now I know they were best used as kitty litter. I can guarantee that, if you are getting rejected regularly, the pages you wrote today will make you want to vomit next year.

The kindness, of course, is that the delusion that our writing is good writing is the thing that keeps us going until the writing really is good.

Please write this on a piece of paper and tape it over your desk: IF I AM NOT WRITING WELL ENOUGH TO GET PUBLISHED, THEN I AM NOT QUALIFIED TO JUDGE THE MERIT OF MY OWN WORK.

A book like this is supposed to be inspirational. It's supposed to make you feel good about your writing, enthusiastic, hopeful. And by now you're probably wondering, "What the hell kind of inspiration is this, Gary, telling me that writing well is hard and that my writing is lousy?"

But think about it. If I told you that your writing is fine, but that the peculiarities of editors and other machinations of the publishing world had conspired to leave you out, I would be telling you that there is no hope. Your fate would not be in your hands. But I'm telling you that constant rejection means you are not writing well enough yet, and that means that you have control of the situation. You, not them. All you have to do is work harder and study more and keep an open mind about your writing. Be persistent, be humble, and be curious, and your writing dreams will come true. I know this for a fact, and that's why I wrote this book.

Chapter Two

Style

It's Not Just What You Say . . .

Once upon a time I wanted to learn about the human brain. On one of my exciting trips to the laundromat I stopped at the library and grabbed a couple of brain books off the shelves without browsing through them. A few days later when I found the time to sit back and look at them, I devised a simple test for deciding which book to read. I picked up the first book, flipped to a page at random, and stabbed my finger at it. I landed on this sentence:

> But does the greater spontaneity and speed of assimilatory coordination between schemata fully explain the internalisation of behavior, or does representation begin at the present level, thus indicating the transition from sensori-motor intelligence to genuine thought?

Then I grabbed the other brain book, flipped it open, poked in my finger, and landed on this:

> If a frog's eyes are rotated 180 degrees, it will move its tongue in the wrong direction for food and will literally starve to death as a result of the inability to compensate for the distortion.

Which book do you think I read?

Which book would you have read?

Both were written by experts on the subject, but unless the reader is also an expert, there is no contest in the fight for reader attention. The second one is just better writing.

The author of the second book used visual images to put what he understands into a form that I understand. I can see that confused little frog's eyes rotating and his tongue shooting off in the wrong direction, while *assimilatory coordination* stuffed into a sentence with *schemata, internalisation,* and *sensori-motor intelligence* leaves me more confused than even that frog.

The second author also won me as a reader for the same reason that you will make more friends in Burundi if you brush up on your Swahili. He spoke to me in my language. The expert who wrote the first sentence spoke to me in his own language.

The author's use of visual images and accessible language should establish more firmly in your mind something you already knew when you picked up this book: Style does make a difference. It's not just what you write that matters; it's *how* you write it.

Although too many editors these days emphasize the story, the content, the subject, over the technical abilities of the writer, good writers *can* make *any* subject interesting, while incompetent writers can make anything dull.

While you should strive to make all of your writing lively, you should know that you're going to have to work harder at it if your raw material is less than thrilling, such as advertising copy, a sales report, or an essay on time management in the insurance industry. One might even imagine a mathematical formula that says writing that works must be well written in inverse proportion to how dull the subject matter is.

Tomorrow morning you can trot down to your local newsstand and pick up some enormously successful paperbacks that are not well written. However, chances are that they will be about matters intrinsically and universally fascinating, such as the sex lives of last year's Oscar winners.

If, on the other hand, to use a ridiculously unlikely example, someone managed to write a bestselling ode to biology, crammed full of thoughts on such sleep-inducing matters as ant behavior, bacteria, mitochondria, and symbiotic relationships, the style would have to sparkle; it would have to be so clear and sharp that it immediately sliced through the reader's resistance to the subject matter. Impossible? Not at all. Such books, rare though they may be, *are* written and *do* succeed. Outnumbered as they are by their ponderous counterparts, they shine like jewels.

One such rarity was written by Dr. Lewis Thomas, who imagined that people in the street might read about biology if he could put what he understood into language they understood. Thomas wrote *The Lives of a Cell: Notes of a Biology Watcher,* won the National Book Award for it, and sold a lot of copies.

Why? Was it because of his credentials as a scientist? Of course not. There are millions of scientists who will never reach a popular audience. They are good scientists, but they can't write like this:

> Viewed from the distance of the moon, the astonishing thing about the earth, catching the breath, is that it is alive. The photographs show the dry, pounded surface of the moon in the foreground, dead as an old bone. Aloft, floating free beneath the moist, gleaming membrane of the bright blue sky, is the rising earth, the only exuberant thing in this part of the cosmos. If you could look long enough, you would see the swirling of the great drifts of white cloud, covering and uncovering the half-hidden masses of land. If you had been looking for a very long geologic time, you could have seen the continents themselves in motion, drifting apart on their crustal plates, held afloat by the fire beneath. It has the organized, self-contained look of a live creature, full of information, marvelously skilled in handling the sun.

Yes, the story is important; the subject matter is the big draw. But it will help immensely if you can learn to write of the "dry, pounded surface" that is "dead as an old bone," the "gleaming membrane of bright blue sky," and the "crustal plates, held afloat by the fire beneath." Thomas's book didn't sell because of what he wrote about, but because of *how* he wrote about it.

I once worked as assistant managing editor of the *UU World,* which you probably never heard of unless you happen to be a Unitarian Universalist. One of my functions in that job was to receive a lot of dreadfully written material about great Unitarian or Universalist historical figures, people like Michael Servetus, Origen, and Francis David. The information I got about these people arrived in the form of church-anniversary brochures, sermons that someone thought would make good editorials, or short histories written for no apparent reason.

These treatises on the giants of liberal religion were not only of scant interest to the general public, they seemed carefully crafted to lull even a dedicated Unitarian Universalist into a state of catatonia. I realized that I had come to think of Servetus, David, and their cohorts as dull, when in reality they were colorful, exciting men who had the misfortune to be chronicled in words not wisely chosen.

I was cured of this misconception when a booklet called *400 Years* showed up on my desk. Yet another history of Francis David and King John Sigismund, this one was nineteen pages long and was issued by the First Unitarian Society of Minneapolis. I'm sure I must have groaned and braced myself for boredom when I picked it up, knowing I would have to read at least three pages before I could in good conscience throw it away. But this one was different. The project had been put in the hands of someone who could write. His name is Edward Darling, and his booklet began:

> During the dark and bloody days of the Emperor Charles V and the vicious, tooth and claw free-for-all between the Holy Roman Empire and the Sultan for the control of eastern Europe, there developed in Transylvania a true-life drama the likes of which the world had never seen. It was an almost incredible happening which is still regarded by scholars as a miracle of history. And it was played out on a stage wide enough to include Buba and Constantinople — although the central action was in the Land Beyond the Forest — Transylvania.

Of course I read on. Wouldn't you? Material I had always resisted now attracted me. How had Edward Darling captured me as a reader?

I read Darling's *400 Years* for the same reason I read the brain book by the author who wrote of the frog that moved its tongue in the wrong direction, for the same reason I read Lewis Thomas's *Lives of a Cell.* Each of these writers presented material I could have gotten a dozen other places.

There was nothing unique about the substance of their work, but "the way in which something is said or done as distinguished from its substance" made all the difference. (That's my dictionary's definition of *style.*) They had all captured me with their style.

Style is not what you write, but how you write it. Style is the form, not the content. The following sentences all have the same content, the same information, but they have different styles.

It could not be used.

It was useless.

It failed to function.

Junk, pure junk!

It was as useless as a rule book at a riot.

So what's the right style? All of them. Voltaire said, "Every style that is not boring is a good one."

As you read books about writing and take writing classes, you will find that *style* is one of those writing terms that never seem to mean the same thing twice. You cannot corral it into one neat definition any more than you can stuff a cloud into a burlap bag. It's vague. It's fluid. It wriggles when you try to grab it.

When I began to outline this section, I came to the disconcerting conclusion that half of everything I wanted to say in this book could legitimately be deposited in a chapter on Style. Some jerk could even come along and nail me good with the argument that *all* writing instruction is about style, because style is the *way* a thing is said, not *what* is said. All writing can be viewed as style because, even though there are other aspects to writing (such as description, dialogue, and characterization), words or phrases can be many different things at one time, depending on how you look at them. This section of the book is about one way of looking at them, a way that is called *style*.

Now that we have a few thousand years of written language behind us, we've begun to notice that some stuff gets read and some stuff gets tossed directly into the wastebasket. If we study enough of both kinds, we begin to see some common denominators; we observe how some words in certain combinations can hold readers and how some turn them off. In other words, writing that works and writing that doesn't work. These observations, especially when applied to writing in general, are called *rules of style*.

The rules of style are not like the rules of arithmetic. Nobody can prove that one way is better than another. But there are valid generalizations about which writing techniques create the most interesting, most compelling reading. No rule of style should be followed 100 percent of the time. Writing is an art, not a science, and there are many times in your writing when the "wrong" way is the right way because of the context, or the mood you are trying to create. But a fair guideline is this: Always obey the rule of style unless you know why you think the writing works better some other way.

Eschew Verbosity

Sooner or later in your writing career, a teacher or an editor will return a manuscript with the notation "too wordy."

Wordiness, as generally used by teachers, editors, and writers, has two possible meanings. One is the second definition in my dictionary: "Expressed in or using more words than are necessary to convey meaning." We'll get to that soon.

The other way you can be guilty of wordiness is by using long words when short ones will do, using rare words instead of common ones, using words that look as if they were erected instead of written.

Such wordiness occurs in this excerpt from my first attempt at a novel, *The Rabbit Knows:*

> So he stood torpidly on the pebbled border of the lifeless highway with his arm outstretched across the corroded asphalt and his thumb sought some sort of concession to his distress, and once again he found himself making nugatory conjectures.

Do you know what *torpidly* means? Do you know what *nugatory conjectures* are?

I didn't, and I wrote that mess.

This sort of wordiness can put your reader to sleep as fast as the wordiness in that sentence I came upon in the first brain book: "But does the greater spontaneity and speed of assimilatory coordination between schemata fully. . . ." Zzz.

Generally speaking, words like these, especially when used frequently, just don't work.

By "words like these" I mean words that are unfamiliar to most of your readers, words that reduce or eliminate the reader's comprehension of a sentence. I also mean words with which the reader is familiar but not intimate, words that add complexity to an idea without returning something in precision or color, words that require the reader to pause and translate. ("Clarence was ambulatory?" the reader says to himself. "Oh. That means Clarence could walk, doesn't it?") The reader should not be spending his time trying to remember what a word means. The word and its meaning should be indistinguishable.

Obscure words don't work because no matter how specific and accurate a word is, it is worthless if your reader doesn't know what it means. In fact, it is worse than worthless, because it might turn your reader away from your writing.

These words don't work because they interrupt the reader with the question "What does that mean?" They create an unexpected noise in his head and remind him that there is a writer at work just as surely as the shattering of glass and the shrieking of an alarm tell him there is a burglar at work.

This sort of wordiness generally results from insecurity, the need to impress people with your vocabulary. I speak from experience, believe me: I'm *still* embarrassed when I read some of my old stories, nugatory conjectures and all.

This sort of wordiness also results from an overdependence on the thesaurus. The thesaurus is a book of synonyms. It's a very valuable tool for a writer. Get one, but don't use it to look up a lot of words that you've never seen before. Use it to look up words that are colorful and precise and mean exactly what you want to say. You know thousands of such words, but they don't always rise to the surface of your brain.

Obviously you will use many words that are unfamiliar to some of your readers. If you tried to stick to words that every single reader understood, you would end up writing about Dick and Jane and Spot.

But, of each word you use, ask these questions:

Have most of my readers seen and understood this word many times before?

Will the readers who don't know the word lose the meaning of the sentence, or will the context clear it up for them and possibly give them a new word?

If they have to look it up in the dictionary, is this the only time they'll need to, or will they spend more time with Webster's book than with mine?

So use simple words. But don't confuse simple with dull. Words are rarely dull by themselves, but, like recollections of birdies on the sixteenth hole, they become dull when you hear them over and over. So when repetition threatens to bore your reader, draw on that treasury of *simple but interesting* words. If *walk* is dull, *stroll* is simple but interesting, and *perambulate* is wordy. If talk is getting wearisome, then have people chat, bicker, or shoot the breeze, but don't let them discourse or expatiate, except on rare occasions. If too many people are getting wet in the rain, have a few get soaked or drenched, but please don't let anyone become moisture laden.

Remember: *Writing gets more interesting as it acquires precision, not length.*

Exercise

Make a list of ten common words that can become dull through repetition (such as *man, book, sat*). For each word try to come up with a synonym that is simple but interesting and a synonym that is wordy. (You may have to hunt through the thesaurus, but don't for a minute entertain the idea that that's "cheating." The writing profession has tools, just as any other does, and you wouldn't think a carpenter was cheating because he used his saw.)

After you've compiled your lists, put the words into sentences. Lock yourself alone in a quiet room. Sit and relax and get yourself into a meditative mood. Read your sentences aloud, and try to get in touch with the subtle effects that words have on your brain, your concentration. Try to feel that split second of apathy that comes when you read a dull word, the apathy that makes you close a book when it occurs again and again. Try to feel that fleeting rush of enthusiasm that comes when you see that someone *sprinted* or people *bickered.* The simple but interesting words are what draw you into a piece of writing and keep you there. Finally, try to feel the subtle tension in your body, the annoyance, the almost imperceptible anger you experience when your reading is interrupted by a noisy stranger like *perambulated, expatiated,* or *torpidly.*

Ultimately, nobody can give you a list of good words and bad words, words that are familiar to your reader and words that are not. But if you read enough, and write enough, and listen to enough conversations, you will develop an ear for words that work and words that don't.

The other definition of wordiness is concerned not with the quality of words, but with the quantity. Many new writers use too many words too often, and all writers use too many words sometimes.

You don't put extra words into a sentence for the same reason you don't tape two toilet brushes to the windshield of your car: They wouldn't serve any purpose, and they would get in the way.

The reason fewer words are better will be clear to you if you can remember walking through the schoolyard and having some smart-aleck kid say, "Hey, which is heavier, a pound of feathers or a pound of iron?" and after you cleverly figured out that they weighed the same, he said, "Oh yeah? Then which would you rather have dropped on your head?"

The reason iron would be your second choice, though it weighed the same as the feathers, is its density. Iron has more weight per square inch. It has more *impact.*

So it is with words. The smaller the number of words you use to contain a thought or an image, the more *impact* that thought or image will have.

Consider the impact of this six-word classified ad:

"For sale: Baby's crib. Never used."

The overemployment of words generally takes three forms: redundant words, wasted words, and weak words.

Redundant words. The dictionary says redundant means "needlessly repetitive," which has led people who are feeling witty to say things like "It's redundant to commit suicide in Kansas," or " 'Boring insurance salesman' is a redundant phrase."

Redundancy occurs when you use two or more words to say something that is already being said clearly by one of them. A "little leprechaun" would be redundant, as would an "enormous giant," a "two-wheeled bicycle," a "long-necked giraffe," or "six a.m. in the morning." "Red in color" is redundant because a thing can't be red in anything but color.

Find the redundant phrases in your own writing and kill them dead. (Get it? If you don't, reread the last paragraph.)

You can sharpen your editing skills on this by watching and listening for the redundancies in advertising, where products often have "long-lasting durability"; in news broadcasts, where situations are often "potentially dangerous"; and in political campaigns, where posters often boast, "like you, he's fed up, too."

Redundancy doesn't always come in neat little two- or three-word phrases, though. Often you will find two words doing the same job in separate parts of a sentence:

"Lenore picked up a weekly paycheck every Friday." (If it happens every Friday, then we know it's weekly.)

"Immortalized in stone, he would live forever."

Wasted words. When you write, don't use extra words that serve no purpose; they slow your writing down. Wasted words frequently show up as overused, meaningless phrases like "in the event of" (if); "on the occasion of" (when); "owing to the fact that" (because); "for a period of a month" (for a month).

Words are also wasted in an attempt to modify that which cannot be modified, as in "*very* unique" and "*slightly* impossible." These phrases seem to be the pets of the educated but insecure, those people who think that more words equals more thought and knowledge. Wasted words proliferate in business memos, government manuals, Rotary Club speeches, grant proposals, and letters from lawyers.

Here is an example of how a lawyer might waste words. It's also an example of the other kind of wordiness, obscure language.

> Herewith enclosed for your consideration are the instruments of liability waiver made mandatory by the requirement that we eschew any litigation contingencies.

Here is the same sentence in English.

> Here are the releases we have to sign so we won't get sued.

Weak words. One of the best ways to improve what you have written is to throw out two or three weak words and replace them with a strong one that conveys the same meaning. Listen to what happens when:

"Lee was a mean woman" becomes "Lee was a shrew."

"He was a generous and thoughtful man" becomes "He was a saint."

"He passed away early in the morning, and people all over America cried" becomes "He died at dawn and the nation wept."

When you can change ten words to seven, or two words to one, the writing almost always will work better.

Here's a tip for finding weak words. Be wary of adverbs ending in -*ly,* such as *rapidly, perversely,* and *lavishly.* They often pop up because you used a weak verb and tried to boost it. Whenever possible, chuck them in the wastebasket and replace them with stronger verbs.

For example, if Stan *jumped suddenly* upon the burglar, your reader will see it better if you say he *pounced* upon the burglar. If Maria *ate* her supper *quickly* in order to keep her date with Mark, your reader will see it better if Maria *wolfed* her supper.

(Note, particularly in the second example, how the stronger verb gives your reader not only a clearer picture of the specific action, but also a stronger sense of the overall mood.)

Exercise

Change these weak verbs into strong, colorful verbs that have more impact.

1. Pulled quickly
2. Picked up impulsively
3. Wrote nervously
4. Hit angrily
5. Looked curiously
6. Closed forcefully
7. Departed quickly
8. Stepped on callously
9. Removed clothes slowly
10. Held lovingly

Pruning your prose is not a chore. It's as much fun as any word game. When you spot the redundancy or weed out the wasted words or come up with a stronger verb, you feel clever. You feel like a writer.

However, don't become a fanatic about it. Don't cross out every word you could possibly do without. Just be sure that every word you use has a job to do.

If the word is doing some work, such as providing needed information, creating a clearer picture, or reminding the reader of something important, then let it stay. But if it's lazy, not earning its keep, throw it out.

There is no perfection to be attained in any of this. Just as you can never pull all the weeds from a garden, you will never eliminate all the useless words from your writing. You can pick up any book or magazine in the world and find words that are just not working.

Use Active Voice . . . Most of the Time

A guy I know hangs around his apartment every evening in front of the television, hoping somebody will call and invite him to dinner. In the afternoon he haunts the mailbox, figuring maybe an invitation or a check will show up from some unexpected source. He dreams about new friends coming into his life, a better job popping up out of nowhere, and he figures he might win a new car someday if a disc jockey calls him up and asks an easy question.

I know another fellow who plays tennis every morning. When he meets a man or a woman he'd like to know better, he gets the phone number and calls the person up. This guy started his own business a few years back, and now he's putting the profits into businesses started by his friends. He also likes to go skydiving.

Which man do you find more interesting, the passive one who lets things happen to him, or the active one who makes things happen?

The active man is more interesting. In writing, too, active is more interesting than passive. Just as you would fix your attention on the active man and ignore the passive one, your reader will fix his attention on the active words and phrases.

New writers often fall into the habit of casting their characters as the passive recipients of some activity, when they should be writing about people or objects doing things, making things happen.

Compare "The Christmas present given to Frank was an electric guitar" with "Frank got an electric guitar for Christmas"; "The result of the accident was many injuries to Bertha" with "When the car crashed Bertha broke her arm, twisted her neck, and dislocated her hip."

A key to finding the active voice is to write about people, not things. "A good time was had by all," for example, is a passive-voice sentence about good times. "Everybody had a good time" is an active-voice sentence about people.

Sometimes, of course, you are not writing about people, but about objects or concepts. Even then your object or concept should take charge of the sentence, become the subject, and work in the active voice.

For example, "Nushka was loved by Garonovitch." If you're writing about Garonovitch, then "Garonovitch loved Nushka." But maybe you're really writing about love. In that case, "Love filled Garonovitch with excitement," and "It was love that made him act so foolishly."

The tip-off to these dull, passive-voice sentences is usually a compound verb such as *was driven* or *were presented.* Cash them in for sharp, short, interesting, active verbs, and your writing will work better.

Exercise

Make these sentences as interesting as that man who plays tennis and goes skydiving by putting them in the active voice.
1. Horseshoes were placed over every doorway by the new owner.
2. Two hundred barrels of industrial waste were deliberately dumped into the Nagana River by Farlo Jennings and his crew.

3. Ceramic bunnies, oragami eagles, and toy wooden soldiers were some of the things fashioned by Henry during the time he was confined to the house with hepatitis.
4. Sixty-two points were scored by the Boston Celtics in the fourth period against the Detroit Pistons.
5. The brothel was the first place they went to when they got to Roselle.

Use Strong Verbs

This is an important rule of style and I've already touched on it in our discussions of wordiness and of active voice. So I'll be brief.

Strong verbs are verbs that are active, vivid, specific, and familiar. They are the engine that runs your prose. Don't use vague verbs that are boosted by adverbs. Don't write, "Buster ate his dog treats quickly," if you can write, "Buster gobbled his dog treats."

Don't use weak general verbs like walk, cry, fall, and touch if the situation calls for plod, weep, collapse, and caress.

Exercise

Make the verbs in these sentences stronger, more vivid, more specific.
1. Raymond killed six hogs last Thursday.
2. The three sisters built the house in the summer of 1969.
3. The president wrote his letter of resignation.
4. Luigi exercised every day in his cell.
5. Spike and Lester held their guns for ten minutes before they entered the bank.

Be Specific

One day recently I drove a car across a barren area in the South.

Can you see it?

On my last birthday I drove a red convertible across the Everglades.

Can you see it more clearly? Yes, you can see a birthday more clearly than "one day recently." You can see a red convertible better than "a car." And you can see the Everglades better than "a barren area in the South." You can see them better because they are more specific. With the second sentence I gave you a clearer, more compelling picture, and I used fewer words to do it.

In our discussion of strong verbs you've already seen that specific verbs like plod and caress are stronger than general ones like walk and touch. The same principle applies to nouns. If I tell you I was bitten by a dog on my way to the post office this morning you can see it. But if I tell you I was bitten by a poodle you can see it more clearly. And it didn't cost me any more words to tell you. I just substituted the specific poodle for the general dog.

Which can you see better — a criminal or a safecracker? A book or a Bible? Cereal or cornflakes?

One way to make things more specific is to modify them with adjectives. You can turn a house into a big house, a little house, a messy house, or a two-family house. But adjectives are not efficient workers; they slow your writing, and they should not be your first choice for any job. (Writing teacher Donald Murray has said, "Any time we use an adjective or an adverb we should feel a little sense of failure.") The best way to get the benefit of being specific is to replace words, not modify them. Replace house with mansion, cottage, hovel, or duplex. Or, if the situation calls for it, make the house a bungalow, a shack, an A-frame, or a brownstone.

Exercise

Here are five sentences containing common general nouns. Try to make the sentences more vivid by adding adjectives that make the nouns more specific. For example, the small tragedy, "Russ drove in too quickly and crushed his daughter's toy," becomes more poignant when you write, "Russ drove in too quickly and crushed his daughter's new toy."

After you've done that, go back and try to make the nouns more specific by replacing them, not by modifying them. For example, "Russ drove in too quickly and crushed his daughter's tricycle."

1. When I was in the sixth grade my friend Marvin and I used to throw *fruit* at each other.
2. Since there was no kindling wood, Ramona used her *magazine* to start the fire.

3. When Keith turned on the high beams he could see that it was an *animal* on the road.
4. The only bettor who had Crazy Bananas in the sixth race was a *man* named Raul Alvis.
5. Nobody could believe that Santos had gunned down three people for such a small *jewel*.

Say Things in a Positive Way

If you write about two teenagers exploring a quarry who come upon a cave and you write, "There was no light in the cave," the first thing the reader will see is the light that's not there. You are writing in a negative way; you are telling the reader what is not true. But if you write in a positive way—"The cave was dark"—you communicate to the reader what you are really trying to show him: darkness.

Writing about what is or was true usually creates a clearer, more interesting picture than writing about what isn't or wasn't true. It works better. (This is another generalization. Practice it, but don't become obsessed with it.)

Which can you see better, "He was not a generous man" or "He was a miser"?

"The painting did not have any flaws" or "It was a masterpiece"?

"He did not treat his kids nicely" or "He brutalized his children"?

"She did not write interesting sermons" or "Her sermons put parishioners to sleep"?

"Phil was not a graceful person" or "Phil was a klutz"?

Tell the reader the truth. Be straightforward. Show her what you want her to see, not what you don't want her to see.

Exercise

Make these negative sentences more interesting by putting them in a positive form.
1. The eggs that they brought to my table were not cooked.
2. *Chariots of Fire* was not a movie that held my attention.
3. Trudy's novel about a plumber was not accepted by any publisher.
4. Gary's examples indicated that he was not of sound mind.

5. By eight o'clock 597 of the 600 opera tickets had not been sold.

Show, Don't Tell . . . Most of the Time

> Marilyn French smiles a lot when she speaks to you, and often she chuckles. She's not as angry as her book would have you believe, but she *is* angry, and sometimes when she's sitting on the couch, smiling, she can express that anger in a very cold fashion.

There is nothing wrong with that passage. It's grammatically correct, it's clear, and it provides information. But if I wrote a whole book or an article that way, you probably would not survive to the end. The paragraph *tells* you that Marilyn French chuckles. It *tells* you that she's angry. It *tells* you that she sits on the couch, smiles, expresses anger.

The problem is that all readers are from Missouri: They want to be shown. As much as possible, *show, don't tell* your readers what you want them to see.

Instead of *telling* my readers the above information in a *Writer's Yearbook* profile of Marilyn French, I wanted to *show* them. Read what happened.

> Marilyn French smiles a lot when she speaks to you, and such statements can rise from her on the crest of a chuckle. Unlike her book, she does not pulsate with anger. But the anger is there—big jagged chunks of it careening through her body to be tossed out when she needs them—and sometimes even as the trace of a smile hangs on her face and her soft round body is coiled like a kitten's on the couch, she can say what she needs to say with all the cold efficiency of a highly paid assassin.

Show, don't tell.

Show means create a picture for the reader.

If you did an interview with Kathleen Turner and she seemed anxious for you to leave, you can tell the reader, "Turner seemed impatient." Or you can show the reader, "Turner looked at her watch constantly. She tapped her foot. 'Are you almost done?' she asked."

You can tell your reader that your character was handsome, or you can show that "women turned to watch him when he came into the restaurant."

Which do you find more compelling: a man who is cruel or a man who whips his dog? A woman who is afraid or a woman who reached for her gun when there was a knock on the door?

Showing in your fiction and nonfiction is more compelling than telling.

This is another example of how important verbs are. Adjectives tell. Verbs show. I made the writing work better by turning adjectives into verbs. I turned the adjective *impatient* into the verbs *looked* (at watch), *tapped* (her foot), and *asked.* What I told with the adjective *handsome* I showed with the verb *turned* (to watch). *Cruel* became *whips,* and *afraid* became *reached.*

So look for adjectives that tell and turn them into verbs that show. Ask yourself: What would he, she, or it *do* because he, she, or it *is*?

A man *cries* because he is *sad*. A girl *crouches* because she is *fearful.* A plane *roars* because it is *loud.*

Exercise

Make a list of five nouns preceded by adjectives that tell. Try to turn the adjectives into verbs that show. For example, if your list were loud man, happy dog, old paint, shiny coin, and sad woman, you might come up with: man roared, dog wagged tail, paint peeled, coin glinted, and woman wept.

Try these first.
1. Old paper   *Cracking parchment*
2. Overworked clergyman
3. Reluctant lover
4. Disgruntled employee
5. Overheated photocopy machine

To make this exercise more fun in my workshops I ask for five nouns and then five adjectives, but I don't tell my students which adjective I'm going to put with each noun. It makes for some interesting combinations. Here is a list of nouns and a list of adjectives. Create as many combinations as you can and turn the telling adjectives into showing verbs.

1. Lunatic	1. Fanatical
2. Nun	2. Skinny
3. Pancake	3. Slimey
4. Sailor	4. High-pitched
5. Writer	5. Distressed
6. Relationship	6. Exuberant
7. Clarinet	7. Turbulent
8. Frog	8. Rich
9. Ocean	9. Club-footed
10. Podiatrist	10. Homicidal

Avoid Clichés and Word Packages

Each sentence you write should smell fresh when it arrives in front of the reader. If the reader has seen your sentence before, it should at least look as if it has been reinvented, not pulled from a shelf in a sentence warehouse.

There are hundreds of sentences and phrases which have been used so many times that they will never again smell fresh. They are clichés like "cute as a button" and "meek as a lamb." They've been used too many times, and they suffer from the same problem that Jack Nicholson has when he tries to take his coffee break at McDonald's: They can't sneak in without being recognized. You must excise these clichés from your writing. Clichés land on your manuscript page when you are too lazy to think, or too timid to take a chance.

You didn't take the time to visualize how the governor might have gotten rid of his new aide, Peterson, when the press revealed that Peterson was a child molester, so you wrote, "When the story hit the front page of the *Times Picayune,* the governor dropped Peterson like a hot potato."

You thought of some clever ways to describe your character's dumbness, but you thought they looked silly, so you played it safe and said, "Clarence was dumb as a doornail."

Review your manuscripts. Look at each sentence, each phrase. Do you really feel as if you made up that combination of words, or at least reinvented it? Or is something that was hanging there in the air for everybody to see and for anybody to grab? Is it fresh or is it stale? Is it something that you and your readers have read a thousand times? Get rid of it. Replace it with something original. I once crossed out "as useless as a refrigerator to an Eskimo" and changed it to "as useless as a pair of inflatable paperweights." I'm not sure if that's good, but I know it's mine.

Exercise

Here are some clichés and overused expressions that writers often reach for when they lack the energy or imagination to come up with something new. See if you can freshen them up; invent original ways of saying the same thing.

1. He's such a good salesman he could sell refrigerators to the Eskimos.
2. Sly as a fox.
3. Old as Methuselah.
4. She burned her candle at both ends.
5. Behind the eight ball.
6. Black as night.
7. Out of the frying pan into the fire.
8. He left no stone unturned.
9. Gilding the lily.
10. That hits the nail on the head.

Remember, there's nothing inherently wrong with these expressions. Most of them are good descriptive phrases. It's *because* they were good that they were used over and over and started to get boring, just as a good song can get boring after you've heard it too often.

Closely related to clichés are "word packages." The novelist Anne Bernays told me that the use of word packages is one of the most common mistakes of her writing students, so I'll let her tell you about them.

"They are somewhere between a cliché and a noncliché," Anne said, "They are verbal formulas that come very quickly to you and you just put them down. For example, a woman in my class wrote, 'I walked the two long blocks to her house.' 'Two long blocks' is a word package. It's easy to say and she thinks she's saying something, but she's not. Were they really two long blocks? Were they longer than any other blocks, or did they just seem longer because she was in a hurry or anxious? Other word packages would be 'by all rights' or 'I felt curiously tired.' They don't mean anything."

Anne, incidentally, admits that she uses word packages in her first and second drafts. That's okay. We all do. First drafts don't have to smell fresh; final drafts do. Go through your manuscript and cut out those phrases that don't mean anything.

Appeal to the Senses

Through the senses of sight, sound, taste, smell, and touch we reach out to the world; we experience. We perceive life with these senses, and our memories are the memories of those perceptions. Writing that works is writing that appeals to the senses. So always in your writing return to the senses. The abstracts you create, the "think" material, float tenuously on the surface of the brain and can be blown away by the ringing of the telephone. But when you appeal to the reader's senses, you give him something to latch on to, an image that can be re-created with the mention of a single word. Sight. Sound. Taste. Smell. Touch. Through these channels you will most effectively reach your reader.

I've talked about the sense of sight in writing. (Show, don't tell. Remember that frog.) Sight is the sense we use most. Even in sleep we use the *sense* of sight to perceive our dreams. But the worlds you want to bring alive with your writing are also rich in other sensory stimuli, the sounds, the smells, the flavors, and the peculiar tactile sensations that come from textures and temperature and motion.

While you can't load every paragraph you write with sights, sounds, and smells, you should return again and again to the senses to remind the reader that this written world is the same one he lives in. It sparkles, it roars, it rubs against him, and sometimes it stinks.

You will find that appealing to the senses works especially well at the beginning of an article or story, when you are leading the reader into your written world. "See," you are saying, "it's made of the same stuff as the world you're in now."

Here are some of the ways I used the senses in an article about apple picking for *Worcester* magazine.

Sight:

> The orchard's office was locked. A sign dangled from the door-knob. "Pickers Wanted," it said. "See the foreman."

I walked around the small brick building into an immense empty orchard. Rows of apple trees stretched away from me for as far as I could see, and on each tree hundreds of red MacIntoshes hung like Christmas bulbs.

Smell:

The air was cool and the sky was clear, the way apple growers like it. I took a deep breath. It was like sticking my nose into an empty cider jug.

Sound:

The foreman was a husky, balding man of about 60, every bit as weathered as the trees he tended. He had a fist for a face, and it studied me from atop a yammering forklift which he jockeyed around the apple trees.

Touch:

There's something very real about an apple. It has the reassuring heft of your first baseball, and the aroma that rises from its flesh is one not soon forgotten. And when you can sit serenely under a shady tree and know that 50 or 60 of those red beauties are just within your reach, it makes you feel as if Mother Nature is going to take care of things after all.

If you interview the governor of Kentucky or a woman who raises ducks, and you want to make your subject real to the reader, consider how you might move through those highly accessible channels, the senses, to bring the person right into the room with the reader.

Did the governor get embarrassed? Or did his face turn red, did his fingers tremble slightly, did moisture rise to the surface of his palms?

Does the duck woman smoke a lot? Or does she have two fingers that are as brown as fresh-baked bread from nicotine stains? Does the air in her office reek with the smoke rising from half a dozen ashtrays?

Think about your subject in a sensory way. Sure, he's a nice guy, he's dynamic, he has accomplished a great deal. But what of the senses? When you shook his hand was it warm or cool, wet or dry? Is he shaped like a tree or a pillow? What sort of sounds does he make? Is his voice harsh? Can you hear his footsteps?

The senses are touchstones for the reader. Return to them often. They work.

In the next exercise I'll ask you to find things that appeal to all five senses within different environments. It's good practice. But in most of your writing, you'll be working mainly with three senses: sight, sound, and touch. Except for eating, drinking, smoking, and kissing, we don't associate taste with most experiences, and if you tried to find a taste or flavor for each experience you wrote about, your writing would not work. The same goes for the sense of smell. Thousands of objects emit a smell, but we usually only think about the stronger smells, such as the scents of flowers, the aromas of food, and the gagging stenches of cigarette smoke and bus exhaust. A specific smell used in the right place can work wonders in making your writing work for the reader. Proust, for example, did a lot with very subtle fragrances — limeflower tea, and so on. But go easy. Too many writers load their prose with every olfactory sensation they can imagine, everything from the pungency of aging pickles to the aroma of freshly picked cotton.

Exercise

For each of the environments below, write a paragraph or several sentences, using all five senses to describe the environment.

For example, if your environment were a "movie theater," you might mention the sight of an usher, the sound of some bratty kid kicking the back of a seat, the smell of popcorn, the taste of a candy bar, and the feel of the floor that is invariably sticky from spilled sodas and discarded wads of chewing gum.

The important thing to remember is that you should use sensory stimuli that are associated with that environment but not with environments in general. If you say, "It was noisy at the baseball game," you haven't gained any ground in trying to engrave the image of a baseball game on the reader's brain. But if the noises you mention are the crack of the bat, the whizzing of a fast ball, the roar of the crowd, the heckling from the bleachers, and the hush that falls over the stadium when one more strike will complete a no-hitter, then you have used "baseball words" to remind the reader of where he is.

1. A coffee shop

2. A fruit stand
3. A rock concert
4. A truck pull
5. A desert

Write Things In Logical Order

It was noon when two men came into the bank. They walked across the lobby to the entrance to the vault. They wore ski masks and carried carbine rifles.

The problem with that paragraph is that the reader saw two men walk across the lobby, but he didn't know they wore ski masks and carried rifles. If he had, he would have watched them more closely.

Always remember how the reader is getting the information. The writer saw two men with masks and carbines walk across the lobby because that's how he envisioned it before writing. But the reader didn't know about the masks and carbines until after the men had walked across the lobby. The reader only knows what's happening when you tell him, left to right, one word at a time.

Make sure you put your words on paper in the order that you want the reader to see the images they represent. Compare these.

"Jack's front teeth broke as his face crashed into the asphalt. He had pitched forward and fallen hard after the Gypsy smashed him over the head with a tire iron."

Exercise

Make the action and information in these passages clearer to the reader by putting the sentences in logical order.

1. Maureen jumped out the window, realizing that the building was on fire.
2. The election in 1982 was a surprise to everybody. Germaine Deacon won it. He had only gotten 42 percent of the vote, but that was enough for a plurality in the three-way race. No black man had ever even run before, let alone won.
3. Dr. Wilson left the office in a rage. When he saw his wife's lawyer he shot him in the head. Wilson had grabbed his .357 magnum before leaving the office.

Put Emphatic Words at the End

Emphasis tends to flow to the end of a sentence, so if there is one word or phrase you want to say a little louder, put it at the end.

If there's been some confusion about which day the writer's workshop will be held, you can best remind people by putting the day at the end of the sentence:

> The writer's workshop, featuring guest speaker Ken Lizotte, will be held on Saturday.

If you want to emphasize the guest speaker you write:

> The writer's workshop on Saturday will feature guest speaker Ken Lizotte.

And if you want to emphasize what is happening on Saturday you write:

> Saturday Ken Lizotte will be the guest speaker at the writer's workshop.

This business of emphasis flowing to the end of the sentence is particularly important when you are trying to be funny. Often a writer loses the humor in his sentence by putting the funny word or phrase in the wrong place, where it loses emphasis. Woody Allen is the master of getting the funniest elements in his sentences to the end, where the reader will automatically emphasize them. The lines in this first set are just the way he wrote them, with the right words placed carefully at the end.

From "The UFO Menace":

> They told me they were from another galaxy and were here to tell the earth that we must learn to live in peace or they will return with special weapons and laminate every first-born male.

From "My Speech to the Graduates":

> No citizen can be wantonly tortured, imprisoned, or made to sit through certain Broadway shows.

From "By Destiny Denied":

> The store is an instant success, and by 1850 Entwhistle is wealthy, educated, respected, and cheating on his wife with a large possum.

Now I will take the humorous element from one and move it up. Because you come to it sooner it is less emphatic, and less funny.

> They told me they were from another galaxy and would return with special weapons and laminate every first-born male if the earth did not learn to live in peace.

Exercise

Rewrite these sentences so that you get the proper punch from the information that should be emphasized.

1. The general called and told us he wanted the team to invade now, instead of waiting for St. Patrick's Day.
2. I couldn't believe that Morty picked me even though he could have had Sarah, or Farrah, or Tara.
3. The formula does cause hair to grow on most men, but it also turns their skin green, which is one of the side effects that the FDA is concerned about.
4. Oscar winner Rita Moreno, who has also won a Grammy and Tony, once won an Emmy.
5. "If you can't get Irmgard to come here by midnight, then you are the one I will have to kill."

Be Suspicious of Newcomers

Writing for publication is not the same as taking an English exam. In the former you're trying to make the writing work for the reader. In the latter you're trying to please the teacher so you'll get an A.

In making your decisions to use marginal words or to use them in questionable ways, don't ask yourself if your high school English teacher would approve. Ask yourself, "Would it make the writing work? Would it help to etch the image I want on the reader's brain?"

If you try to keep track of all the words that are jargon, slang, or colloquial, all the words that are "unacceptable" or "improper usage," and to edit them from your work, I can promise that you'll turn into a raving lunatic and you'll be locked up in a state hospital where you'll spend the rest of your life howling through the bars of your window, "*Contact* is not a verb. *Like* is not a conjunction. *Upscale* doesn't mean anything."

We do need consistent rules of usage. We also need to forbid some words entry into our language. Words and the forms they take must be consistent in order to be recognizable. If a word means something different every time you see it, it has no meaning at all.

It's true that the indiscriminate acceptance of new words could ruin our language and reduce it to a general shorthand lacking both nuance and beauty. It's true that jargon, particularly when it originates on Madison Avenue, can scrape your nerves and triple your pulse rate as it's jammed down your eustachian tubes by people who have buckets of cash to pay for moronic TV commercials and vulgar billboards.

But it's also true that our language is rich with words that were once considered unacceptable, words that were once shunned and scorned, but are now employed to say what no other words can say. They've earned their way into our language.

I think the problem is that many teachers, editors, and writers approach the issue of jargon and slang not in a practical way, but as a moral crusade. They see new words as Huns swooping down from the hills to rape our mother tongue.

But even these vigilantes don't always agree on just who the bad guys are. Language laws cannot be enforced. There are too many opinions, disagreements, and special cases. If you try to always be "right," you'll end up crazy instead.

My advice is that you look at words of dubious reputation not as interlopers or criminals, but as job applicants. They want to join the language. They want to be part of your writing. So ask yourself if they work. Are they worth the space they occupy? Will they do the job they are hired for? Listen to them carefully. How do they land upon the ear? Give them a trial period. If they work well, keep them. If they don't, you know what to do. Of course, you should maintain high standards. Don't latch on to every new word that comes down the pike, just as you wouldn't hire every bozo who drifted into the personnel office. But listen to each word. Give it a chance.

For me there are words that just don't work. My friend Jan called recently to tell me she'd been named as "facilitator" for some group or other. I immediately lost interest. Then there are the people who are always "orientating" themselves, which sounds to me as if they are getting oriented while rotating.

On the other hand, if some girl grabbed the money and "split," I can see her fleeing, and if a man tells me his divorce trial was a real "bummer," I know exactly what he means. These words work for me, so I expect them to work in my writing.

Don't Force a Personal Style

Your personal writing style is what makes your description of a one-legged gnu different from mine. Since we both have the goal of showing the reader a one-legged gnu, the different ways we do it won't be crucial, assuming we both understand the basics of writing that works.

There are some writers, however, who develop a style as specific as their thumbprints. The writing of journalist Tom Wolfe, for example, can be spotted without a byline. Anyone familiar with Wolfe's work would quickly recognize this passage from "Las Vegas (What?) Las Vegas (Can't hear you! Too noisy) Las Vegas!!!!" which appeared in *The Kandy-Kolored Tangerine-Flake Streamline Baby* (Farrar, Straus & Giroux, 1965) as Wolfe's or the work of a clever imitator.

> Hernia, hernia, hernia, hernia, hernia, hernia, hernia, hernia, hernia, hernia, hernia, hernia, hernia, HERNia; hernia, HERNia, hernia, hernia, hernia, hernia, HERNia, HERNia, HERNia; hernia, hernia, hernia, hernia, hernia, hernia, hernia, eight is the point, the point is eight; hernia, hernia, HERNia; hernia, hernia, hernia, hernia, all right, hernia, hernia, hernia, hernia, hard eight, hernia, hernia, hernia, HERNia, hernia, hernia, hernia, HERNia, hernia, hernia, hernia, HERNia, hernia, hernia, hernia, hernia
>
> "What is all this *hernia hernia* stuff?"
>
> This was Raymond talking to the wavy-haired fellow with the stick, the dealer, at the craps table about 3:45 Sunday morning. The stickman had no idea what this big wiseacre was talking about, but he resented the tone. He gave Raymond that patient arch of the eyebrows known as a Red Hook brushoff, which is supposed to convey some such thought as, I am a very tough but cool guy, as you can tell by the way I carry my eyeballs low in the pouches, and if this wasn't such a high-class joint we would

take wiseacres like you out back and beat you into jellied madrilene.

At this point, however, Raymond was immune to subtle looks.

The stickman tried to get the game going again, but every time he would start up his singsong, by easing the words out through the nose, which seems to be the style among craps dealers in Las Vegas — "All right, a new shooter . . . eight is the point, the point is eight" and so on — Raymond would start droning along with him in exactly the same tone of voice, "Hernia, hernia, hernia; hernia, HERNia, HERNia, hernia; hernia, hernia, hernia."

Everybody at the craps table was staring in consternation to think that anybody would try to needle a tough, hip, elite *soldat* like a Las Vegas craps dealer. The gold-lame odalisques of Los Angeles were staring. The Western sports, fifty-eight-year-old men who wear Texas string ties, were staring. The old babes at the slot machines, holding Dixie Cups full of nickles, were staring at the craps tables, but cranking away the whole time.

Hunter S. Thompson is another contemporary journalist whose style is like a signature on every subject he touches. For this he gets the benefit of loyal fans who flock to him for something they can't get elsewhere. (On the other hand, he might be writing himself into a corner, because his style consists of a very subjective view, reams of exaggeration, flights of fancy, and outright fiction in the midst of fact, which turns a lot of people off.)

This passage from Thompson's *Fear and Loathing in Las Vegas* (Random House, 1971) shows his approach to the same city.

A week in Vegas is like stumbling into a Time Warp, a regression to the late fifties. Which is wholly understandable when you see the people who come here, the Big Spenders from places like Denver and Dallas. Along with National Elks Club conventions (no niggers allowed) and the All-West Volunteer Sheepherders' Rally. These are people who go absolutely crazy at the sight of an old hooker stripping down to her pasties and prancing out on the runway to the big-beat sound of a dozen 50-year-old junkies kicking out the jams on "September Song."

It was some time around three when we pulled into the parking lot of the North Vegas diner. I was looking for a copy of the Los Angeles *Times,* for news of the outside world, but a quick glance at the newspaper racks made a bad joke of that notion. They don't need the *Times* in North Vegas. No news is good news.

"Fuck newspapers," said my attorney. "What we need right now is coffee."

I agreed, but I stole a copy of the Vegas *Sun* anyway. It was yesterday's edition, but I didn't care. The idea of entering a coffee shop without a newspaper in my hands made me nervous. There was always the Sports Section; get wired on the baseball scores and pro-football rumors: "Bart Starr Beaten by Thugs in Chicago Tavern; Packers Seek Trade" . . . "Namath Quits Jets to be Governor of Alabama" . . . and a speculative piece on page 46 about a rookie sensation named Harrison Fire, out of Grambling: runs the hundred in nine flat, 344 pounds and still growing.

"This man Fire has definite promise," says the coach. "Yesterday, before practice, he destroyed a Greyhound Bus with his bare hands, and last night he killed a subway. He's a natural for color TV. I'm not one to play favorites, but it looks like we'll have to make room for him."

Indeed. There is always room on TV for a man who can beat people to jelly in nine flat . . . But not many of these were gathered, on this night, in the North Star Coffee Lounge. We had the place to ourselves — which proved to be fortunate, because we'd eaten two more pellets of mescaline on the way over, and the effects were beginning to manifest.

Don't worry about your personal writing style. It's not something that Tom Wolfe has and you lack; it's just that his is more distinctive. In time you will fall into writing patterns, you'll develop a habit of doing it this way more often than that way. You don't have to consciously cultivate a style. Just learn to write well, and your style will emerge.

No doubt there is a moron somewhere typing up his theory of "writing style analysis," which says that if you use a lot of short sentences you can plan on dying young, and if you're stingy with the commas you're probably a Pisces. Well, maybe. But it's best not to get analytical about your writing style. Just as you cannot acquire peace while yearning for peace, you cannot acquire style by shoving your writing under the microscope and carefully scrutinizing it. If you peer too closely at your style you will end up parodying yourself. Your writing voice must flow from you naturally, just as your conversational voice does.

Most important, whether your writing style is subtle or obvious, don't feel that you're stuck with it. The writing won't work if there's a clash between form and substance, between *what* you're writing about and *how* you're writing about it. You should be able to change your writing style on a whim, and you must be able to change it to suit the material.

Remember that your primary goal as a writer is not to leave your imprint on the page. Your goal is to *make the writing work,* make it do what it is supposed to do, cause laughter, tears, fright, anger, curiosity. . . .

Keep It Simple

Here are the beginnings of three novels:

> The book of ballads published by Von Humboldt Fleisher in the Thirties was an immediate hit. Humboldt was just what everyone had been waiting for. Out in the Midwest I had certainly been waiting eagerly, I can tell you that. An avant-garde writer, the first of a new generation, he was handsome, fair, large, serious, witty, he was learned. This guy had it all.

> I wasn't born yet so it was Cousin Gowan who was there and big enough to see and remember and tell me afterward when I was big enough for it to make sense. That is, it was Cousin Gowan plus Uncle Gavin or maybe Uncle Gavin rather plus Cousin Gowan. He—Cousin Gowan—was thirteen. His grandfather was Grandfather's brother, so by the time it got down to us, he and I didn't know what cousin to each other we were. So he just called all of us except Grandfather "cousin" and all of us except Grandfather called him "cousin" and let it go at that.

> On the day they were going to kill him, Santiago Nasar got up at five-thirty in the morning to wait for the boat the bishop was coming on. He'd dreamed he was going through a grove of timber trees where a gentle drizzle was falling, and for an instant he was happy in his dream, but when he awoke he felt completely spattered with bird shit.

Consider those three paragraphs. Look at the style. Are they weighted with symbolism? Are they lined with beautiful metaphors? Are they knotted into great and complex poetry? Are they deep? Do they mean so much that they must be read three times to be understood?

No. They are all simple, direct, unpretentious. The style in each is unadorned, and every sentence is like an arrow aimed at exactly what it means to say. Each author is trying to do just one thing, tell a story.

The three paragraphs are the work of Nobel Prize winners. The first is from *Humboldt's Gift,* by Saul Bellow, the second from *The Town,* by William Faulkner, and the last from *Chronicle of a Death Foretold,* by Gabriel Garcia Marquez.

Now you know the secret of good writing style. And you also know how to get to Stockholm.

COFFEE BREAK

The adjective, no doubt, is the most maligned part of speech, and for good reason. For every adjective that is improving a sentence, ten are being written to the detriment of the sentences they inhabit. In *The Elements of Style,* William Strunk suggests that adjectives are "the leeches that infest the pond of prose, sucking the blood of words."

Adjectives identify some distinctive feature of a noun; they tell you what color it is, how it's shaped, what size it came in and how fast it moved. Adjectives do great work when they are needed. But too often they are brought in when they are not needed. The careless writer drags them in to provide information that would have greater impact if it came directly from the noun. (After all, isn't meeting Woody Allen a lot better than meeting a guy who knows Woody Allen?) So before you write a noun that is modified by adjectives, ask yourself if a noun can convey the information without help. Can your "sprawling homestead" become more impressive as an "estate"? Can your "tall building" become more visual as a "skyscraper"?

I'm harping on adjectives here because I am rereading *The Summing Up* (Pocket Books), by Somerset Maugham, a writer whose vendetta against the adjective once inspired him to write an entire book without adjectives.

"I wanted to write without any frills of language," writes Maugham, "in as bare and unaffected a manner as I could. I had so much to say that I could afford to waste no words. I wanted merely to set down the facts. I began with the impossible aim of using no adjectives at all. I thought that if you could find the exact term, a qualifying epithet could be dispensed with. As I saw it in my mind's eye, my book would have the appearance of an immensely long telegram in which for economy's sake you had left out every word that was not necessary to make the sense clear."

Maugham found that to neglect adjectives altogether was to drain much of the color from his writing. But, though his response was extreme, his intentions were admirable. When you take a pencil to what you have written, you should be searching for adjectives you can remove, not places to insert new ones.

Once in a while a writer will publish a memoir which, while not officially designated as a book about writing, will contain more sage advice about the writing craft than many of the books that are so designated. *The Summing Up* is one of those books, perhaps the best. Another such book is *One Writer's Beginnings* (Harvard University Press), by Eudora Welty. Ordinarily you could safely bet the farm that a book like this — a seventy-five-year-old woman reminisces about her childhood in Mississippi — would grovel in obscurity for as long as it took to go out of print. But, incredibly, *One Writer's Beginnings* was on all the bestseller lists, clearly a message of hope to all of us.

It's a marvelous book by a woman who has won the Pulitzer Prize, the American Book Award, and a good many other honors for her fiction. So after I reread Maugham's tirade on the adjective, it occurred to me that Welty must know a thing or two about using adjectives. I thought I'd take a look, not to see what she had to say about them, but what she did about them.

I turned to a page at random and counted adjectives. I found twenty on the page, which contained 370 words. After I discounted the necessary adjectives, needed for clarification, not just enhancement (such as "I'd felt as a *younger* child" or "is never likely to be at home in *organized* religion"), I had fifteen adjectives.

Now it was time for the true test. Were Welty's fifteen adjectives "sucking the blood of words"? Should she feel "a tiny sense of failure"? Could they be compressed into stronger nouns that would make her tight writing even tighter?

Perhaps. But not by me. I could not find the nouns that would improve "a *little* book bound in *thin* leather, falling apart." And I certainly couldn't come up with a word that carried the information of *sheep-cropped* grass. As far as I could see, Welty had not used any adjective that was not carrying its own weight. I thought I would list the rest of her adjectives as a test for you to see if you could beat my score. But I have a better idea. Don't test your ability to eliminate adjectives with Eudora Welty's writing. Test it with your own.

Chapter Three
Grammar

Crusaders and Communicators

After this book is published I will receive at least seventy letters from readers, generously pointing out that in my chapter about grammar I made five grammatical mistakes. Most of these letters will be kind, well meaning, and clever. But many will be disturbingly hostile, and they will end with something like: "You dare to call yourself a writer! Why don't you learn the language first, turkey!"

I know this will happen because it has happened before. It happens to anybody who says anything about grammar in public. There is a vociferous, and possibly dangerous, fringe group in our society that takes grammar just a bit too seriously. So, in the matter of English grammar, my first bit of advice to writers is: Calm down, relax, don't get crazy. Grammar is important to writers, but it's nothing they should develop ulcers about.

There are two large groups of people who are wrong about grammar, and generally speaking, neither group produces good writers.

One group comprises people who think they can ignore the rules of grammar altogether and still write successfully by scribbling any combination of words that occurs to them, while announcing to the world that ignorance or laziness is really artistic freedom.

The people in the other group are those who discuss grammar as if it were some sort of religion that must be rigidly followed even if clarity, wit, style, and poetry must be sacrificed. They would rather be right than write well.

Both groups make the same mistake. They view grammar as a master, when they should look upon it as a servant.

The grammatical anarchists, convinced that grammar is a tyrant, are saying, "I ain't letting no grammar push me around." The grammatical religionists, certain that grammar is a god, say, "I will worship grammar and put no other writing consideration before it."

My second bit of advice: When you think about grammar, think about being a communicator, not a crusader.

If you are a writer who is concerned about the quality of his grammar, I have good news and I have bad news.

First, the bad news.

To succeed as a writer, you must know, respect, and obey the rules of grammar in your writing. If editors or writing teachers have consistently found grammatical errors in your writing, the flaw in your work is not minor. It is fatal. Good writing and good grammar are not twins, but they are usually found in the same places.

The rules of grammar exist to help you write well, not to sabotage your work, and you cannot write well without them. The rules of grammar organize the language just as the rules of arithmetic organize the world of numbers. Imagine how difficult math would be if three and three equaled six only once in a while or a tenth was equal to 10 percent only when somebody felt like it. Grammatical rules about tense, gender, number, person, and case create for us all a literary currency that we can spend anywhere the language is spoken. Grammar is a system of rules for speaking and writing a given language, and the system was not created just so that English teachers would have something to harass you about. It exists so that we all can communicate well, and when you blatantly violate portions of the system, you are chipping away at the stability of the whole.

Here's some more bad news. If you use poor grammar, people will think you are stupid. Right or wrong, people generally regard poor grammar as indicating ignorance, and if you write, "Two men was hit by a car in Williamstown on Thursday. Both of them had been drinking," your writing will be ignored or ridiculed. Even if an editor were willing to correct those grammatical mistakes, the fact that you made them destroys your credibility with him. If your grammar is that poor, he has to worry about the accuracy of your facts, the source of your information, and whether or not you are saying what you mean to say. He cannot take your work seriously. Would you hire a carpenter who didn't know how to use a ruler?

Poor grammar also disturbs the reader. It make a funny noise in his head that breaks the reading spell, just as your spell was broken when I used the plural verb *make* with the singular subject, *it*.

Poor grammar confuses the reader. If you write, "The boys arrived at camp with their parents and every boy was required to put their name on a sheet of paper that was passed around," your readers are going to see the plural pronoun *their* and assume it refers to a plural antecedent, *parents;* then they're going to see the singular *name* and wonder why each boy has only one parent. The sentence should say, "every boy was required to put his name on a sheet of paper that was passed around."

Mistakes That Hurt

The examples I have given so far involve what I, and any editor, would call significant and unforgivable grammatical mistakes. If you consistently make mistakes like the ones below, you almost certainly have many more writing problems that are not related to grammar, and I will explain why later.

Mistakes of tense: The boy rises from his bed early and sneaks down to the stream where he was met by the fetching Becky O'Shea.

The writer started with the present tense (rises, sneaks) and slipped into the past tense (was met).

Mistakes of number: Politics are my favorite subject.

The writer used a singular subject (politics) with a plural verb (are).

Mistakes of case: We're going to have a showdown with they.

They is in the nominative (also called subjective) case, and it's being used as an object in that sentence. It should be the objective case, *them.*

Also among the serious, significant grammatical mistakes I would include those of gender (Bart entered the room and put her books on the table) and person (Gary sat at his desk, turned on his typewriter, and then I started to write this article). If you can even *imagine* making mistakes like those, you'd better brush up on your grammar.

In addition to those major grammatical mistakes, there are a good many minor mistakes to be made, and nobody's hands are completely clean. We all have a few grammatical rules that we can never quite nail down. Many people cannot remember the difference between *who* and *whom.* (*Who* is nominative case, and *whom* is objective case, as in "Who is going to the prom with you, and with whom did she go last year?") Many writers use *like* as a conjunction (She walks like she's got a train to catch), even though most grammarians insist it be used only as a preposition (It looks like a luxury car and it rides like a dream). And almost everybody gets confused about *lay* and *lie*. (And with good reason. *Lay* means to put something down, and *lie* means to recline, but the past tense of *lie* is, would you believe, *lay*.)

Minor mistakes like these might confuse, disturb, or disgust your reader, depending on which mistakes you make, how often you make them, and who the reader is. It's arbitrary. When I wear an editor's hat, I don't mind a writer using *who* instead of *whom,* or occasionally using *like* as a conjunction. On the other hand, I would be inclined to reject the writer who consistently used *like* as a conjunction (even though Shakespeare did it), or who wrote, "I lied down for a nap."

Mistakes That Help

When it comes to minor grammatical mistakes, editors don't all draw lines at the same place. But all editors have a limited number of grammatical mistakes that they will forgive, so you should at least aim for grammatical perfection except when you can improve the writing by breaking a rule of grammar.

But keep in mind that good grammar, even perfect grammar, does not guarantee good writing any more than a good referee guarantees a good basketball game.

"It is my objective to more fully utilize my management expertise than has heretofore been the case," is acceptable grammar, but poor writing because it is poor communication. The sentence should read, "I'm looking for a better job." On the other hand, "I ain't got no money" is terrible grammar, but could be good writing in some context, by communicating *exactly* what the writer wants to communicate.

There are many writing situations in which inferior grammar makes for superior writing. You could use poor grammar to reveal the character of a narrator, as Mac Hyman did in *No Time for Sergeants*.

> The thing was, we had gone fishing that day and Pa had wore himself out with it the way he usually did when he went fishing. I mean he went at it pretty hard and called the fish all sorts of names — he lost one pretty nice one and hopped up in the boat and banged the pole down in the water which was about enough to scare a big-sized alligator away, much less a fish, and he spent most of the afternoon after that cussing and ranting at everything that happened.

You could use poor grammar in an essay or an opinion piece to establish tone: "Mike Tyson and Buster Douglas go at each other tonight in the Centrum and it ain't going to be pretty."

You can also use faulty grammar to characterize people, places, and events or to establish a casual, conversational tone. In this example, poor grammar does both jobs: "Moose asked every guy in the bar if they had seen Helen. Nobody knew nothing. Moose looked like he was going to tear the place apart." There are three grammatical mistakes in those three sentences, but they are all intentional and they are all doing some work.

Whenever you knowingly use poor grammar you should ask yourself two questions. The first: Is my meaning clear? If the answer is no, rewrite. The second question: What am I getting in return for the poor grammar? If you can't answer that, don't use the poor grammar.

Many grammatical errors occur because the writer tries too hard *not* to make a mistake. Instead of trusting his ear for language, the writer reacts to some traumatic correction in childhood. Most of us, for example, once said, "Jimmy and me are going to the movies," and had some impolite adult snap at us, "It's Jimmy and I are going to the movies." Many people were corrected so often that they now change all their *me*'s to *I*'s and write things like "The contract was given to Jimmy and I." (It should be "Jimmy and me." *I* is nominative; *me* is objective.) Or, having been bawled out for saying, "I played bad," when he should have said, "I played badly," the kid turns into an adult who writes things like "I feel badly about your loss," when he means that he feels bad about your loss. The problem is that the writer recalls the specific words involved, instead of the pertinent rule, which was not explained.

They Keep Changing the Rules

Even if you know all the rules of grammar, you're covered only for today, not tomorrow. The rules change. Grammar is a living thing; it grows to meet new needs.

An obvious example of this is something called the degenderization of language. The feminist movement has successfully lifted our consciousness about the fact that English pronouns of unspecified gender are always male, a fact that contributes to the idea that males are the regular folk and females are something else. It is good grammar but poor feminism to write, "A doctor should always clean his stethoscope before checking someone's heart."

Several solutions to the problem have been suggested. Among them are *he/she, his/her,* and *s/he*. None has really caught on. What is catching on, however, is "A doctor should always clean their stethoscope," an error in number that is perpetrated by people who would rather offend grammarians than feminists. It's good feminism but bad grammar and I don't like it. In fact, to be perfectly honest about it, I hate it. But I'm starting to get used to it, and it seems to be earning its way into the language. If it proves to be made of hardy stuff, I will welcome it.

The point is that it's bad grammar today, but it might be good grammar ten years from now. Today's rules have no better shot at immortality than *thee* and *thou* had.

While you should accept the fact that changes do occur in the language, you should also resist each change every step of the way. Change should not come easily. It must be tenacious. New words and constructions seeking entry into the language should be met by a mighty army of grammarians saying, "It's wrong," and the rest of us saying, "It just doesn't sound right," so that the trendy, the senseless, and the merely pretty fall dead on the battlefield, and only the truly valuable survive. Change, if I might switch my metaphor, should come gradually and rarely, or the language will fall like a table that has all its legs removed at once, instead of replaced one at a time.

Terms

Do you know what modal auxiliaries are? Can you explain the difference between determiners and adjectivals? I sure as heck can't and I've sold sixteen books and a thousand short pieces. I can certainly identify a verb, a noun, or an adjective when I see one, but I know many successful writers who can't even do that. So don't berate yourself because you don't know all the grammatical terms. Writers don't need to know the names of all the parts in their typewriters. And the fact that you've forgotten how to diagram a sentence doesn't necessarily mean your grammar has deteriorated.

You'll also be happy to know that if you have a few grammatical idiosyncrasies, you are in good company. Carlos Baker writes of Ernest Hemingway, "It was a special trademark of his personal style to use *nor* instead of *or* after a previous negative. In easy defiance of the grammarian's rule, he regularly retained the final *e* when adding *ing* or *able,* as in *loveing* or *comeing* or in the phrase immortalized in the title of *A Moveable Feast.* He did not give a damn about the distinctions between *who* and *whom, lying* and *laying.* 'The last thing I remember about English in high school,' he once wrote, 'was a big controversy on whether it was "already" or "all ready." How did it ever come out?' "

And Andy Rooney writes in one of his columns: "I know a lot about using the language. Still, there are times when I'm stumped. I was wondering the other day what part of speech the word *please* is in the sentence, 'Please don't take me seriously.' "

Seriously is how most of us took our English teachers. They were well meaning, most of them, but they were hired to teach us good grammar, not good writing.

If English teachers are sometimes wrong, that gives them something in common with the strictest grammarians who, on occasion, also don't know what they are talking about. Take, for example, the *which* vs. *that* controversy. Do you know the difference? Most sincere grammarians will insist that *that* be limited to restrictive clauses (the ones that define), as in, "The TV that is in Room 117." And *which,* they'll tell you, should be used only for nonrestrictive clauses (those that describe something but don't define it), as in, "The Eiffel Tower, which is extremely tall, needs a paint job." This dictum sounds nice, but it's wrong. *Which* has been at home in restrictive and nonrestrictive clauses for ages and it has been put there by the best of writers. Use your ear, not your rule book.

If it pleases you to know that even grammarians make grammatical mistakes, it should please you more to know that *you* probably don't make many significant grammatical errors. I say this because I have been teaching creative writing to adults for years, and out of each class of twenty I rarely have more than two students who seriously need grammar review. Incidentally, I even know *why* you're not making a lot of grammatical mistakes, but I'm saving that for later.

However, if you are making a lot of significant grammatical mistakes, you probably don't know it. The fastest way to find out is to give thirty pages of typed manuscript to somebody who knows grammar. Ask him what grammatical mistakes you are making. If you can write thirty pages without occasionally making those major mistakes in tense, case, number, etc., you can write thirty thousand pages the same way and you don't have what I would call a significant problem with grammar. So get to work on the minor problems, of the *who* vs. *whom* and *like* vs. *as* variety. You can look up the rules in a good, conversational grammar book. And if you can't remember the rules, look them up when you need them while you're writing.

But if you *are* making those significant grammatical errors that I spoke of—if you repeatedly misuse tense, gender, case, number, or person—then, as I said earlier, you have a serious writing problem that goes far beyond grammar. And that, friends, brings us to the crux of the matter.

Trust Your Ear

Truly knowing about grammar in the way that is relevant for a writer is not a matter of book learning. It is not a matter of knowing the names for the parts of speech. It's not a matter of remembering rules you were given in high school. It is, quite simply, a matter of music. You know when someone has made a grammatical mistake the same way you know when someone is singing "White Christmas" off-key. You know because you have heard it on-key so many times, and even if you can't tell whether the singer is sharp or flat, you know that "it just doesn't sound right."

When I want to write the past tense of *ring,* I don't say to myself: "Ring? Isn't that one of the two hundred irregular verbs that take odd forms in the past tense?" I simply write *rang* because it sounds right and *ringed* doesn't sound right. That's what *I* do and that's what *you* do.

To know good grammar is to be able to hear when something just doesn't sound right.

For most of you, this is good news. If you've developed a pretty good ear for the language, you're probably not going to get into too much grammatical hot water. But if you constantly make those major grammatical mistakes, you have not developed a true ear for the language, and chances are you are also not properly tuned into the subtleties and connotations of words, the rhythm of sentences or the sour note in a sentence or paragraph, and you are a lot further (or is it farther?) from being a good writer than you thought. You must go back and take a course in grammar, but this time learn it with your ears, not with your eyes.

And the rest of us must not get too smug just because we have good ears for language. We should remember that we are not merely users of the language. As writers, we are its guardians. Grammatical rules are born of usage and so, ironically, we who are most worried about the rules are the ones who in the long run *make* the rules. We should not make new ones lightly.

So strive most of all for good writing, but make proper grammar your rule and improper grammar your exception. Don't give easy access to every bizarre construction or chunk of senseless jargon that comes whistling down the pike. Never violate a rule of grammar unless you have a good reason, one that improves the writing.

But never choose good grammar over good writing. There is nothing virtuous about good grammar that does no work. Your goal is good writing. Good grammar is only one of the tools you use to achieve it.

Chapter Four
Music

Writing Is a Symphony

Writing is not a visual art. It is a symphony, not an oil painting. It is the shattering, not the glass. It is the ringing, not the bell. The words you write make sounds, and when the sounds satisfy the reader's ear, your writing works. Note that I said "satisfy," not "please." We writers want satisfied readers, not necessarily happy readers. If your reader's heart starts to pound and his palms begin to sweat because you have placed in your horror story a word that startles him like a shriek from the attic, he is not happy, but he is satisfied.

I can't teach you everything you need to know about sound in writing. To a large extent you just have to develop a good ear for writing, and nobody can help you do that. If you're not feeling confident about this, consider the fact that you probably hear dozens of grammatical mistakes even though you don't know the grammatical rule that's being broken. That's because you have developed an ear for grammar. You know something's wrong because it sounds wrong. The same process applies to your writing. If you write every day you will develop that ear to the point where you know that "it just doesn't sound right." Eventually you will begin to understand *why* it doesn't sound right.

Writing Should Sound Like Conversation

You are perhaps having some auditory difficulty in perceiving my attempts to achieve communication with you. Let me make a few adjustments here. Okay, can you hear me now? Is it clear? Sure it is. That's because I've created a sound you like, one you recognize and easily comprehend. It's the sound of conversation.

The effective writer satisfies his reader by creating sentences and paragraphs that sound like conversation. My first wordy sentence at the beginning of this section created an unsatisfactory sound, not because you didn't know the meaning of the words, but because the words were not primary words; that is, they were not words that reveal their meaning instantly. You needed time to stop and think "Auditory—what does that mean?" But I didn't give you time. I kept talking, adding more words that required a second for translation. And so my words became as meaningless as the static on a cheap radio. If I had continued that way, you would have stopped listening.

So good writing sounds like conversation because it uses the simple primary words of conversation, words that say what they mean and say it immediately. Good writing, like conversation, also uses a variety of sentence length which we'll discuss. And good writing contains the frequent breaks or pauses of conversation. When we talk we rarely use a sentence of more than twenty-five words. We say, "I went to Watertown yesterday. Ran into Ron and Marcia. Marcia looks great. Ron's got this job working for some kind of school for the blind right there in Watertown. I'm not sure what he does. Publicity, I think. I'll tell you one thing, though, I'm never going to drive through Watertown on a Saturday again, not with all that traffic. Horrendous!"

Good writing *sounds* like conversation. It doesn't duplicate it. The person in conversation is always working in the first draft and he has no word limit; he does not choose his words with great care and he does not economize the way a writer must. The speaker says, "I saw this fox. . . . It was brown and had a long tail. Anyhow, it came over to where Buddy, that's Jim's dog, was sleeping. You remember Buddy. Jim's dog, the one that's always sleeping on the back porch of his cottage up in—what's the name of that town? Winchendon—that's it. Anyhow, this fox came up to where Buddy was lying and just sort of jumped over him real fast and then he went dashing off into the woods. There's some beautiful woods up there. I found out later that the fox does this all the time."

The writer has to make every word count, so he writes, "The quick brown fox jumps over the lazy dog."

Also remember that being conversational in your writing does not mean being chatty. Here is an example of a writer trying to be chatty, not conversational:

Want to learn more about being an equine practitioner? Hey, no problem! Get to know some. They'll talk. They'll share. They'll fill you in on what it's all about. They'll give you valuable tips. After all, they've been around. They've seen it all. They know what can happen.

That, of course, is not the way my friend Ron Trahan wrote it in his book, *Careers for Horse Lovers* (Houghton Mifflin). He wrote:

One of the best ways to learn more about the career of an equine practitioner is to become acquainted with one. Most are usually willing and eager to discuss their careers. Their information can be invaluable. After all, they've successfully combated and surmounted all of the problems typically encountered.

Vary the Length of Your Sentences

The fastest way I know to make this point is with something I've written before, in *Writer's Digest* and in my book *One Hundred Ways to Improve Your Writing* (New American Library, 1985).

This sentence has five words. This is five words, too. Five word sentences are fine. But several together become monotonous. Listen to what is happening. The writing is getting boring. The sound of it drones. It's like a stuck record. The ear demands some variety. Now listen. I vary the sentence length and I create music. Music. The writing sings. It has a pleasant rhythm, a lilt, a harmony. I use short sentences. And I use sentences of medium length. And sometimes when I am certain the reader is rested I will engage him with a sentence of considerable length, a sentence that burns with energy and builds with all the impetus of a crescendo, the roll of the drums, the crash of the cymbals, and sounds that say listen to this, it is important.

So write with a combination of short, medium, and long sentences. Create a sound that pleases the reader's ear. Don't just write words. Write music.

Example: *WRONG* (All long sentences.)

My first love was a girl named Nancy in the first grade who had long black hair and always wore adhesive tape over one frame of her eyeglasses. Nancy was as toothless as a toad but she had a smile that could send cramps careening through my body for hours and I loved her with passion beyond measure from the heartbreaking distance of three seats back and two rows closer to the windows. In the second grade Nancy was ripped from my life by selfish parents who were bent on moving to California, so I never had an opportunity to make a fool of myself with her. So, my first real intrusion into the world of boys and girls together came years later and it was a hellish experience which drained me of courage with women for the next twenty years.

Example: *WRONG* (All short sentences.)

The great trauma occurred in 1957. I was a thirteen-year-old fool. I lived in Boston, Massachusetts. Specifically, I lived in Roslindale. Roslindale was a lower middle class section. The houses there had small backyards. The neighbors all drove Fords. The girl was Deborah Wallace. She was also thirteen. She was wonderful.

Example: *RIGHT*

Deborah had arrived in my life two years earlier, shyly presenting herself to Miss McCormick as the new girl who had just moved to Roslindale. Deborah was so lovely in her yellow taffeta dress. She was as soft as wet modeling clay. I knew at once that I was in the grip of mature and eternal love. I imagined that if I touched her we would fly to a wondrous world where school was unthinkable and corporal punishment absolutely forbidden.

The monotonous sound that you hear in the first two examples is the sound you will make in the reader's head if you write several sentences in a row that have approximately the same length. The ear must have variety or the mind will go out to lunch. You wouldn't listen to a singer who sang the same song over and over. You wouldn't watch a movie that played the same scene fifteen times. And you won't read something that makes the same noise sentence after sentence.

Here are some numbers for you: 25, 14, 12, 3, 21, 33, 28, 8, 12, 35, 51, 16, 33, 4.

Those are the numbers of the words in the first fourteen sentences of Mark Twain's *The Adventures of Huckleberry Finn*, a book that sold well. I rest my case.

Exercise

Rewrite the following so that you end up with a more satisfying variety of sentence lengths.

It was a story that shocked the nation. In April, 1989, police discovered thirteen bodies. The bodies had been mutilated. Among them were Texas college student Mark Kilroy. There was evidence that the victims had been sacrificed. Also, they had been ritually tortured.

Four members of a satanic drug ring were captured. Many others were at large. Among them was Adolfo Constanzo. Constanzo was a mysterious Cuban American. He was from Miami. Constanzo was the gang's ringleader. Also at large was Sara Aldrete, a tall and attractive honor student at an American college who, it was said, lived a double life: friendly college girl by day, ritual killer by night. There was talk of Satanism, of cannibalism, of police payoffs, of more bodies buried in shallow graves, and much of this would turn out to be true. Like most people, I was at once horrified and mesmerized by the news coverage of this story because there is something about the word "Satanism" and the idea of such rituals that makes us all lean a little closer to our newspapers and ask questions.

When I decided to write a book about the tragedy, I knew that I would have to write it fast because the terrible deaths in Matamoros were falling into the folklore of the Mexican countryside so rapidly that the facts had to be retrieved quickly, before they became indistinguishable from legend. I flew to Mexico and Texas where I visited the scenes and wrung whatever information I could from whatever sources were available, and I ended up, as journalists inevitably do, with an intriguing, but imperfect body of information.

Vary the Construction of Your Sentences

Wolf raised the flag.

Ollie North and Gordon Liddy swapped pistols.

The big green billboard on Colorado Avenue swayed in the wind, then toppled over onto Sturge Thibedeau's new Cadillac convertible.

Those three sentences are of different lengths. But they are all constructed the same way. Each begins with the subject, moves directly to the predicate, and ends with the object. When we first learn to write, we are taught to put the elements of a sentence in that order. It is the most logical, most easily understood construction. Most of your sentences should be built this way.

However, just as there should be variety in the length of your sentences, there should be variety in their shape. You should vary the sentence construction in a way that creates a pleasant music. The subjects, the predicates, and the objects should all, from time to time, dance to surprising places.

If several sentences in a row are constructed the same way they will create a drone that will bore readers. Here's an example.

> She slipped into a window seat in the nonsmoking section and placed a slim black case on her lap and leafed through its contents. She latched the case once the plane was in the air, then she glanced briefly at the sunlit Manhattan skyline, let her head fall back, and closed her eyes.
>
> Anne Ellis, thirty-two, was a senior editor at Castle Press, a highly successful publishing house on lower Park Avenue. She was flying to Washington to meet with a man named Hamilton Carver. Every sizable publishing house in New York had sought a meeting with Carver for years. Carver was a financier, developer, and womanizer who was surrounded by a battery of lawyers and a cadre of bodyguards and he had played as large a part as any man could in changing the face of the eastern seaboard of the United States in the years since 1960. Little was known of his personal life.

That's my rewrite of the first chapter of Douglass Wallop's novel, *The Other Side of the River* (W.W. Norton). I would have to go on quite a bit longer to make it really boring, but I think in those two paragraphs you can begin to hear the monotonous sound created when several sentences in a row are constructed the same way.

Now listen to the difference when variety of construction is added to the music. This is how Wallop wrote those first two paragraphs.

> Slipping into a window seat in the nonsmoking section, she placed a slim black case on her lap and leafed through its contents. Once the plane was in the air, she latched the case, glanced briefly at the sunlit Manhattan skyline, let her head fall back, and closed her eyes.
>
> At thirty-two, Anne Ellis was a senior editor at Castle Press,

a highly successful publishing house on lower Park Avenue. She was flying to Washington for a meeting with a man named Hamilton Carver. A meeting with Carver had been sought for years by every sizable publishing house in New York. Financier, developer, womanizer, surrounded by a battery of lawyers and a cadre of bodyguards, Carver in the years since 1960 had played as large a part as any one man could in changing the face of the eastern seaboard of the United States. Little was known of his personal life.

Exercise

Rewrite the following so that you end up with a more satisfying variety of sentence constructions. After you've done it, read the first paragraph of Truman Capote's *Breakfast at Tiffany's*.

I am always drawn back to places where I have lived. I am drawn to the houses and their neighborhoods. I had my first New York apartment in a brownstone in the East Seventies during the early years of the war, for instance. It was one room crowded with attic furniture, a sofa, and fat chairs upholstered in that itchy, particular red velvet that one associates with hot days on a train. The walls were stucco, and a color rather like tobacco-spit. There were prints of roman ruins freckled brown with age, in the bathroom too. The single window looked out on a fire escape. My spirits heightened whenever I felt the key to this apartment in my pocket. It was still a place of my own, despite its gloom. My book, jars of pencils and everything I needed was there. I felt that I could become a writer.

Experiment with Parallel Construction

Though several sentences in a row with the same construction can bore the reader, there are times when you will deliberately build two or three consecutive sentences the same way to create a sound and an emphasis that serves your purpose. This is known as parallel construction.

Jerome Kern could have written, "Fish got to swim, and flying is something that birds have to do." Instead, he, being a composer and needing to make his words work with music, used parallel construction: "Fish got to swim, and birds got to fly. I got to love one man til I die."

Here is an example of how you might use parallel construction in a travel article.

> *Without parallel construction:*
> Worcester County is a wonderful place for a vacation any time of the year. Mt. Wachussett is available for skiing. Golf courses are easy to find. Several lakes in the area offer fishing opportunities. The foliage in Worcester County is among the most beautiful in the area.

> *With parallel construction:*
> Worcester County is a wonderful place for a vacation any time of the year. You can ski in Worcester County. You can golf in Worcester County. You can fish in Worcester County. You can view beautiful foliage in Worcester County.

Parallel construction means setting up two or more sentences or phrases in a row so that they will make a similar sound. Why? Because you want to remind the reader that they are alike. Sentences that are built alike land on the ear the same way and they gain a cumulative credibility. Often it's as if you make a statement and then provide the reader with a list of corollaries to prove you're right. Listen to what happens in this passage from my Marilyn French profile. In the first sentence I make a statement. In the next four sentences I use the parallel construction of *they* followed directly by a verb to prove I'm right.

> The stories woven into this novel, which she insists is not autobiographical, are of women enduring from one mundane moment to the next. They have babies. They clean diapers. They pinch their bodies and paint their faces for parties down the street, and they swap souls with other women over coffee in the kitchen. They go to college when their thighs have fattened and spots of gray cling to their fluffy black hair, pressing their lives into an elusive mold called liberation.

Parallel construction makes a nice sound. It works. Use it, but don't go crazy with it.

Exercise

Try to improve these paragraphs by using parallel construction.

When I was in high school I dated two girls from Hong Kong. I had another girlfriend who was black. And for a while there I was going out with an Eskimo girl.

Massachusetts leads the nation in the production of cranberries. Hawaii, of course, is known for sugar. Mushrooms are the big thing in Pennsylvania. Florida produces oranges.

When Sidney got home from the truck pull he found that the walls of his house were covered with a mysterious green slime. Upstairs in the family room, the new TV was surrounded by the same green slime. Knots of the green slime also covered the dog's bed, the new video camera, and Sidney's golf clubs.

Read Your Work Out Loud

Each word you write will make *sounds* in the reader's head. So in your writing you should strive for that organization of sounds known as *music*.

Writing works when it plays the tune you want it to, the way you want it played. Just as the sound of each instrument contributes to the quality of an orchestra, the sound of each word you write contributes to the quality of your story.

Of course, the sound of each word varies depending on where it is heard, just as the sound of an electric guitar could be euphonious in a soft rock band but jarring in the midst of the New York Philharmonic.

So read everything you write aloud, and imagine that your ear is a sensitive drum lying on its side. In your mind watch each word fall to the skin of the drum and listen for the sound it makes.

Does it fall softly, like a silk scarf floating onto the surface, where it barely whispers? Does it comes quickly out of nowhere, like *pit* or *rap*, seeming to puncture a tiny hole in the drum? Is it a three-foot length of steel chain crashing down, like *manufacturing*, or does it sweep across the drum and gently subside, like *esoteric*? Does it make a ping or a thud? Does it clamp right down on the surface, like *imbed*? Or does it bounce a few times, like *imitate*, before it settles down?

Reading out loud will return to you the true sound of your story. You will hear the sour note of the word that's "just not right." The drastic changes in tone will call out to you for editing. You'll notice that you are breathless at the end of one long sentence and you will know that you must break it up into two or three. Listen for the music, the variety, the emphasis. You will discover that some of your sentences could be taken two different ways and that a single word or even a comma can eliminate the wrong one. And you will see that a sentence like "Who knew that Lou cued Sue, too?" might not look funny, but it sure makes a funny and distracting noise in the reader's head.

If you feel as if you are losing your ear for what you have written, try reading it out loud in sounds, not words. You might hear a sound that you don't like. If that doesn't work, put the manuscript away for a few days and then read it out loud, possibly with another listener. But before you do any of these things, go back and reread the tips in this chapter.

The music of your writing, like its style, is not something you sit down and plan syllable by syllable. It is more like learning to play piano by ear. For the most part you learn to do it without thinking about it. As long as you can truly hear what you've written, you probably won't compose a lot of harsh and grating noise.

Exercise

Sometimes when I can't think of what to write, I think instead of what sounds to make. Passages, especially opening paragraphs, come to me as noises, like dada dada, dadum. Dee, dee da deedeedee, da da. It sounds ridiculous, but it works, and that's what counts. Then I start creating sentences, and when I can't think of a word or phrase I'll plug in some nonsense words just to maintain the rhythmic flow. In time it evolves into something readable. I'd like you to try the process in reverse. Take this opening paragraph from *Freedom at Midnight* by Larry Collins and Dominique Lapierre (Simon & Schuster, 1975) and read about half of it not as words but as sounds. Read it as a bunch of dadees and dumdums, or hum a tune to it.

It was the winter of a great nation's discontent. An air of melancholia hung like a chill fog over London. Rarely, if ever, had Britain's capital ushered in a New Year in a mood so bleak, so morose. Hardly a home in the city that festive morning could furnish enough hot water to allow a man to shave or a woman to cover the bottom of a wash-basin. Almost without exception, Londoners had greeted the New Year in bedrooms so cold their breath had drifted on the air like puffs of smoke. Precious few of them had greeted it with a hangover. Whiskey, in the places where it had been available the night before for New Year's Eve celebrations, had cost eight pounds — thirty-five dollars — a bottle.

Use Complete Sentences Often. Fragments Rarely.

Ninety-nine percent of the time you should use complete sentences in your writing. The reader expects a subject and a predicate to greet him every time he begins to read a sentence. He listens for them. If he doesn't hear them he is disturbed. Something just doesn't sound right. Awkward. Like here. And here. Sentence fragments. See? Not good.

However, there is that other 1 percent of the time when sentence fragments can make the sound you want. Here is an example.

> This lunatic called on Friday and told my answering machine that I would be dead by the end of the month. He called again on Saturday. Same message. After the third call I was worried. Real worried.

Those sentence fragments draw meaning from the sentences near them, and they create a nice rhythm by using fewer words than a complete sentence. But you should use sentence fragments like those only when you are certain that you are getting something in return.

Exercise

In the following paragraph try to improve the writing by rewriting and including sentence fragments.

"We'll have to have lunch sometime," Helen had said to me. She had said it just like that. She had said it as if we were casual friends. I couldn't believe she was suggesting lunch and nothing more. I had expected to marry this woman. I really wanted to marry her. And here she was saying we could maybe share a tuna salad sandwich or something. I was stunned. I was really stunned.

In these next paragraphs try to improve the writing by getting rid of the sentence fragments and replacing them with sentences.

The Bloated Belly Beer Drinker is found everywhere. All over the world. The creature is most commonly found in a particular section of Boston. Dorchester. Because conditions are favorable there. Plenty of bars. Soggy pizza. Good TV reception. The BBBDs find Boston ideal.

It was once believed that the Bloated Belly Beer Drinkers comprised a much larger portion of the population. Ninety-two percent. A figure derived from a sampling of litter on American highways. Figure was discarded when it was learned that BBBDs litter at a far greater rate than the rest of the population.

Don't Repeat Uncommon Words

If you use a common word like "and" or "her" or even "house" six times in a paragraph, nobody is going to notice.

But if you write, "Jackson made several inflammatory remarks during the debate. The final resolution had an inflammatory effect on the nation," you will make a disturbing sound in the reader's head. When the reader hears that second "inflammatory," she will say to herself, "Hmm, I think I've heard that word recently." It will sound familiar and it will remind her that she is reading.

The repeated words don't even have to be that close together to disturb the reader. Listen for the disturbance in this example.

> Today the Electrics, one of the best hockey teams in the state, have talent, equipment, a regular schedule, and a shot at a national championship. But they were a moribund bunch indeed when Westcott first took over as coach.
>
> Westcott had come over from Castel, a small Pennsylvania

town made moribund by the layoffs in the steel industry. He was glad to have the job.

When you heard moribund twenty-one words after the last time you heard it, you were reminded of the writer at work.

After you use a word like "inflammatory" or "incandescent" or "inelegant" or "moribund," you certainly don't have to retire it for the rest of the story, but generally several paragraphs should pass before the reader hears it again, unless you are obviously repeating it for effect, such as, "Jackson's remarks were inflammatory. Wilson's remarks were inflammatory. In fact, everybody's remarks were inflammatory."

COFFEE BREAK

One of the most common mistakes beginning nonfiction writers make is confining themselves to the material they have specifically collected for the story. The writer interviews the head of an advertising agency. On the way out, the writer picks up the agency's brochure about itself, and maybe a couple of samples of its prize-winning ads. Then he goes home and writes the story, drawing only from that shallow well of material. He ignores the rest of the world.

If you want to write exciting, lively nonfiction, reach out to the world around you and bring back material. It doesn't necessarily require any special research. Just draw from life.

If you are writing an article about private detectives in your city, you might note that the life of a real private detective is "not as glamorous as *Moonlighting*, or as dangerous as *Magnum, P.I.*" If your subject is executive salaries, you might note, "Of course, that sounds like a lot of money, but it's only a fifth of what Don Mattingly will earn this year playing first base for the Yankees." Writing about red tape? Well, maybe, "The company's annual report made James Joyce's *Ulysses* read like a nursery rhyme by comparison."

When you draw quotations, anecdotes, allusions from the worlds of television, movies, sports, literature, and current events, you are reaching into the world shared by you and your reader. This shared experience makes your story more attractive.

One way I reach into the world around me is by stretching my left arm about two feet from my word processor to my bookshelf.

I was asked to improve someone's article on the perseverance required in selling insurance. One of the ways I did it was by playing the text off a rhyme, which I got from *Rhyme and Verse*, one of eight thin volumes in Jacob M. Braude's *Complete Speaker's and Toastmaster's Library* (Prentice-Hall). I found it under "Perseverance":

"The man who quits has a brain and a hand
As good as the next, but he lacks the sand,
That would make him stick with courage and stout
To whatever he tackles and fight it out."

The author of that rhyme is not known, but it sounds as if he knew a thing or two about selling insurance.

Using appropriate anecdotes is another way of pulling outside material into your story.

When I wrote an article about wealthy people in my area and the qualities that contributed to their wealth, I used this anecdote from the "Stinginess" section of Edmund Fuller's *2500 Anecdotes for All Occasions* (Dolphin):

> The young journalist was sent to get an interview with the old Scotch merchant. His paper wanted a human interest story on how the merchant had accumulated his riches. "Well it's a long story," said the old man, "and while I'm telling it we might as well save the candle." He blew the candle out. "Never mind about the story," said the reporter. "I understand."

By far the most common device for enlivening your articles with outside material is the quotation. Earlier I used the example of a writer writing about an advertising agency, because I had such an assignment recently. To make my article livelier, I used several quotations I found in *Peter's Quotations: Idea for Our Times*, by Laurence J. Peter (Bantam). Here is how I integrated some quotations from that book into my article, along with a few pointers about using quotations.

Usually I try to avoid using a name that I'm sure is not familiar to my audience. You sound pretentious when you make several references to obscure figures. In this case, I simply found a way to acknowledge that the name was not well known.

> "Advertising is what you do when you can't go see somebody."
> So said Fairfax Cone, whom most people have never heard of.
> Perhaps that's because he didn't advertise.

Quotations also add credibility by association. Mentioning an important name somehow suggests that he agrees with what you have to say.

> "Few people at the beginning of the 19th century needed an ad man to tell them what they wanted," said John Kenneth Galbraith. But times have changed. People have needs, but they don't always know there are products that meet those needs.

Sometimes, if a quotation is obscure enough, I will steal it and reword it if necessary.

Some people say that advertising encourages people to live beyond their means. Perhaps. But then, so does matrimony.

While you should certainly have a copy of *Bartlett's Familiar Quotations* on your bookshelf, I think you'll probably get more mileage out of a book like *Peter's Quotations.* If you use Bartlett's, you'll find yourself quoting Longfellow, Hale, and Grant all the time. With Peter's your article will have a more contemporary look with quotations from Woody Allen, Simone de Beauvoir, and Robert Benchley, who once said, "The surest way to make a monkey of a man is to *quote* him."

Chapter Five

Pace

Travel Light

The paperback dictionary I always keep within arm's reach says that *pace* means "the rate of movement or progress." As we discuss it here, I am thinking about the overall pace of your article, story, or book. But I'm also thinking about the pace of that story at any given sentence or paragraph. A few slow passages in an otherwise fast-moving story can be as distressing to a reader as a few long traffic jams in an otherwise fast trip. So along with pace, we'll be talking about proportion and balance, and avoiding traffic jams.

When an editor says, "I hate the pace of your story," or words to that effect, he sometimes means that the pace is too fast, or it's inconsistent and jarring. But 90 percent of the time he means the pace is too slow. The story drags. It's boring.

Your story has got to move fast. But that doesn't mean that you have to mount your reader on a rocket and hurl her through space. A nice, leisurely horse and carriage ride can also be pleasant. "Keep the story moving" means that your story should always feel as if it is moving with maximum efficiency. If it's a horse and carriage ride, fine, but don't make it feel as if the horse is near death and the wheels are square.

It's all a matter of luggage. Yes, luggage. If you don't believe me, just walk down the street with two loaded suitcases in your hands, then walk down the street without them. Luggage can slow down any vehicle, whether it's a horse-drawn carriage or a Ferrari. So what are you going to do, drive to Pennsylvania without any clean shirts? No. You're going to drive to Pennsylvania without your tool kit and your silverware and all the other things you don't need in Pennsylvania. In order to make your story move at maximum efficiency you must get rid of the excess luggage.

Rich description, detailed characterization, and extended dialogue are not necessarily excess luggage. They can be very valuable luggage and you don't want to toss them out on the highway just for the sake of a faster pace. What you do want to jettison is the luggage you don't need. We're talking junk here, ugly, heavy, worthless junk. That's what makes cars sluggish, and that's what makes stories sluggish.

I find junk in all of the manuscripts I read, including my own first drafts.

Most of the junk comes in the form of unnecessary words. As we discussed earlier a word is unnecessary if it is not doing any work, if it's doing work that doesn't have to be done, or if it's doing work that's being done by other nearby words.

Sometimes you might write a piece of fiction or nonfiction that is well told, well structured. But because you have burdened it with so many unnecessary words, it can be compared to a sleek and beautiful racing car that has been buried under so much junk that it can hardly move faster than forty-five miles per hour. Your job then is to shovel away all those unnecessary words, all that junk, so that the readers can enjoy a fast ride in your beautiful car.

Exercise

The following sentences contain typical mistakes. See if you can quicken the pace of these sentences by getting rid of unnecessary words. Can you see what's wrong with these sentences?

1. Raymond thought it would take his entire lunch hour to pick up the new chainsaw, but for some reason today there was only a handful of shoppers.
2. Linda, wondering what Raymond planned to do with the chainsaw, strode to the liquor cabinet and poured herself a stiff drink from one of the bottles.
3. As Raymond passed through the lingerie department on his way to Tools, a whiff of expensive perfume almost got his attention.
4. It almost seemed to Linda that Raymond scheduled Gloria's visits for times when he knew that Linda wouldn't be home.
5. Raymond was able to climb the drainpipe and sneak into Gloria's dormitory room.

6. Raymond and Gloria proceeded to wrap the chainsaw for Linda's surprise party.

How did you do?

In the first sentence, the phrase "but for some reason" is meaningless. Take it away and you still have all the information.

In the second sentence, "from one of the bottles" adds nothing. Of course the drink was from one of the bottles; it certainly wasn't poured out of a drawer.

In the third sentence, the word "almost" is junk. The perfume must have gotten Raymond's attention or he wouldn't know that it was expensive or that it was there.

In the fourth sentence, "almost" is the culprit again. Does the writer mean it "almost seemed," or does he mean "it seemed"?

In the fifth sentence, the writer doesn't mean that Raymond "was able to climb." He means "he climbed." Don't have people "able to" do things when you can have them do them.

In the sixth sentence, the word "proceed" is junk. They didn't proceed to wrap it; they wrapped it. Don't have people "proceed to" or "begin to" do things when they can simply do them.

Perhaps you're thinking, "Geez, Gary, you're kind of a fanatic, aren't you?"

No. It's just that each of these words and phrases weighs about as much as a quarter-inch nail. Not very heavy. But try filling the back seat of your car with crates of quarter-inch nails and see how fast you go. You're never going to catch every unnecessary word. They grow like weeds in your manuscript. But you must be constantly vigilant. I've given you a few examples of unnecessary words that can keep your story from running at maximum efficiency. You can probably think of hundreds of others.

The Opening

You must get your story off to a good start. Editors will not read through several slow pages to see if things pick up later. The first few paragraphs are the most important. That's when the reader decides if he's going to stay for the ride. You must set a fast pace as soon as the starting gun is fired. Remember, this doesn't mean you have to go at breakneck speed. It means you must move with maximum efficiency while carrying all the luggage that's *necessary* for your particular story. You must write a good lead.

Many writers make the reader feel as if she were at the bottom of a steep hill, by beginning with background. Many college professors, despite the fact that they are unable to write a single coherent sentence, set out to write biographies, and the first thing they do is bludgeon the reader into boredom with long and intricate explanations of who was married to whom and which immigrant Scottish sheepherder fathered the girl who would marry the man whose daughter would become the mother of the fellow the book is about . . . zzz. A lot of novice novelists do the same thing.

I discussed this tiresome practice with Justin Kaplan, one of the nation's top biographers. Kaplan, who won the Pulitzer Prize and the National Book Award for *Mr. Clemens and Mark Twain*, said, "All that genealogical stuff bores the crap out of me. I mean if you don't even know a person to begin with, how are you going to keep his grandparents straight? A lot of biographies are just plain abysmal."

What's abysmal in biographies is abysmal in all other writing. Kaplan might as well have said, "If you don't even *care* about a person to begin with, why would you want to keep his grandparents straight?"

Make the reader care.

That's how you get your story off at a fast pace.

When I wrote an article on the Solcotrans blood bag for *Family Circle* magazine, I could have begun with a lot of background information, explaining what the bag was, when it was developed, and so on. But I knew my reader would be carried along by my story if I got him involved first, if I wrote a lead that made him care about my subject. I began:

> Do you ever worry that someday you might need an operation and there won't be enough blood in the blood bank to save you? Or it will turn out that you have some rare blood type, difficult to replace? Or you'll get contaminated blood?
>
> I do. Everybody does.
>
> These are nasty little fears, but they are not unrealistic in the age of AIDS. Blood supplies are diminishing all over the country because donors believe, incorrectly, that they can get AIDS from giving blood. And people who are going to receive blood have a higher rate of anxiety, fearing that they will get contaminated blood.

But what if you didn't have to depend on other people's blood? What if you could have transfusions of the best blood of all? Your own.

You can.

Now here is a very different lead. It's one of my favorites, the first paragraph from Scott Spencer's novel *Endless Love.*

> When I was seventeen and in full obedience to my heart's most urgent commands, I stepped far from the pathway of normal life and in a moment's time ruined everything I loved—I loved so deeply, and when the love was interrupted, when the incorporeal body of love shrank back in terror and my own body was locked away, it was hard for others to believe that a life so new could suffer so irrevocably. But now, years have passed and the night of August 12, 1967, still divides my life.

That lead does what a lead should do. It makes the reader care and it makes him ask questions. What on earth could the narrator have done at age seventeen? The narrator says, in effect, "I did something bad and I was punished." The author makes you care enough so that you want to stick around and find out exactly what happened. Another reason that I like the lead is that it is a little bit old-fashioned; it has the comforting quality of a fairy tale or the pirate tales we read as children. I think there is an instant of loneliness just before we pick up a book, and we're looking for an author to say, "Here I am, and I'm going to tell you a story." Spencer does that with the very first sentence.

Even though that paragraph from *Endless Love* is a good example of a fictional lead, there is something far more important that I want you to see in it, and that's why I'm going to use it again in a little while.

Make Things Happen

A fast pace means that something happens, then something else happens, and then another thing happens. Things just keep happening. There should be no long passages during which nothing happens. Even the horse-drawn carriage keeps moving; it doesn't stop. Putting it another way, if nothing is happening, why are you writing about it? You don't come home from work and describe to your spouse all the moments during the day when nothing was happening.

A few years ago a friend of mine named Steve Lowe gave me a section of manuscript from his novel in progress, *Aurora*. I took the pages home and read them, but I didn't have to read many to tell Steve why his manuscript would be rejected. Here is a passage:

> Sunrise began to paint its kaleidoscope of pastels on the desert of New Mexico. The cool August morning gave way rapidly to rising temperatures and to the gray-violet outline of butte and cactus. These forms, hidden for hours in darkness, now appeared in changing hues of pink and orange. Step by step, the sun's palette distributed its gentle splendor onto a vast canvas of still-ness.
>
> All night long the man-made glare of white light shone from massive staging platforms and block-shaped buildings that made up Section IV of Holloman Air Force Base. The strong white dots from these lamps now became less and less intense as the sun set to work establishing its light and warmth over all of the base's 160 square miles. When the sun showed its full shimmering roundness on the eastern horizon, the white lights faded in inten-sity and surrendered their usefulness. Observing this regular changing of the guard on the flat expanse below, the night's fingernail moon shone brilliantly against its borrowed setting of fragile indigo. It, too, began to fade, in obedience to the sun's powerful daily magic.

I used to write like that. Everybody used to write like that. We all begin as youthful writers no matter how old we are when first we write, and we are filled to the brim with poetic ways of describing things, especially sunsets and girls we yearn for. Desperate to im-press, and convinced that we are clever, we write passages that have no pace at all. From the first word to the last, the reader has not moved an inch. Nothing has happened. It's all description.

Description is the thing that makes what's happening more vivid; description should never be the thing that's happening.

When you write anything, don't "get around" to the people and the action. Put them right on every page in every paragraph. Descrip-tion is worthless if the reader doesn't care about the thing being described. Nobody cares if "Sunrise began to paint its kaleidoscope of pastels on the desert" unless there is on that desert some person they can identify with. Now be honest, do you really care what the weather is like in New Mexico right now? Probably not, unless you are in New Mexico, or have friends there. Well, of course I said all of this to Steve Lowe. And the next time I saw him he had rewritten the book seven times and sold it to Dodd, Mead, which published it in hardcover. It was later reprinted in paperback by Gold Eagle Books. This is how it starts.

> A mixture of snow squalls and chilling rain churned its way from the sharp peaks of the Canadian Rockies and whirled southward to Evergreen, Colorado. Institute Director Dennis Covino watched the storm, seeking solace in the September swirl of gray and white. Darts of rain pecked at the wall-sized window, making him edgy yet grateful; at least it gave him an excuse to turn his attention away from his animated guest. He palmed the desktop, turning toward the fat man, William Hendley of Hendley International Industries, who waved home another point, grabbing at the air above his bald head like a magician preparing a finale. Let it be the finale, the director thought. Wind it up, please God, wind it up.
>
> "Make no mistake, Doctor," Hendley continued. "The other side is still years — I might say light years — ahead of us in celestial research, and you know it. This project will send chills down their spines. Like the moon landing. We get there first. It'll freeze them in their tracks. We are needed, both of us, to keep the other side honest."
>
> Covino nodded. "The other side," he thought. Never "the Reds" or "the Russians," just "the other side." Devils versus angels.

In the passage I gave you from the unpublishable version of *Aurora* nobody did anything. In this passage from the published novel, there is only one sentence in which nobody is doing anything. Pace is people doing things, things happening, and the more things that happen on a given page, the faster the pace.

So what about nonfiction? Can "things happen" in nonfiction; can "people do things" in, let's say, a travel article about a train ride from Boston to San Francisco?

Sure. Just by coincidence, I happen to have written an article on that very subject and here is an excerpt from it.

> To get the most out of a cross-country train ride you must be a shameless voyeur. You roll through the small American towns and across the sprawling countryside and for a moment the people who live there are trapped beneath the glass of your window,

caught doing whatever it is they do when the train rolls by. If you are fascinated, as I am, by the houses we build, the signs we put up, and the way we wait for a bus, you can sit for hours composing on the canvas of your windowpane paintings that Estes or Rockwell or Wyeth would be proud of. There are the old men snatching cups of coffee in smoky diners, the teenaged girls feeling, at last, sexy, as they stand out by the drugstore, and, in a thousand backyards, boys tossing footballs, not knowing that a passing stranger on a train can see them pretending to be Joe Montana. There are endless images that you can never see from a plane. Or even from a bus because, surprisingly, people live a lot closer to the railroad tracks than they do to the highways.

The sky got cleaner west of Chicago and through the twilight hours Gail and I watched Iowa, an immense patchwork quilt of farms, always the same yet always changing in the contours of its slight hills, in the movement of its livestock, and in the way it absorbed the oblique sunlight that passed through scattered clouds. Miles slipped by with no dwellings on them and then, in the exact center of nowhere, a house would appear with smoke flying from its chimney and a light glowing in its kitchen. I imagined that in each house there was at least one dreamer who smiled when he heard the distant passing of the train.

Though this is a piece of nonfiction, not about any specific person, it is still filled with images of "people doing things" (old men drinking coffee, boys tossing footballs) and "things happening" (skies get cleaner, miles slip by, smoke flies from chimneys).

All of which brings us back to Scott Spencer and that first paragraph from *Endless Love*.

Many times when I tell a student that a page or several pages in his manuscript have to be cremated because they have no signs of life, he tells me that he reads lots of published books like that. "What about James Michener?" he says.

It's true that a few successful authors write pages of description that move with all the speed of a slug worm and get them published, either because their prose is so unusually compelling or their reputation is so lofty that the reader knows his persistence will be rewarded. But usually when a new writer thinks he has read published work that is as static as his own, it is an illusion. He is mimicking what he thinks he read, but a closer inspection will show him that there's a lot more going on in the published work. Scott Spencer is a fine example. Here, again, is the first paragraph from *Endless Love.*

> When I was seventeen and in full obedience to my heart's most
> urgent commands, I stepped far from the pathway of normal life
> and in a moment's time ruined everything I loved—I loved so
> deeply, and when the love was interrupted, when the incorporeal
> body of love shrank back in terror and my own body was locked
> away, it was hard for others to believe that a life so new could
> suffer so irrevocably. But now, years have passed and the night
> of August 12, 1967, still divides my life.

Spencer is using a rich and somewhat passive style here and it
would be easy for the reader to imagine that she had read some lovely
prose but not much "story." The illusion is that the pace is slow and
the prose still satisfying.

But just how slow is the pace? How much really happens in that
paragraph? Well, a kid *steps* away from a pathway, then he *ruins*
everything he loves, he *loves* deeply, then some love *gets interrupted,* and a body *shrinks* back, then another body *gets locked
away,* and others can't *believe* something, and a life *suffers,* and
then years *pass,* and a night *divides.*

All that in just ninety words.

Look at your own writing. Listen to it. Ask yourself: Are things
happening or are they just being? If they are just being, the pace is
not fast enough.

Exercise

See if you can pick up the pace of the following by eliminating
some sentences.

I dashed out of Crevin's cellar and ran to Nora's to tell her the
news. I couldn't tell Ma, because she was at work and I knew that if
I'd gone to Foshey Bones with my tale the old lady would have locked
me in a closet until Currie had bled to death. Foshey Bones had
one of those deep dark closets that always smell like old boots and
mothballs. It was behind the pantry downstairs and the door on it
creaked like an old bicycle pump.

Nora, figuring Old Crevins would be too befuddled to do anything
right, called an ambulance. Later she talked to one of her policeman

friends . . . a short, Scottish guy who had a face that was red, like he'd been sunburned . . . and found out that Currie had gone through surgery and was in a ward at Boston City Hospital. The hospital on Harrison Avenue was a big scary place where all of us kids had gone for tonsils and tooth pullings.

Nora came over to smoke cigarettes and drink coffee and make absolutely certain that she was the first to tell Ma what had happened.

"Shot?" Ma said when Nora told her. "Oh, my God. I knew something like this would happen."

Ma was stunned. Her face went white. Her hands trembled. She opened her mouth as if to say something else but couldn't get it out. She fell into a chair without even taking off her spring coat. It was a ratty-looking old coat, gray and threadbare, but she was attached to it. Ma was already convinced that we had moved into the crime capital of the world. This didn't help.

Proportion

Okay, so things shouldn't just *be* in your stories; things should happen.

But how often?

That question perplexes many writers. How often should something happen? Ned walks into a room and you want to say a few things about Ned before Ned does something. But how many things should you say about Ned? Should you tell the reader everything that Ned is wearing? Should you tell the reader where Ned was born? How much can you tell before something else should happen?

What are the proportions?

A woman recently sent me a novel in which she had three paragraphs of details about a character cutting his finger and then bandaging it. I told the author that if the character eventually developed gangrene and died because of the cut, then perhaps those paragraphs would have been in proper proportion to the significance of the information they contained. She would have covered some ground with the fuel she had burned. But since the cut was a minor point, she had spent far too many words. She hadn't gotten good mileage.

It would be lovely if there were a magic formula I could give you. But then writing wouldn't be art anymore; it would be some weird thing that's done the same way by all the people who know the magic formula. So I can't. But we can do some exploring together.

Your story is made up of what we'll call "story events" and "additional information." The story events are the things that happen, that make it a story, the things you say when you're telling somebody about the story. Like this:

"See, this guy named Joe is in jail for a couple of days for vagrancy and he overhears another guy talking about a robbery he pulled off and how the cops never found the cash, because he has such a clever hiding place. So Joe figures that this guy is just dying to boast about his clever hiding place if he can find someone who won't go and steal the money. So Joe pretends that he's in for murder and will probably be in prison for life, and he flatters the guy and the guy reveals the hiding place. So when Joe gets out two days later he goes to get the money, only the dead body of the guy's wife is also there and Joe gets sick and runs away."

Additional information is the description, the details, the background.

The pace of your story is set by the number of story events. The more story events you have per page, the faster the pace of the story. If every sentence were a story event, the thing would fly by, but it wouldn't really be a story. It would be a summary, like the one about Joe.

The additional information is as necessary to your story as costumes, sets, and lights are to a stage show. But if the story events are continually interrupted by thirty lines of description, detail, and background, the story will be a flop.

Some learning writers set too fast a pace. But most of them move too slowly. They put in too much description, detail, and background. Or, putting it another way: junk. They don't know when to stop.

So let's compare a typical unpublished manuscript with a typical published one.

Ted is a Florida writer who sent me a 100,000-word novel called *At the End of the Killing.* He's got a lot of talent, a good eye, and terrific story sense. His story is in excellent shape these days, but when he sent it to me it moved slower than a check from a publisher, which, believe me, moves pretty slowly. "Dear Ted," I wrote. "You have sent me a good 50,000-word novel. Unfortunately, you have smothered it to death under another 50,000 unnecessary words."

Ted laughs about his overwriting now, but I don't think he was amused when I told him to cut 50,000 words out of his novel.

Here are 600 or so words of the novel as Ted originally sent it to me. I will italicize the story events. Everything else is additional information.

> *Dan ran his eyes down the street, then across the street to the apartment buildings nestled in the gloom.* He would not know which building to enter until he crossed the street and checked the numbers.
>
> Cold wind swept a paper bag past his feet, then over his shadow, made full by the insipid rays of the street lamp above him. He stepped back to the corner of the building, to kill the shadow, to still the biting wind.
>
> Above the buildings he could see the incandescent splendor of a thousand stars — twinkling and glistening, they appeared to him as brilliant white diamonds clinging to invisible fingers. Diamonds reminded him of words from a Beatles' song his daughter used to sing around the house: Lucy in the Sky with Diamonds. She said the words implied an LSD trip. *The box in his hand made Dan wonder about the trip he was on.* Delivering a package at ten o'clock was absurd. But Peter had insisted on it, saying the man would not be home until this hour.
>
> Dan studied the buildings again. He would cross the street where he stood and hug the buildings for warmth while searching for the address. It was a freak cold wave cutting its way through Miami on this last day in March. The weatherman had promised that it would break by noon tomorrow.
>
> Eerie light danced and swirled in the cavern of air space between the rows of facing apartment buildings, the product of a fierce but futile battle for supremacy being waged by the half moon and the street lamps. Under this eerie light the street lay brooding. The street gave it off as though it were shimmering heat produced by the blinding midday sun. The brooding of the street lapped over the sidewalk and touched Dan's feet.
>
> Far away the urgent scream of a police siren rent the night air. Dan stomped his feet to warm them, then told himself to relax. The Machiavellian effect of the street was only an illusion, given the late hour and the cold. He turned his watch to the street lamp and noticed that six minutes yet remained until the hour of ten. He would cut the minutes in half and then cross the street.
>
> He thought of Peter, how noticeably Peter had aged in the four months since they had last played golf together, the bags

under his eyes darker, more pronounced, a new furrow creeping from the corner of his left eye toward his cheekbone. *Responding to a call from Peter, he had arrived in Peter's office at three in the afternoon*, surprised to find Peter less than his usual effervescent self. *Peter had wasted little time addressing the purpose of his phone call, the box resting on the edge of his desk. Would Dan Curtiss be so kind as to deliver the box?*

In the first paragraph Dan is standing on the street with a package in his hand. Seven paragraphs later he is still there. That would be okay if those seven paragraphs were filled with story events in flashback or in Dan's memory. But they are not. They are filled with the streetlights, the weather, etc. Ted could quicken the pace of this material by deleting everything but what I italicized.

> Dan ran his eyes down the street, then across the street to the apartment buildings nestled in the gloom. The box in his hand made Dan wonder about the trip he was on.
>
> Responding to a call from Peter, he had arrived in Peter's office at three in the afternoon. Peter had wasted little time in addressing the purpose of his phone call, the box resting on the edge of his desk. Would Dan Curtiss be so kind as to deliver the box?

Can you hear the difference in the pace? The second version is at top speed. You certainly don't have to write everything like that, but keep in mind that your reader is reading to see what happens next, not about lights, brooding streets, and weather.

Now here's the first six hundred words from published material of the same type, Robert Parker's bestselling Spenser novel *A Catskill Eagle* (Delacorte). Again, I'll italicize the story events.

> *It was nearly midnight and I was just getting home from detecting. I had followed an embezzler around* on a warm day in early summer trying to observe him spending his ill-gotten gain. The best I'd been able to do was catch him eating a veal cutlet sandwich in a sub shop in Danvers Square across from Security National Bank. It wasn't much, but it was as close as you could get to sin in Danvers. *I got a Steinlager from the refrigerator and opened it and sat at the counter to read my mail. There was* a check from a client, a consumer protection letter from the phone company, a threat of a field collection from the electric company, *and a letter from Susan. The letter said:*

*I have no time. Hawk is in jail in Mill River, California.
You must get him out. I need help too. Hawk will explain.
Things are awful, but I love you.*

Susan

And no matter how many times I read it, *that's all it said. It was
postmarked San Jose.*

I drank some beer. A drop of condensation made a shimmery
track down the side of the green bottle. Steinlager, New Zealand,
the label said. Probably some corruption between the Dutch Zee-
land and the English Sealand. Language worked funny. *I got off
the stool very carefully and went slowly and got my atlas and
looked up Mill River, California. It was south of San Francisco.* Population 10,753. I drank another swallow of beer. *Then
I went to the phone and dialed. Vince Haller answered on the
fifth ring.* I said it was me.

He said, "Jesus Christ, it's twenty minutes of one."

I said, "Hawk's in jail in a small town called Mill River south
of San Francisco. *I want you to get a lawyer in there now.*"

"At twenty minutes of fucking one?" Haller said.

"Susan's in trouble, too. *I'm going out in the morning. I
want to hear from the lawyer before I go.*"

"What kind of trouble?" Haller said.

"I don't know. Hawk knows. *Get the lawyer down there right
now.*"

"*Okay, I'll call a firm we know in San Francisco. They can
roust one of their junior partners out and send him down,* it's
only about quarter of ten out there."

"*I want to hear from him as soon as he's seen Hawk.*"

Haller said, "You okay?"

I said, "Get going, Vince," and hung up.

I got another beer and read Susan's letter again. It said the
same thing. I sat at the counter beside the phone and looked at
my apartment.

Bookcases on either side of the front window. A working fire-
place. Living room, bedroom, kitchen and bath. A shotgun, a rifle,
and three handguns.

"*I've been here too long,*" I said. *I didn't like the way I
sounded in the empty room.* I got up and walked to the front
window and looked down at Marlborough Street. Nothing was
happening down there. I went back to the counter and drank
some beer. Good to keep busy.

The phone rang at four twelve in the morning. My second
bottle of beer had gone flat on the counter, half finished, and I

was lying on my back on the couch with my hands behind my head, looking at my ceiling. *I answered the phone*, before the third ring.

At the other end, a woman's voice said, "Mr. Spenser?"
I said yes.
She said, "This is Paula Goldman. I'm an attorney with Stein, Faye, and Corbett in San Francisco and I was asked to call you."

As you can see, Parker doesn't allow too much additional information to get between story events. He keeps things moving. There are a lot of story events there, and I didn't even italicize the ones we're hearing for the second time. Parker doesn't stop to describe the curtains and couches in Spenser's apartment, he doesn't tell us how Spenser met Susan, or who exactly Hawk is. He puts us in the car and starts driving at a pretty good clip. He will drive us by everything he wants us to see, but you'd better bring a sandwich because he won't stop anywhere for lunch.

If this particular passage were written down as a paragraph-by-paragraph formula showing the proportion of "story event" sentences to "additional information" sentences, it would look like this:

Event. Event. Info. Info.

Event. Event.

Event.

Event. Event. Event. Event. Event. Event.

Event.

Info. Info. Info. Info. Info. Info. Event. Event. Info. Info. Event. Event. Info.

Info.

Event. Event.

Info.

Info. Event.

Info.

Info. Event.

Event.

Event.

Info.

Info.

Info. Info. Info.

Info. Info. Info. Info.

Event. Info. Info. Info. Info.
Event. Info. Event.
Event.
Event.
Event. Event.

As you can see, there are only two paragraphs that have more than one sentence and no story events.

I've used a published detective novel here to show fast pace because it was an unpublished detective novel that I used to show slow pace. Keep in mind that a detective novel like *A Catskill Eagle* is usually faster paced than the average novel. I haven't put this here as a formula for you to follow. It is just an example for you to measure yourself against. Take something that you have written and write the formula the way I have with Parker. Your proportions of events to additional material don't have to be the same as Parker's, but they should be a lot closer to that than to the example I gave you earlier.

A good pace means that the reader can hear the author saying, "This happened and then that happened and then this happened and then that happened and then. . . ."

Exercise

If you've written fiction, pick out five pages of a story or novel and underline the story events as I have in these examples. Listen for the sentences that say, "This happened and then that happened." Those are the story events.

When you are done, count the sentences that contain story events and the sentences that don't. Ask yourself if the results are closer to Ted's writing or to Robert Parker's.

Then, just think about it.

Story Events in Nonfiction

Your news story, magazine article, or nonfiction book is made up of story events, just as fiction is. The difference is that the story events in nonfiction don't add up to a plot; they add up to a body of information. But the generalizations about pace still apply. Keep those story events coming.

Sometimes in nonfiction, story events come in a logical, chronological sequence, as they do in fiction. For example, "I met Roseanne Barr in her trailer on the set. She came to the door, carrying a dish-cloth in her hand. 'I ain't got no coffee or nothing for you,' she said. She tossed the dishcloth aside. 'Don't hardly use these things no more.' "

But most nonfiction story events don't come in such neat little packages. When you are writing articles about the mating habits of mice or about high-tech medical diagnostic tools, most of your story events are sentences or phrases that are like a series of illustrative snapshots that you flash before the reader. These snapshots would be a hodge-podge in a work of fiction, but in nonfiction the rules are different. The story events don't have to build suspense, reveal character, etc. They just have to make an orderly contribution to the collection of information.

Here's an example:

A bottle of milk breaks, and then a guy gets through life, but then he sees a broken bottle and he realizes he won't live forever. Then some guy explains something and some people are going to be brought back to life, but nobody can find the cure. Then something won't work and a guy dies of cancer, and he's frozen, and something can't be repaired, then something else can't even be imagined, then some people get submerged in nitrogen and a guy bets his microscope and some worms don't give anybody a chance.

Those are all story events; they create a sense of forward move-ment. The movement is not toward a story ending like, "And in that golden moment I realized that Nushka Resnikoff had saved me from the Chinese bandits and that I would make her my wife," but toward a complete body of information. The events are from the beginning of an article I wrote about cryonics. It goes like this.

> Do you know why a bottle of frozen milk breaks?
>
> "Water expands when it freezes," says Dr. Roy Andersen, a professor of physics at Clark University. "Ice occupies more room than water, so the glass breaks."
>
> You can probably get through life without this information, but the next time you see a broken bottle of frozen milk consider this: the fact that the bottle breaks is one reason why you proba-bly won't live forever.
>
> Andersen uses the analogy of the milk bottle to explain why he thinks cryonics won't work. "Cryonics," a word which has not earned its way into the dictionary, is the practice of freezing the

newly dead, so that they can be brought back to life when a cure is found for whatever killed them.

As a legitimate science, its reputation among scientists ranks somewhere between phrenology and soothsaying. The reason?

"It simply won't work," Andersen says. "The body is mostly water. When you freeze a body the same thing that happens to the milk bottle takes place. The water expands and the cells are destroyed."

In other words, if a man died of cancer and was frozen, the discovery of a cancer cure would only begin to solve his problem. Scientists would also have to find a way to repair all those cells they destroyed when they froze him. And that, says Andersen, is a technology which can barely be imagined at this time. Virtually all of his colleagues would agree.

Nonetheless, there are at least five dead people in Berkeley, California, who would argue with Andersen if they could. They are at a place called Trans-Time, Inc., comfortably submerged in liquid nitrogen, and they died fully confident that they would be returning someday. While Andersen would gladly bet his microscope that these people will stay dead, he would probably have to agree with Curtis Henderson, founder of the first cryonics society in the country, that their chances of coming back are "better than the worms and the crematorium are going to give you."

So make sure that your nonfiction, as much as your fiction, has "something happening," and try to have at least one story event in each paragraph.

Exercise

Here is a short profile of police chief Joseph McNamara that appeared in *Gallery* magazine (Nov. 1989, no byline). After you've read it, make a list of all the things that McNamara *did* that were mentioned in the profile. Then make a list of all the things he *is* in the profile.

Then write a profile of similar length about your closest friend, including approximately the same number of things your friend did and things your friend is.

Joseph McNamara — He is the strong-willed chief of police from

San Jose, California, and the only police official in the U.S. with a Ph.D. from Harvard. Born in New York City, he is a former Harlem beat cop (as was his father) who worked his way up through the ranks.

He left the NYPD to become police chief of Kansas City, Missouri. Early into that administration, McNamara caused a departmental ruckus when he attended the funeral of a young black man killed by one of his officers, claiming, "it was the right thing to do." The move divided the department, but solidified the black community behind the new chief. Soon after, however, McNamara moved to his current post in San Jose, where he is passionate about the need for law enforcement to be given a stronger hand.

McNamara also is a noted author, having written two best-selling novels (*The First Directive* and *Fatal Command*); numerous newspaper articles; and one nonfiction book, *Safe and Sane*, a guide to protecting your family.

But, for the most part, McNamara contends with the burden of being a police chief. Last year, a drifter opened fire on a San Jose street. He eventually was killed, but not before one of McNamara's men lay dead, the result of a tragic crossfire. "We must control guns in this country," the chief stresses. "Criminals are armed for war. The cop must be given a fair chance."

McNamara is a logical choice for a federal post or, if he's willing to put aside the writing for a while, an elected slot in a conservative state such as California. Either way, he will be a major force.

Transitions

For a few frantic years during my childhood, I had my heart set on a life of crime. And when my friend Cliffie Cummings and I fantasized about all the daring heists we would pull off, we always agreed that we would make our getaway in a dark blue Ford sedan.

Eventually I turned to a life of writing instead of crime, but seldom does a workday pass when I do not think of that dark blue Ford. And I remind myself of what Cliffie and I knew even then: If you want to get from one place to another without being noticed, you drive a Ford, not a Maserati.

Whether you write fiction or nonfiction, you will make thousands of getaways during your career . . . getaways from one scene to another or from one subject to another. You want to make most of those getaways without being noticed. You will not use a Ford, however. Your means of transportation will be the transition.

A transition in writing is a word or group of words that moves you from one place to another. The "place" might be the location of a scene, a spot in time, or an area of discussion. The transition should be quick, smooth, quiet, reliable and logical, and it should bring to itself a minimum of attention. An example of such a transition occurs in the last sentence of my third paragraph: "Your means of transportation will be the transition."

By equating the subject of one paragraph (transportation) with the subject of the following paragraph (transitions), I made it appear as if we were smoothly continuing a discussion of transitions, though in fact the word *transition* had not even been mentioned up to that point. I used that sentence to make one paragraph *flow* into the other, instead of making an obvious and distracting leap.

Transitions occur throughout your writing, not just where paragraphs meet. But the gap between paragraphs is a "danger zone" where you risk losing readers unless you guide them carefully. If I had not used a transitional sentence, the change in paragraphs would have looked like this.

> You will not use a Ford, however.
> A transition in writing is a word or group of words that moves you from one place to another.

Readers would be jarred, confused. It sounds to them as if I'm changing the subject. Readers may continue even though they are annoyed. But what if I did this five more times in the same article?

If you're still not sure which of your words are transitions and which are not, it isn't because your wits are dim. It's because transitions, like most writing tools, often do two or more jobs at the same time. For example, "Winter arrived in waves of white violence" is a transition. But it is also description because it tells you something about the winter. The phrase "Winter arrived" would be a complete transition by itself.

So, to get your mind clearly focused on what a transition is, here are some common transitions. I call them "simple transitions" because they usually do just one job. They get readers through those danger zones, and introduce them to a new time, place, or subject.

Transitions of Time: "The following week." "In December." "By the time Poogie arrived." "After the prom." "Twenty years later."

Transitions of Place: "On the other side of the mountain." "In Black Eagle, Montana." "Meanwhile, back at the ranch." "When we got to Daniel's place."

Transitions of Subject (or to a different aspect of the same subject): "Consequently." "In this manner." "On the other hand." "In contrast to." "Despite all this."

(One other common type of transition doesn't require the use of words at all, but rather spaces, such as skipped lines, new chapters, etc.)

As you study these simple transitions, searching for common denominators, notice that most, not all, of them begin with prepositions. But all do have one thing in common. *They all make a connection between what the reader has just read and what he is about to read, by implying the relationship between those two bodies of information.*

The examples I've given you are perfect transitions. They're short and direct. You should use them often and you can generally be certain that they are doing the job.

But they are not enough.

If you expect to hold reader attention, you must consistently find new and entertaining ways to deliver your messages. A story in which every tenth sentence contains a phrase like "five minutes later" or "in the meantime" will give readers the sense that they are being nagged by somebody in the other room. They will either turn to the words of another writer, or skim through your material to get it over with quickly. So you must be, in a word, creative.

Before I offer tips to help you invent smooth transitions, I want to tell you some of the things you should *not* do.

Don't Use Long Transitions

A great way to destroy the pace of your fiction and nonfiction, and put your reader into a coma, is to use long transitions.

A transition should be short, direct, and almost invisible. In the manuscripts that I read I find that many writers are afraid of leaving something out, so they account for every moment.

Lenny meets Irving at the Paddock Lounge on Friday night and they decide to hijack a bagel truck. They work out their plans and they go home. The bagel hijacking is scheduled for Tuesday. A good transition would be, "On Tuesday they met in the parking lot of Louise's delicatessen. The bagel delivery truck showed up exactly at ten o'clock."

But the writer thinks that the reader is going to notice that Saturday, Sunday, and Monday are missing, so to explain she writes something like this:

> On Saturday Lenny was still thinking about the bagel hijacking. How many bags of bagels would there be, he wondered. When he got to the rope factory he avoided talking with his colleagues for fear of giving anything away. At lunch he didn't go to Danny's Grille, the regular place where all the guys usually gathered. Instead he went to The Clinton Cafe. Should I order a bagel, he wondered. No, it would look suspicious. Instead he ordered a grilled cheese and tomato sandwich on whole wheat toast and a glass of chocolate milk. Irving was all right, he thought, a nice guy, sharp. When the five o'clock whistle blew at the rope factory Lenny went straight home. There was a Knicks game on, so he watched it. At ten o'clock he went to bed. It was hard to sleep, thinking about bagels. He read for a while. Then he turned off the light, rolled over, went to sleep.
>
> On Sunday morning he woke up at. . . .

This sort of thing erodes the pace of your story. It is a sedative. You are not writing a calendar. If it's of no significance to the story, the reader doesn't care what happened on Saturday, Sunday, and Monday.

Even writers who are comfortable writing, "On Tuesday morning they met in the parking lot of Louise's delicatessen," are often uncomfortable with the simplicity of a transition that can cover three thousand miles or twenty years in a few words. They suspect that large amounts of time or space demand large amounts of words. Wrong. "Forty years later they met on the other side of the world," is a perfectly good transition. Or even, in a science fiction story, "Eighty million years later they met on a planet which didn't even exist when they were first introduced." There are no limits to the amount of time and space that can be covered by a simple transition. You should jump over everything that's not important, no matter how long it took or how much space it occupied.

Write this on a piece of paper and hang it over your desk:

A STORY IS NOT EVERYTHING THAT HAPPENED. IT'S EVERY IMPORTANT THING THAT HAPPENED.

AN ARTICLE IS NOT EVERYTHING THAT'S TRUE. IT'S EVERY IMPORTANT THING THAT'S TRUE.

Don't Write a Scene When a Transition Will Do

If you have written an entire book that is moving too slowly, chances are you have written dozens of unnecessary scenes that should be replaced by simple transitions.

I received such a book from Ruth Rosing, a California writer who sent me a biography-in-progress of her late husband, Val Rosing. Val was an interesting guy, a womanizer, a gambler, the roller skating champion of Russia, and one of the most acclaimed opera singers and producers of his time. Ruth had done a fine job with her book, but she knew the pace was too slow.

I read it for her and I found that the story would speed along for ten or so pages and then hit a wall. That was because, like many writers, Ruth was writing scenes when she should have been writing transitions.

Val Rosing traveled often, and Ruth had the habit of taking the reader to the train station, putting him on the train with Val, showing him the scenery through the window, and so forth, when she should have gotten Val from place to place with a simple transition

"Dear Ruth," I wrote "You have a tendency to write entire scenes when all you need is a transition. If Val goes from Switzerland to Russia you should write, 'Val went to Russia,' and then get on with what happened in Russia, unless something happened along the way this is important to your story, or reveals character. If the trip from Switzerland to Russia was uneventful, then don't include it. When you use several paragraphs to make a transition that could be made in a single sentence you are driving with your foot on the brake."

Ruth replaced all those unnecessary scenes with transitions and the book now has a much faster pace. Look at your manuscripts. Do you have unnecessary scenes? Do you have long passages when nothing eventful happens? Get rid of them. Here's another sign for you to hang over your desk:

WHEN YOU WRITE A STORY LEAVE OUT THE BORING STUFF.

Don't Explain When You Don't Have To

New writers often write long-winded and unnecessary transitions because they're afraid that the short phrase hasn't said enough. They try to *explain* when they should simply *acknowledge.*

For example, let's say a writer needs to get his character, Sam, from a scene in Sam's apartment to a scene at a church, and nothing important to the story is going to happen between those two places. A simple and obvious transition would be "Sam drove to the church." The writer simply acknowledges that Sam did get from the location of one scene to the location of another, and goes on with the story. It might look like this.

> As Sam placed the books back on the shelves, he felt a tear form at the corner of his eye. He knew he would miss this apartment.
> Sam drove to the church. Susan was waiting for him and she was not smiling. "Where have you been?" she asked.

Simple. But many new writers, suspicious of the easy and the obvious, go on to explain in a clutter of unnecessary words with something like this.

> Sam moved slowly down the stairs of the apartment building. He walked across the street and climbed into his car. He turned the ignition key and put the car in gear. Then he pulled out into Maple Street traffic. When he reached Wilder Avenue he took a left and drove for three blocks. At Warren Street he waited for a red light that seemed to take forever. Finally he got onto Carver. He could see the Bethany church up ahead.

Reading this sort of thing is just like waiting for that red light to change. You're eager to get moving again. The writer doesn't need all of this because his reader is familiar with the routine of starting an engine, turning the wheel, etc. "Sam drove to the church" is short-hand for all of that. The transition does all the work.

Don't Acknowledge When You Should Explain

Many writers try to force transitions to do work that should have been done by the writer elsewhere in the story or article. They misuse the transition in a way that is the reverse of what I have just discussed. They *acknowledge* when they should *explain.*

Years ago I heard a true story, which I've tried to track down in order to demonstrate this point. I couldn't find the story at the library, so I'll just dredge it up from memory as best I can.

In the 1930s, a writer wrote adventure serials for one of the London monthlies. At the end of each installment the hero (we'll call him Ben) would be in some dreadful situation. Of course, thousands of readers would wait eagerly for the next issue of the magazine to see what would happen. At the end of one installment, the writer had Ben trapped at the bottom of a twenty-foot pit with no tools, no ladder, and no one around to hear his cries. I'm sure the pit was dark and the walls were slippery, and let's throw in a couple of snakes for good measure. For a month people all over London discussed Ben's plight. How would good old Ben get out of this mess? Unfortunately, the writer of the serial was wondering the same thing and by the time his deadline arrived, he had not come up with any brilliant solution. So he began his episode with, "After Ben got out of the pit, he proceeded to walk toward the city," a transition that, no doubt, put his readers into a lynching spirit and did serious damage to his writing career.

The writer did not make his getaway without being noticed. His transition was a bright red Maserati with the words *GETAWAY CAR* painted all over it. Of course, he got caught.

"After Ben got out of the pit" would be a perfectly decent transition if climbing out of a twenty-foot pit were as routine an activity as, say, eating dinner. The reader will accept your acknowledgment of changes in time or place only if those changes could have been accomplished in *normal, routine ways*, or in unusual ways that you made believable earlier in your story. (If you tell us on page one that Superman can fly, we will have no trouble accepting the transition, "On Tuesday, Superman flew to Chicago.")

So, as you read your manuscript in search of flaws, stop at each transition and ask yourself: Did anything unusual or hard to believe happen in the gap covered by this transition? If the answer is yes, go back and lay some foundation so that when the transition comes along, readers will accept it easily and be transported without asking a lot of questions.

Do Not Use Transitions to Conceal Information

As a writer, you have entered into a covenant with the reader. The whole writing-reading process depends on the writer and reader each having faith that the other will not violate the terms of the covenant. If the covenant were written out, it would contain a clause concerning transitions that would look like this:

> Reader agrees that a transition such as "Sam drove to the church" can encompass all the routine acts of starting a car, taking left turns, etc.
>
> In turn Writer agrees not to use such transitions to deprive reader of information which is rightfully his.

In other words, don't write something like:

> After the wedding, they stood out on the church steps, posing for the photographer. Suddenly Sam clutched his chest. The violent heart palpitations that had so frightened him during the drive to the church had returned. He heard Susan say, "What's wrong?" and then his world plunged into darkness and he felt himself falling.

Your reader got into the car with Sam and accepted quick passage in the belief that this was an ordinary drive to the church. He didn't see a sign of any heart palpitations then, and if you now say that there were some, you shatter the reader's belief that "Sam drove to the church" tells him all he needs to know.

Don't Write Transitions That Distract the Reader

In general, your writing improves as your words become more specific. If you can make your character trot, dash, or lope, the writing will be more effective than if she simply "runs." She will get more attention because the more precise word will focus her more sharply and provide more information about her state of mind or the situation. However, in writing transitions your goal is somewhat different. You don't want to attract attention. You want to show the reader point *A* and point *B*, but the passage between the two should be quick and uneventful.

If you want to get Diana from a scene at home with her husband to a scene with Penelope, her neighbor across the street, and you write, "Diana dashed across the street to Penelope's," you will distract your reader with the vivid picture of Diana dashing and you will also occupy him with the question, "Why is Diana dashing?" You will, in effect, have created an unnecessary scene. The best way to get Diana and the reader across that street without being noticed is by using a bland verb that nobody looks at twice (*Diana went across the street*), or a phrase that tells the reader that the trip has already taken place (*When she got to Penelope's house . . .*). This second type of transition often will jar your reader unless you have "pointed" to it. I'll explain that later.

Now let's see how this sort of unnecessary visual distraction can muck up an entire scene.

This is an example from a story by one of my students. In her story, two characters, Jan and Linda, were talking to each other at a party. She wanted to get Jan alone into a conversation with Jim. She had to create a transition between these two conversation scenes, but she also had to get rid of Linda in the process. So she wrote:

> Linda was called away by Mrs. Briggs to join in a game of charades, and Jan drifted across the room to where Jim waited.

The problem here is that as the reader moves into the Jan-Jim conversation, he still has that unnecessary game of charades imbedded on his mind. In fact, he might be distracted enough to glance across the room at the game of charades all through the Jan-Jim dialogue. (Imagine that you are carrying on a conversation in a room where a game of charades is being played.) The game of charades should never have been brought out and flashed in front of the reader's eyes. The writer should have written, "Linda was called away, so Jan . . ." or "When her conversation with Linda ended, Jan . . ." Keep it simple.

Up to now I've given you some "don'ts" about transitions. Here are some "dos," some tips to help you write transitions that work.

Point to the Transition

Anybody who has carried on a secret affair or pulled off a surprise birthday party knows the value of this advice. If you leave the house in the morning, saying, "It looks like I might have to work late at the office tonight," nobody will get suspicious when you call at five and say: "Hi, hon. Bad news. I'm afraid I was right about having to work late tonight." You create an expectation and then you fill it.

Transitions in writing often work the same way. If you write, "After the PTA meeting, Gloria flew to Düsseldorf, West Germany," the reader is not going to go along calmly. He will stop and say, "Hey, wait a minute. You mean my friend Gloria has been planning this trip to Düsseldorf and she never even mentioned it?" Your reader will find the transition hard to take. But if you had pointed to the transition with something like, "Gloria had a hard time concentrating on the meeting. She kept thinking about the excitement of two weeks in West Germany. She glanced at her watch nervously. The plane for Düsseldorf was leaving at midnight," the reader will climb aboard that plane without a second thought.

Use Key Words

It doesn't do any good to point to a transition if the reader doesn't remember the "pointer," the word or words you used to create the expectation. In my last example, the word *Düsseldorf* filled the expectation easily. It is precise and memorable, and it doesn't carry many other connotations to confuse readers. Those qualities make it a good key word for transitions.

For example, let's say you are writing a magazine article about Joel Asher, a movie star who was murdered, and you are tracing the events of his last week. It was the final week of filming a movie and in paragraph six you write, "A little after ten a.m. on Friday, Ann Wright, the producer, invited Asher to a wrap-up party to be held that night at her house." Then you cover other events and you don't get to the party until paragraph fifty-four. You begin that paragraph, "The wrap-up party began at nine o'clock, but Asher didn't show up until almost midnight." The reader will accept the transition easily and get oriented quickly because the only time he saw that word, *wrap-up*, was when the invitation was extended. Expectation of this event was created. If you began paragraph fifty-four with, "The party at Ann's began at nine o'clock," your reader might become disoriented because he has seen "Ann" in several places, perhaps even at another party.

Use Bridge Words

My friend Nicky, who is nine years old, came into the living room the other day to tell me about a Tom and Jerry cartoon. It seems that Tom was concerned about Jerry stealing cheese from the refrigerator, so Tom very wisely stretched barbed wire across the kitchen to prevent theft. At this point in this story, Nicky looked up at me and said, "Speaking of barbed wire," and he went on to tell me about a geography class quiz that included a question about barbed wire.

At age nine, Nicky has already learned that one of the demands we make of speakers and writers is that they show us what connects the current topic with the topic of a moment ago. Metaphorically, our demand might look like this: "I won't believe you have taken me across the river until you show me the bridge that you used." So writers and speakers use "bridges," similar words or phrases, one on each side of the river, to imply a connection.

In routine conversations, we don't ask much in the way of bridges. We will accept anything from Nicky's awkward "speaking of barbed wire" to the even more desperate, "This stalk of celery reminds me of my brother Larry. Larry would never eat his celery. He's out in California now. I ought to give him a call."

Readers, however, are not so tolerant. They expect you to lead them along a route that is straight and smooth. They want to cross bridges that are well built and well placed, not bridges that creak and sway because they were thrown together helter-skelter on a whim.

Make Transitions Seem Logical

When you write fiction, your scenes usually emerge from something that happened in a previous scene. So fiction, when it is well written, is usually connected by transitions that are logical, even if they are not smooth. In nonfiction, however, you don't usually have the built-in logic of "time moves forward," or "events cause consequences," and so on. What you usually have before you start to write nonfiction is a list of subjects you want to write about, and you must find transitions to link them. But you're writing about something specific. You're not just some guy eating celery and rambling on about his brother. So it's not enough simply to convince your reader that subject E can be associated in the mind with subject D. You must also convince him, with your bridge words, key words, or other transitional devices, that the subject is relevant to the matters at hand, that it is a *logical* progression.

In the March 1982 issue of *Esquire*, Frank Rose wrote an article called "Walking on Water," an update on the California surfing scene. Here's how he used a bridge word to make a logical transition from a discussion of sponsors to a discussion of media.

> Unfortunately, like the good surfing spots, most potential sponsors have already been taken.
> The scramble for sponsors makes surfers especially media conscious.

Rose made a smooth transition here because he chose the logical bridge words, words that were specific and memorable as key words and words that, unlike Nicky's "barbed wire," represent *the subject we have been talking about.*

So, whether you see your transitions as getaway cars or bridges or hard-working donkeys or any other means of transportation, keep in mind always that the trip should be as short and uneventful as possible. You want your reader to be so enthralled with where you have taken him that he doesn't even know how you got him there.

Chapter Six

Description

Description Is a Slave, Not a Master

Description is the most overrated aspect of writing by beginners. Long before they develop story sense, most writers, including me, strive for some sort of poetic beauty with description. They choose their adjectives with great care. They agonize over every adverb. In voluminous detail they inform the reader about the slope of the snowy mountain, the color of the lover's hair, the sparkle in the eye, the majesty of the prairie, the yellowing of the pages, the peeling of the plaster in the attic. And what is very difficult to see when you're starting out as a writer is that if you haven't created a fast-moving story or a fascinating piece of nonfiction, nobody gives a damn about the slope of the mountain.

Description is a slave, a helper, an enhancer, and if there is nothing to enhance, description serves no purpose.

Imagine this. You walk into a theatre in Greenwich Village. The stage is bare. There is no set, no actors. How long will you sit there staring at the empty stage? Now imagine that actors in plain street clothes strut onto the bare stage and they talk to each other, they act out a compelling story. Now you're hooked. You will sit there in front of that bare stage as long as the story is interesting. Now imagine that behind the actors a great and colorful set appears. Suddenly the actors are in costumes. Lights come on. Props arrive. Windows, doors, stairways, all take their natural place in the story. Now the story is even more interesting. Now imagine that the actors leave. Suddenly, there are no people, no voices, no conflicts. All that's left is that beautiful set and the props. How long are you going to sit there staring at it?

"Not very long, Gary," is the correct answer.

The description you write is like that beautiful set. It is only there to enhance the actions of the actors. Without the actors and the story it is worthless.

Keep Description Short

Have you ever wondered why some of the highly touted classics, the allegedly great books of the ages, are often as dull as cold pancakes?

One reason is too much description. It wasn't too much description then, but it is now.

"How's that, Gary?"

Well, consider the kangaroo, for example. Let's say that in 1817 some schoolmarm from Scituate, Massachusetts, took a voyage to Australia and came back to write about her adventure. No doubt she would include the kangaroo in her story, and if she could write well, a lengthy description of a kangaroo could be quite fascinating. Not too many people in Scituate had seen a kangaroo, or even a picture of one, by 1817. The writing would have worked.

If a descendant of that woman went to Australia today and came back and turned out long descriptions of kangaroos, you wouldn't read them. You'd say, "What does she think I am, an idiot? I know what a kangaroo looks like."

In fact, just about everybody knows what a kangaroo looks like. They've seen them in zoos, in movies, and on *Wild Wild World of Animals.* Just the word *kangaroo* is enough to describe a kangaroo.

Unless you are writing science fiction or telling tales from some exotic land, chances are the reader has seen one of everything you describe. He will not tolerate long descriptions of things he can already see. Imagine how you would describe an airplane to an African tribesman who had never seen one. Then imagine how much shorter your description would be if you tried to describe it to the average American.

The reader's brain holds an enormous catalog of pictures. He has seen an infinity of images on television and in movies, photographs, and real life. He knows how a vast number of things function, how they relate to one another. You don't have to describe them all.

For example, let's take aviation again, because it has gone from the unknown to the commonplace during the past century. What if your story takes place at an airport and you want to set the scene by creating a picture of a busy airport before you put your characters into action. Fifty years ago you might have gone on for pages, describing a runway as a long strip of land that airplanes roll on before they fly, explaining that a stewardess is a woman who wears a particular type of uniform and serves coffee on the plane. And you might write a long description of the control tower, since nobody would have seen 112 airport movies at that point.

Today you might begin the same story:

> La Guardia at noon. Businessmen and harried stewardesses rushing for the gates. Airplanes, too many of them, lined up on the runways. Porters and hustlers and gypsy girls with cookies and flowers for sale all working the terminal while the public address system crackles with flight numbers and in locker 301 the contents of a black suitcase tick off the last seconds in the lives of thirteen people.

How are the stewardesses dressed?
What color are the airplanes?
Do the porters have uniforms on?
What's in the black suitcase?

You can answer these questions and dozens more without further description, because you've *seen* all these things, either in real life or on television.

Keep description short. Aim for that density I talked about earlier by using a few carefully chosen words. The reader already has most of the pictures. You're just telling him which ones to look at.

The advice to work with images already in the readers' heads applies not just to readers in general, but also to specific groups of readers.

For example, if I had written an article about stock car racing for an auto magazine, I wouldn't have spent many words describing the general atmosphere of stock car races. That would have been commonplace to my readers, and they would have turned to the next article quickly.

But I didn't write my article for a car magazine. I wrote it for a weekly entertainment magazine, specifically for readers who had never gone to the stock car races, but might like to try it. My description goal, then, was to show what the regular fan takes for granted and to show it in terms the general public is familiar with. I wrote in part:

Stock car racing is an experience with a mood and texture all its own. A carnival atmosphere clings to the speedway, whether it's slick and modern or crumbling at the corners. The smell of hot dogs and candied apples rushes to meet you in the parking lot, and when you get inside you are greeted by the roar of anxious engines. A kind of sweet nostalgia rises up from the infield and latches on to the breeze sweeping through the bleachers. Grease and noise that would horrify you at home take on a poetic luster, and even if talk of hemispherical head engines and four-barrel carbs means nothing to you, you get caught up in the enthusiasm that other people are feeling about these things.

When you are describing things and places the reader has seen, keep description short by reminding him of the pictures he has on file.

When you are describing things and places the reader has not seen, keep description short by using pieces of the pictures he has on file to create new pictures.

Exercise

For each item on the following list, write a paragraph describing it to someone who has never seen one.

Then for each item write a sentence or two that includes the short description you would use for the average reader. For example, if you were writing a short story in which a reporter showed up with a tape recorder, you wouldn't say that the tape recorder had a play button, a record button, a fast-forward button, and a long cord that the reporter could use to plug it in. That would be ridiculous. But you might write, "He came in carrying a gray portable tape recorder, about the size of a dictionary. It looked as if it had been banged around a few times."

1. A hot-air balloon
2. A fashion show
3. A modern kitchen
4. A gun
5. A national political convention

Putting Description in Motion

Another shortcoming of those big blocks of description that so infatu-
ated readers a century ago is that they're static. They just sit there.
They don't move.

The writer shows you the sunset, and gives you a list of colors in
the afternoon sky. Then he shows you the clouds, even tells you
what animals they're shaped like. Then he sketches the trees in the
foreground, specifies the color of the dirt, points out the assorted
wildlife, and finally describes a pair of lovers snuggled down under
one of those trees.

It's a photograph in words.

That was fine when people didn't have photographs. But today
they not only have photographs, they have television and movies.
They also have cars they can drive to thousands of places from which
to view real life. They have movement. Their pictures move, and if
you are going to capture reader attention your pictures have to move,
too. So think of your description not as a photograph but as a motion
picture.

Description that moves is description that works.

There are two ways you can set your description in motion. The
first, which you can always do, is to put the description itself into
action by using active verbs and pictures of movement. The second,
which you can usually do, is to sprinkle the description throughout
the action of the story.

Keep in mind that *motion* doesn't necessarily mean that something has moved from Point *A* to Point *B*. It means that things are
doing something instead of *being* something.

Here are some items I employed to dress the stage in a category
romance I once wrote: Dark wooden cottages. Spruce and pine trees.
Charcoal. A wide sky. An asphalt road. Sand on the street. A green
wooden cottage.

And here are the descriptive paragraphs putting those things in
motion.

> "It's lovely," Carol said. She stared out at the quiet streets of
> dark wooden cottages. Most of them were surrounded by spruce
> and pine trees and built facing south to catch the sun in front
> and the shade in back. People in shorts sat on lawn chairs reading
> paperbacks. Kids tossed Frisbees in the yards. Burning charcoal

sent the smell of barbecued burgers wafting across the road and through the open windows of the car.

As they neared the end of Lower County Road, the sky seemed to grow wider, and the asphalt road all but disappeared under a layer of sand. Bonnie took a wide left turn where the road ended, and pulled to a stop in front of a green wooden cottage.

To make your description more active, be on the lookout for the verb "to be." When you see "is," "was," or "were," it might be an opportunity to bring the description to life either by giving an object something to do or by letting it interact with a person. For example:

Passive description: There are two tall oak trees in the yard.

Active: Two oak trees tower over the house.

Interactive: When Joanne was a kid she used to climb the two tall oak trees in front of the house.

Exercise

Here is a list of environments and some of the things in them that you can use for description. With each one, try first to make the descriptions move by using active verbs, by making the things *do* something. Then try to make the description move before the reader's eyes by putting a character into the scene and revealing the objects through his actions. I'll do the first one as an example.

1. A church containing carpets, pews, and candles.
2. A bagel bakery containing bagels, bagging machines, and aluminum pans.
3. A view of Switzerland containing trees, mountains, and railroad tracks.
4. A house on the night before Christmas, containing silence, stockings, and dreams.
5. A health club containing a swimming pool, a basketball court, and Nautilus machines.

For number one I asked myself first what my descriptive objects do. I decided that carpets can lie, line, or cover; candles can glow, stand, line, or shrink; and pews can fill, cover, crowd, or face. I decided to move my descriptive objects past the reader's eyes by writing, "The carpets stretched all the way to the altar," "The candles glowed on both sides of the sanctuary," and "The rows of empty pews waited for the morning worshipers." When I put a person into the scene I wrote, "He walked on the carpet." "He lit a candle." "He slipped into a pew."

You do the others. Some are quite difficult, but they will help you think of description as a motion picture instead of a photograph.

Use Details That Work

Every person, place, thing, or action that you describe will have many qualities, such as weight, color, texture, speed, thickness, sound, and temperature. You certainly don't have to rattle off a whole list of them to capture your reader. It takes very few words to create a picture if the words are chosen carefully.

If your goal were simply to show the reader a picture, you could describe the weight of an object, or its color, or its texture—almost any fairly vivid detail—and the reader would see it. But writing that works doesn't just show the reader a picture. It also gets him to look at it in a certain way.

For example, if I just want you to see the trousers that a man is wearing I could tell you their color (blue), the fabric they are made of (denim), or the price he paid for them ("He came in wearing eighty-dollar jeans"). But description usually involves greater goals than that, and if I wanted you to look at the pants as an aspect of this man's sexuality, his attractiveness, the detail I choose might be *tight*. It doesn't take any more words to write "tight jeans" than it does to write "blue jeans" or "denim jeans." But I have gotten more for my words by choosing the detail that does the work I want it to do.

For another example, let's say that there's a car in your story. There are hundreds of details about that car, and you could use almost any one of them to show the car to your reader. Tell him it is a Chevrolet Monza and he will see it. Tell him it has a flat tire and he will see it. Tell him the hood is up and he will see it. The reader will extend the lines.

But when you write a story or article, you have more in mind than simply creating pictures. You want to plot, you want to characterize, you want to editorialize, you want to evoke feeling. Establish your goals, and then choose the descriptive details that will work toward those goals.

If your goal is to characterize the driver as reckless, you might describe the car as being "pitted with dents."

If you're trying to show a typical middle-class suburban family, you might mention that the car is a "station wagon."

If your piece concerns ecology or consumerism, the car might be a "gas guzzler."

If you're trying to be funny, the car might be a "pile of scrap metal on wheels."

Any one of these will show the reader a car, but each will get him to look at the car in a specific way, and that specific view is what reveals information about a character, situation, or subject.

Exercise

Think of a person, either someone you know or a public figure. Now think of two unrelated characteristics of this person, such as that he is handsome and he is poor, or that she is intelligent and she is greedy.

Next, using three sentences, describe the person coming into a room so that your description communicates that first characteristic to the reader.

Again, using three sentences, describe the person coming into a room in a way that communicates the other characteristic.

Don't Borrow Description

The key to coming up with original description is to STOP and THINK.

Sometimes your story needs a cop to come to the door so, without even thinking about it, you write, "A burly policeman came to the door."

This is the time to stop and think.

Does this police officer have to be burly? Did you even stop to think about what burly means? Walk to that door. Open it. Take a good look. There is an individual policeman there, not a clone of fifty that you saw on television last month. Is he really burly, or is he slight? Does he wear eyeglasses? Does he have red hair? Maybe he is a she. Imagine this person off duty, wearing street clothes. Now put the uniform back on. What do you see? Describe it.

The same thing with places. Maybe you want your teenaged boy to find a canvas bag full of stolen money buried on the beach. Automatically you make it a sunny day with the smell of salt in the air and waves rushing to an uncluttered shore. Because that's the way beaches are in the stock descriptions that have been etched into your mind. That's fine for some beaches. But is that what you really want, or are you just not thinking? There are rainy days on the beach, too, and you can't always smell the salt, and quite often the shore is littered with seaweed or that other disgusting stuff that looks like knots of dead snakes.

There's nothing wrong with a beach that has a blue sky and sunshine, but make sure it's *your* blue sky and *your* sunshine. The point is, think. Put yourself on that beach. Don't just mimic all the other beach descriptions. *Experience it for yourself.* It is the skinny, red-headed police officer and the cloudy day at the beach that make your writing believable.

In writing nonfiction, even though you usually have seen or experienced what you are describing, it's easy to slip into the habit of typing stock description unless you really look at what your are seeing. You are not just describing what you see. You are describing *how* you see it. And if you don't make your own observation, you'll be making somebody else's.

I once interviewed Bobby Riggs, the tennis player. It would have been easy to repeat the stock description of him as a cocky male chauvinist. But I wanted to see him with my own eyes. So before I interviewed him, for a while I watched him operate in the lounge of a tennis club. The image that came to my mind was of a whirlwind, a little storm, and that's how I described him at the beginning of my article.

> Bobby Riggs has a way of storming into a town. It's the way he's come into hundreds of towns since his gravy days of playing Margaret Court and Billie Jean King.
>
> He arrives, all noise and motion, a little wound up munchkin of a man tossing Sugar Daddies, signing autographs, ribbing the gals, and grinning behind his eyeglasses because people still rush to pump his hand.
>
> He still craves action and attention. He's still an admiration junkie and if he can't get it on television in front of forty million

people, he'll get his fixes one or two at a time in places like Westboro.

Anne Bernays, the novelist, once said something to me which I think is particularly appropriate in a discussion of description.

"I've learned," Anne said, "that nice writing isn't enough. It isn't enough to have smooth and pretty language. You have to surprise the reader frequently; you can't just be nice all the time. Provoke the reader. Astonish the reader. Writing that has no surprises is as bland as oatmeal. Surprise the reader with the unexpected verb or adjective. Use one startling adjective per page."

I smiled at her and she knew what I was thinking. The word "startling" had surprised me. It was a startling adjective.

I have found this tip very helpful. When I write I try to keep that word "startling" in mind. I know I can't startle my reader with "a burly police officer." But a police officer who stutters or wears a hairpiece or a skirt . . . that will keep my reader interested.

Exercise

1. Describe a poolroom without mentioning the green felt, the clack of the balls, or the haze of cigarette smoke.
2. Describe a professional basketball player without mentioning his height.
3. Describe the ocean without mentioning waves or boats.
4. Describe the place where you are now, without using "is," "are," "was," or "were."

Use Imagery in Description

In writing, imagery means the creation of one image to stand in for another image, or a series of other images, or a concept that cannot be explained without imagery.

The important thing about imagery, as we discuss it, is that it is representational. "The bull walked into a china shop" is not imagery, because you are saying there really is a bull and a china shop. "The man was like a bull in a china shop" is imagery because you are using the images of a bull and a china shop to show us something else, the clumsiness of a man.

There are a lot of reasons why we use imagery in our writing. Sometimes the right image creates a mood we want. Sometimes an image can suggest connections between two things. Sometimes an image can make a transition smoother. We use images to show intention. *(Her words were fired in a deadly monotone and she gunned down the three of us with her smile.)* We use imagery to exaggerate. *(His arrival in that old Ford always sounded like a six-car pileup on the Harbor Freeway.)* Sometimes we don't know why we are using imagery; it just feels right. But the two main reasons we use imagery are:

To save time and words.

To reach the reader's senses.

By working with familiar images that are already implanted in the reader's mind we can save ourselves from long explanations.

Take, for example, Martin's blind date with Gloria last night. When Gloria greeted him at the door her face fell because she, apparently, was expecting someone more handsome, and perhaps taller. During dinner his explanation of how umbrella handles are made just seemed to bore her. And when he tried to charm her with humor she told him that she really didn't like crude and stupid jokes. At the door when he tried to kiss her goodnight, she turned her face away and he ended up kissing her barrette.

All of that is what happened. But when Martin tells you about it, he doesn't want to go into all the details. He wants to show you that he failed with Gloria, but since his failure is spread over a long period and several events, he searches his mind for an image that will compress failure into an instant. He thinks about a baseball player, whose failure occurs in the fraction of a second that it takes for the third strike to whiz past his bat. Martin says, "Last night I struck out with Gloria," and we all know what he means. That's using imagery to save time.

We also use imagery to make things sensate that are not sensate. Something is sensate when it can be perceived by the senses. That is, it can be seen, heard, touched, smelled, or tasted. If it cannot be seen, heard, touched, etc., it is not sensate. Readers respond much better to the sensate, and so imagery helps us translate the abstract, the vague, the amorphous, into the concrete, easily understood world of the senses. For example, a common visual image for the abstract feeling of being in love would be, "He felt as if he were floating on a cloud." A sound image for the same thing could be, "He heard trumpets play whenever she approached him."

If you can't describe your character's feelings of nausea, use sight, touch, and taste and say, "Montgomery felt as if he had swallowed a seat cushion."

If Montgomery is depressed and you can't find words to get that feeling across, you might use the image of a black bag thrown over his head, or a pane of glass slipped between him and reality. If he is elated, he might feel as if he has a new engine. If he is confused, his mind might be like a junkyard.

Much of the imagery that we use is so common in writing and in speech that we don't even think of it as imagery. That is, we don't translate it; we accept it literally. For example, instead of describing all the mistakes and bad luck that plagued a man's job over a period of months, we say, "His career went down the drain."

Similes

You are using a simile when you say that one thing was like something that it's really very different from, usually to show some common quality. If you said that the pen in the gossip columnist's hand was like a pencil because it was made of wood and had an eraser, that would not be a simile. That would just be a handy way of describing the pen. But if you said that the pen was like a dagger, which he used to slice up the reputations of Hollywood's biggest stars, that would be simile. A pen is not really like a dagger at all, but you have made that connection to achieve a strong image for the reader.

Many similes have become clichés. The wise man is like an owl, the clever man is like a fox. The bad news hits him like a ton of bricks, and when he's feeling good he drinks and dances like there's no tomorrow. The word "like" is the tip-off that you have written a simile.

Exercise

Try to come up with similes for these:
1. A surly editor.
2. A new car that won't start on a cold morning.
3. A piggy bank that has been smashed open.

4. A hammock that has been well used over the years.
5. An author who has suddenly gotten rich.
6. A cupboard filled with canned vegetables.
7. A priest who has been having an affair.
8. A tool that is useless.
9. A song that is boring.
10. A teacher who gives too much homework.

Metaphors

Author Ted Cheney says that the difference between a simile and a metaphor is that the simile admits to being a figure of speech. That's a good explanation. The simile has "like" in it; the metaphor does not. In a metaphor we say that something *is* something else. We say that a woman's life was a river which meandered across the countryside, never rushing, never overflowing. We say that Herman and Rebecca's marriage was a war, and today Herman was on the offensive, storming Rebecca's fragile barriers.

Metaphors tend to be longer than similes. The woman who is like a river might have a "placid surface." She may "nourish everything that came to her shores." The couple at war may "shoot each other with words" or "call a truce." You are carrying on the metaphor for as long as you pretend that a woman is a river, a marriage is a war, or that anything is something else.

Exercise

Here is a list of subjects and metaphorical ways you might write about them. I'll do the first one as an example.

1. Death as a metaphor for a lost pennant.
2. Being a miner as a metaphor to show that writers really do work hard.
3. Escape from prison as a metaphor for women's liberation.
4. Military strategy as a metaphor for lovemaking.
5. A hurricane as a metaphor for a marriage in trouble.

Here is how the first one might show up on the sports pages:

The Red Sox pennant hopes died suddenly yesterday afternoon at four o'clock. Death came when Yankee slugger Reggie Jackson launched a towering three-run homer into the centerfield bleachers. Jackson's sixth-inning blast gave the Yankees a seven-run lead, and from then on there was clearly no sign of a heartbeat in the pennant hopes, which had been critically ill since a nine-game losing streak in late August. The mourners came to the plate, Yastrzemski, Rice, Fisk, but there was not a twitch or a twitter from the corpse.

Funeral services were held at this morning's Fenway Park press conference, with manager Don Zimmer reading the eulogy. "We just didn't have the pitching," he said.

This year, with several key players nearing retirement age and few good prospects coming up, New England's pennant hopes will be buried just a little deeper than usual.

What Works and What Doesn't?

There are other terms for some of the types of imagery writers use, but I won't go into them here. The best discussion of them can be found on pages 172-184 of Ted Cheney's *Getting the Words Right* (Writer's Digest Books, 1983). Here I've just covered a few of imagery's terms to make sure you are clear on what imagery is. Now we can talk about what sort of imagery does or does not succeed in satisfying readers.

This is a tough lesson to teach. The experienced writer recognizes ineffective imagery when she sees it, but she can't always explain what's wrong with it. However, there are several types of ineffective imagery which can be described, and by exploring them, perhaps we can get a better general sense of what works and what doesn't.

Cliché Imagery

Earlier, when I gave you a list of similes, I said that many of them had become clichés. That is true for imagery in general. Here are some examples from manuscripts I have read.

> When he kissed her it was the Fourth of July, fireworks exploding all around her and bells ringing.

> He was broad shouldered, and the muscles on his stomach were like a washboard.

> When he awoke the morning after the party, Harriman felt as if his head had been stuffed with cotton.

Those images are not inappropriate. They are not farfetched. The problem with them is that they are clichés. They have been used so often that your reader has probably seen them several times before. So when she sees them in your work she will be reminded that she is reading. She will see the writer at work.

Look at the imagery you have used and ask yourself, "Is this mine? Did I make it up? Did I really think about it? Or did I merely mimic something I had heard or read someplace else?" Examine each image and ask yourself where it is coming from. If it is not coming from you, get rid of it.

Extended Imagery

Just as many jokes that are hilarious in fifty words bomb miserably at a hundred words, many images won't work unless they are compacted into few words. Writers often invent interesting images, but destroy the effect by spreading the image too thin.

Consider this:

> With his secondhand Remington portable in front of him and the urge to write a novel burning inside him, Brandy Firth began to explore his inner world. At first apprehensively, later with confidence, he followed the trail of each ambition that dwelled within him until he came to a clearing. He climbed the mountains of his fears until he could stand atop each one and look for miles. He pushed back the thickets of confusion, hacking away with a machete of common sense. Each day he mapped out some new inner territory, which he would navigate alone. He felt like a pioneer crossing areas that had never been seen before. From time to time he was ambushed by some anxiety he hadn't known was there, and when he tried to pull back his wagon, the horses would often become confused and begin galloping desperately across years of memories that had been hidden behind a range, or forgotten on some barren prairie. He brought few supplies on these forays into his emotional wilderness, just his faith, and his curiosity and . . .

You get the idea. The imagery of the inner self as territory for exploration works okay. And the overall image is acceptable to the reader for several sentences. But as the writer continued with the image it became exaggerated and then ridiculous. The writer simply overdid it.

It is important that imagery not seem to be more important than the thing it stands for. If you say that Clarissa's smile was like the sunrise, then you've given us a nice sense of her smile in a few words. But if you say that her smile was like the sun rising over a long green meadow in spring, when the birds are singing and the air is still cool over the damp grass, etc., etc., the sunrise takes center stage and the smile is forgotten.

Images Too Similar

The cheetah ran like a gazelle.

What's wrong with that image is that it only repeats what the reader would have had in mind, anyhow—an animal with speed and grace. The image is too similar to the thing it is standing in for. Imagery has got to bring new information to bear on the thing it stands for. It has to give the reader a new way of looking at things. If it just repeats his old way of looking at information, then it is doing no work.

If you write an article on ice hockey and you say that being at a hockey game is like being at a football game, you haven't created any fresh imagery. You've only transferred the same images: competition, a crowd, the smell of hot dogs, etc. The reader doesn't know any more than he would know without the imagery. But if you say that being at a hockey game is like being at a prize fight, then you have created an image concerning the violence in hockey. You've suggested that in hockey a fight is the main event, that the crowd likes to see the punching, that there is a certain amount of bloodlust, perhaps even some betting on the outcome of fights. The imagery brings something new to the hockey game.

Reaching for Images

Imagery should appear to come naturally. If your image is so specific or so remote that the reader becomes aware of it as an image, he will also be aware of you as a writer and the imagery won't work.

Listen to what happens in your mind when you hear these images.

> The buttons on Doris's coat were small and square like the little gray buttons you use to store telephone numbers on one of those new phones with built-in computers.

> Tish was much smaller than her sisters, like a xylem cell that had been produced in the latter part of the year.

Those images are too obviously the work of a writer sweating over a typewriter. The writer who reaches that far to come up with an image will be as obtrusive as the dinner guest who reaches all the way across the table for the salt shaker.

Mixed Imagery

Generally, a collection of disparate images close together on the page will not work. At best, they will have the effect of sketching on the reader's mind a writer dreaming up images. At worst they will make you look like a buffoon.

An example of this would be the mixed metaphor:

> Her love life had long been a desert on which nothing grew until she met Ted Ross and the waves of passion carried her to a shore she had never even seen before.

Here, we begin by saying that her love life is a desert and we end up saying it is an ocean. That's a mixed metaphor. Once you enter a metaphor you must be true to it until you have left it. There is nothing wrong with using the desert metaphor in Chapter 1 and the ocean metaphor in Chapter 6, but if you mix them or even use them within a few paragraphs of each other, they will be disturbing and, perhaps, unintentionally amusing.

The same goes for similes, though the reader can be a little more forgiving. You could use two, sometimes even three, different similes close together, but don't push your luck beyond that. For example, in the pace chapter of this book, I compared unnecessary words to "luggage" at one point and to "junk" at another. You allowed me that, I hope. But if I had also said that unnecessary words were "like garbage," and a few paragraphs later "like handcuffs," and later "like anchors," the chapter would begin to sound like a comedy routine.

Think About Qualities

In trying to come up with good imagery for your stories, don't make the mistake of thinking literally. An apple is literally like a pear. Both have roughly the same shape and weight, they both grow on trees, they are both fruit, both edible, both juicy, and so forth. But one would not work as an image for the other. You would have more luck saying that an apple has the heft of a baseball, the color of a lady's cheek, or that it dangled from the branch like a Christmas bulb.

Imagery is not merely an attempt to show something more clearly.

It's an attempt to say something specific about that thing, such as "Hockey is a violent sport." Do not use imagery until you know what it is you are trying to say, and then choose an image that has the quality which will best convey that message.

Now let's take, for example, a cornfield and apply some imagery.

If you wrote, "The corn was as high as an elephant's eye" the reader might recognize that as a line from a Broadway song, and the effect would be of a cliché, unless the reader thought you were specifically alluding to the song.

If you wrote, "The rows of corn were as straight as the lines on a seersucker suit," you would be reaching for an image which would distract the reader. It would not work.

If you wrote, "The cornfield was a wheat field waiting to be harvested," you would create a metaphor so similar to the thing it is standing in for that the reader would be totally confused.

If you wrote, "The rows of corn were like soldiers standing at attention," you would succeed in showing certain qualities of corn-stalks, the erectness, the stillness. If the corn had been beaten in all directions by a windstorm you might change the simile to "soldiers in combat," to show the wreckage, the disarray. If the corn had been picked, the stalks might be compared to something naked to show that quality.

And you would be mixing your images if you wrote, "The corn had been harvested. Like pennant hopes it would be planted again next spring, but for now a chapter had ended."

Exercise

For each of the items below, come up with three qualities or characteristics that might be used for imagery in your story. I'll do the first, as an example.
1. A computer
2. A golf ball
3. A peignoir
4. Hair
5. A book
6. Eyes
7. An umbrella
8. A rock star

9. A cat
10. Africa

The computer, I might say, is like a brain and I could use imagery concerning thinking or education. Perhaps it "was like the highly intelligent friend he had always wanted, but had never met."

The computer screen glows. Maybe it is "a green light, telling him to go."

And a computer has complexity. "Sometimes it seemed like a simple dinner date with Helen was more complicated than all the computers he had ever worked on."

COFFEE BREAK

If words are employees, as I like to think of them, they are most like handymen. They can disclaim. They can warn. They can remind. They can do hundreds of things, because they have many talents.

A word has meaning, yes, but it also has shape, size, length, sound, characteristics such as rarity or familiarity, and a variety of connotations that have clung to it long before the writer picked it out. Because words, individually and in groups, can perform many chores, you must choose your words carefully, making sure each is pulling its weight and that all are working well as a team. Otherwise they'll do jobs you don't want done. Then they aren't working—they're goofing off.

A continuing theme of this book is the *total writing process,* the relationship between form and content. Form results from words' grouping together. They can be combined in endlessly varied patterns, and each pattern will influence the reader's feelings in a different way. Style, sentence length, sound, punctuation, and other elements you might not have considered—this is the hidden work of words.

It's important for you to know, or at least wisely guess, what a word or an arrangement of words will bring to a reader besides meaning.

Once your story or book or article is published, you have no control over how your readers read it. So you must know what a word will "say," not just with its dictionary definition, but with the noise it makes and the ways it's been used in the past.

One of the ways words work is by causing the reader to connect things in his mind, to associate. Many of the words you use will cause him to make associations. Use words deliberately for this purpose when you can, and edit from your writing all words that elicit associations you don't want made.

These associations cross many lines. A symbol can be associated with something tangible, the figurative with something literal. Something visual, such as punctuation or white space, can be associated with something abstract, such as loneliness.

Here is an example of how your writing style can be *associated* with the pace of your action.

Think about a disagreement turning into an argument, and then to a fight. As the conflict escalates, things happen at a faster pace. We start off saying, "I think you are mistaken on this issue," and finish with, "Drop dead."

By quickening the pace of your sentences, shortening them, you can play on the reader's association of faster pace with hotter tempers:

"Coleman swore at Bernstein and told him never to come back into the store. Bernstein shook a fist at him and once again demanded his money back."

They argue for a while. Tempers rise and sentences get shorter:

"Coleman glowered across the room. Bernstein burned with rage."

A little more writing at this pace, and by the time they come to blows, you've pared your sentences down to just a few words:

"Bernstein punched. Coleman kicked. They spat. They clawed. Bernstein screamed. He crashed to the floor."

By translating the pace of the action into the pace of the sentences, you get the reader to connect the two in his mind.

Now let's consider a distinctly different way of using words to get the reader to associate.

I've cautioned you against wordiness, but a small dose of wordiness could be useful when creating a pompous character that you want the reader to associate wordiness with. Consider this:

> Gary thought he was clever, but in truth he was a dreadful writer. His prose was a thicket of overgrown words, and it seemed that he and his twenty-pound dictionary waged constant war against clear and simple language. So he stood torpidly on the pebbled border of the lifeless highway, and once again he found himself making nugatory conjectures.

That would be more than enough for the reader to associate Gary with wordiness, to connect Gary and wordiness in his mind.

The words you write also have an appearance. They look like something. They have length, size, shape. They are surrounded by white space and interrupted by little marks called punctuation. The appearance of your writing is one more quality you can use to make it work.

One reason dialogue is so popular is that it is sparse writing afloat in a sea of white space. The typical book browser riffles through the pages of a novel and is attracted by the white space he sees flashing by. Without reading the actual words, he is hooked by the look of the writing.

The white space on a page can also be used to influence the meaning of words. Consider this:

> She had come at last to the end of her marriage. Stan was not coming back, and though she'd known that for months, she knew it now at a deeper level. This feeling that had been growing on her had at last pierced the marrow, and as she stood staring dumbly into an empty bureau drawer that once held his socks and shirts, she gave it a name.
> Loneliness.
> She was lonely, and for the moment there was nothing; nothing in the world that could end it.

What could be lonelier than one word all by itself on a line?

Italicized words, such as I have used throughout this book, can make one word in a sentence a little weightier, a little more emphatic, and an exclamation point—judiciously placed, of course!—can certainly enhance the meaning of a sentence. Use exclamation points sparingly, and never use more than one at a time. Don't use exclamation points to call further attention to something you wrote that you think is clever. If it's clever, the reader will notice. If it's not clever, an exclamation point will only make things worse by tipping off the reader that it's *supposed* to be clever. Using exclamation points that way is much like laughing at your own jokes.

The most immediate and practical place for you to consider the visual impact of what you write is in the neatness and cleanliness of your manuscripts and query letters to editors. You could write another *Gone With the Wind,* but if it comes in tattered at the edges, stained with instant Sanka, and crisscrossed with black lines that explain what's supposed to go where, it ain't gonna get published. Mainly because it ain't gonna get read.

Your manuscript has to compete with hundreds of others for the attention of an editor who reads all day. The look of it tells him a lot about your attitude toward your writing. It should be attractive to look at. Use a fresh ribbon. Leave plenty of white space in the margins. Double-space. Stay away from gimmicks like purple paper and red ribbons. In short, make anything you send to an editor as visually appealing as possible. However, don't turn into such a lunatic that you retype a page because it has one typing error. A few pencil corrections won't ruin the looks of an otherwise neat manuscript, but many will.

When you get to the publishing stage, a variety of visual elements that you have no control over come into play. There are hundreds of typefaces and sizes, weights of paper, and an infinite number of ways your story or article can be arranged in print. You won't have a voice in these matters unless you happen to be a big-deal writer who's hauling down heavy bucks for the publisher. Patience, my friend, patience.

Chapter Seven
Voices

Voices in Nonfiction and Fiction

If you search long enough you will find short stories and articles in which there is no "voice" but the author's, no words between quotation marks. But you won't find many. Writing that works owes much of its success to those words—either real or imagined—spoken by other people, other characters.

In nonfiction those words come in the form of *quotes,* the actual words of a person who had something to say about the subject at hand. Sometimes the quotes take the form of a conversation between two or more people, but usually they're the words of an individual replying to a question asked by the writer.

In fiction the words of other people are called *dialogue,* conversations usually between two people, though characters do sometimes talk to themselves or to people who aren't there or who don't reply.

Certainly there are other differences between the spoken word as presented in nonfiction and fiction. But of greater importance to the writer are the *similarities* between nonfictional quotes and fictional dialogue.

Quotes and dialogue both break up the page visually and attract readers.

Quotes and dialogue both create space for opinions other than the author's.

Neither quotes nor dialogue automatically becomes interesting just because it sounds as if somebody is really talking. The writer's goal is to create the illusion of spoken language pouring forth naturally from the speaker. But that language must be so packed with drama or information or wisdom that a real listener would lean forward to catch every word.

Of course, not every quote can be the epitome of pith, nor can every exchange of dialogue cut directly to the core of an issue. But the writer can strive always to use the words of other people in the best way at the best times.

Why Quote?

"The most common mistake I see among writers of nonfiction is that they don't use quotes. Without quotes, the writing moves too slowly," an editor once told me. "If I don't see several quotes in an article I will reject it."

Let that be a lesson to you.

Of course, there are many lively published articles that have no quotes in them, but usually they are short. Most articles written without quotes are as slow as sludge; the only thing fast about them is the speed with which they are rejected by editors. If you can quote the man on the street, the expert on your subject, or the person you are writing about, you will usually make your article livelier, faster paced, and more salable.

Selecting Quotes

Ninety percent of the research you do comes in the form of quotes. Either somebody said it to you, or you read it. The only research that doesn't arrive in the form of quotes is your personal experience.

Logically, then, your entire article could be written in quotes. You could excerpt a book you read, follow the excerpt with the words from an expert, toss in a man-in-the-street view, a few appropriate lines from a poem, and maybe some statistics from the bureau of something or other. *You* wouldn't actually say anything. Chances are you'd end up with an article six times as dull as a Tuesday afternoon in Elgin, Illinois.

That's because you would have overlooked the most important expert in any story. The communications expert. You. The people you talk to say good stuff, but they don't say stuff good. They have interesting things to say, but they don't always say them in an interesting way. They might know about home computers, but they don't know about active verbs, showing instead of telling, being specific, varying sentence length, characterizing, and all the other techniques of writing that works. That's your area of expertise. You are the writer.

There is no scientific method of choosing which words to quote and which to use as background information. You use quotes in a story for all of the reasons that you use any other words: variety, sound, association, and so forth. There is no "right" time to throw in a quote. You have to train your ear and your eye to get a sense of how many quotes an article can accommodate, and that depends pretty much on how interesting your speaker is.

But when you do quote, to create that rhythm, that balance, use quotes that serve a specific purpose and can accomplish it better than you could with your own words.

When to Quote

There are no absolute rules about where you should sprinkle quotes to give your articles a steady and lively pace, but here are some guidelines:

1. When you haven't quoted for several paragraphs and the page is starting to look like one big block of print.

2. When you want to reveal something about the speaker's character. Here is how I quoted a woman who was a chaplain at a nursing home as part of her studies to become a minister. (Note also how I broke up the quote to get the best rhythm.)

> "It isn't just so that I can minister to them," she explained. She stops, and lines of weariness crowd around her eyes. She shrugs her shoulders. Living the traditional woman's role while also pursuing a taxing career that is not at all traditional for women can be exhausting. She smiles.
>
> "Sometimes," she said, "they minister to me."

3. When the speaker has said something in a way that is funnier, more colorful, more succinct, or just generally more interesting than the way you might cover the same information.

Compare

> Eydie Gorme says she doesn't like most of the music of recent years. She feels that the lyrics are asinine and ridiculous and that radio stations have very low standards.

with

"I think the music of the last fifteen years is horrendous," she says, "I can't stand the ridiculous, asinine lyrics coming out of human beings' throats. Radio stations insist on playing computerized crap."

4. When the information is a lot more significant because of who is saying it.
Compare

Donahue is sure that flying saucers will land in Elgin, Illinois, sometime next July, and that an army of bite-sized Saturnites will imprison that town for the next twelve years.

with

"Flying saucers will land in Elgin, Illinois, next July. I'm not guessing. I know," says Walt Donahue, Director of President Bush's commission on extraterrestrial life forms. Mr. Donahue, generally regarded as the nation's most informed and respected UFO researcher, says, "I've got proof that an army of bite-sized Saturnites plans to imprison Elgin for the next twelve years."

5. When the material has emotional, not just informational, content. If a woman says, "I have a son," don't quote her. If she says, "I love my son," or "I hate my son," or "My son has a drug problem and I feel so helpless," then quote her.

So select quotes that work hard for you, that do some job beyond providing the surface information. If the person you interview is a butcher, a baker, or a candlestick maker, it is highly unlikely that he is going to be able to put information into a concise, exciting, colorful, readable form better than a trained professional writer like you. So use the gems he gives you, but remember that you'll find most of them in piles of raw wordage that you have to refine. That's what you get paid for.

Trim the Quotes

If you quote every word a man or woman said, you will burden your article with tons of unnecessary luggage. Speakers are wordy. They are always speaking in the first draft. Remember, you are aiming for maximum efficiency. That means getting the most work out of the fewest words, which includes quotes. Don't change the speaker's meaning. Just throw away the words you don't need.

For example, if you ask the outgoing mayor what was the most exciting event in his forty-year political career, he's likely to say something like:

"Oh, gee, I don't know. There's been so much. It's all been so exciting, really. I remember my brother Ralph one time telling me how much he envied my life in politics, for all the excitement. I mean, every two years your job is up for grabs; it's a real crap shoot. But the most exciting, huh? Oh, I don't know. Had a lot of excitement around here the day Councilman O'Meara left a bag of cash in the men's room. But you can't print that. The police strike of 1972. I guess maybe you could say that was the most exciting thing."

The mayor's recollection of the most exciting event is just not worth that many printed words, so when you write it, it will come out like this:

"It's all been exciting," says Mayor Forbes, "but the police strike of 1972 was the most exciting event."

The quote works because it is the simple and complete answer to the question. Interviewees ramble; writers should not.

Exercise

Here are some words spoken to me in interviews. Try to turn them into strong quotes by eliminating the extra words without changing the speaker's meaning.

1. "You know I had this feeling come over me that I just wanted to do awful things, to get up and maim that person for life. I wanted to make him suffer, hurt him badly, so that he would feel, oh, I don't know . . . punished, I guess, for what he had done. I really had a strong need for revenge, if you see what I mean. I wanted to get even."
2. "I think competence is the most appealing quality in a man. It's the thing that turns me on. It's the thing I look for when I meet a man. Is he good at what he does? That's the sexy quality, that ability to do a thing well. And he knows it. He's confident about it; that's part of the exciting quality."
3. "I don't know if I could have gotten out. I don't know if I could have made it. I think they had one of those doors with a buzzer. You know the kind, where the guy checks to see who's there and he pushes a button that unlocks the door. It breaks a circuit

or something, I think. Anyhow, I wasn't thinking about escaping. I was thinking about what lies I could tell. The counselor was okay, he was a pretty good guy. He let me smoke."

4. "We want to do our music. People come up to us at clubs and concerts and they have requests for all kinds of things. They ask for the Rolling Stones or jazz stuff, or other kinds of music that you just wouldn't believe, music that has nothing to do with us. Things we never even thought of doing. We want to do the music that we like, the music we believe in. If we can't do the music we believe in, then it's just not worth it. It's not worth it to do music we don't care about. We don't want to do music we don't believe in."

5. "There was, oh I don't know, maybe two hours or more of pounding on the wall, very loud, too. It made an awful racket, this pounding. And sometimes there was a noise on the floor, a kind of thumping. A lot of thumping and pounding could scare the hell out of you. Sometimes you'll go by a room and see a shadow. Nothing real, nothing solid, you know, just a kind of shadow, but when you go back there's nothing there. Just nothing."

Don't Describe Quotes

When you quote a person, don't slow the pace by taking time to describe the quote as having been "exclaimed" or "uttered" or "opined."

" 'I think the country is in a dreadful mess,' she opined," doesn't do any more work than " 'I think the country is in a dreadful mess,' she said."

The second sentence moves faster because there is no reader resistance to the simple word *said* whereas *opined* takes an extra second to process.

There are times when you will get some added meaning from an "exclaimed" or an "announced," but generally the quote should contain its own tone of voice.

Don't Repeat Information in Quotes

When I first became a newspaper reporter I had a bad habit of stating something, and then repeating it in quotes. I often wrote things like this:

Mayor Keane told the City Council last night that he will not support the bond issue for a new recreation center.

"I've decided not to support the bond issue for a new recreation center," Keane told the council. "If we don't have the cash on hand for a new recreation center, then that's tough cookies," he said.

If a runner had to run every yard twice like that, you can see that it would slow his pace. So don't do it.

Balance the Quotes

What's the right amount of butter to put on an ear of corn? Whatever it takes to make the corn taste best. Nobody can tell you the exact amount, but we can all agree that a pound is too much and a pinch is too little.

It's the same thing with quotes. Work for a balance that is pleasing to the eye and to the ear.

I have in front of me an article called "Meet a James Garner You'll Hardly Recognize," by Mary Murphy (*TV Guide,* Dec. 13, 1986). Let's see, paragraph by paragraph, how Mary balanced her quoted and nonquoted material. Keep in mind that a profile like this would normally have a lot more quotes than, say, an article about the talking frogs of Ecuador.

1. No quotes
2. No quotes
3. Half quotes
4. All quotes
5. All quotes
6. All quotes
7. No quotes
8. No quotes
9. Half quotes
10. About two-thirds quotes
11. No quotes
12. Half quotes
13. No quotes
14. Half quotes
15. No quotes
16. About 10 percent quotes
17. No quotes

18. No quotes
19. All quotes
20. No quotes

There are fifteen more paragraphs, but you get the idea. Notice that Mary never writes more than three paragraphs of quotes in a row, or more than two paragraphs in a row without quotes. I'm not saying you should adopt that particular formula, but it does give you an example of a nice balance that creates a pleasing pace.

Exercise

Read three or four magazine articles with a highlighter in hand. Highlight all the quotes.

Now study them. With each, ask yourself why the writer quoted at that particular point instead of summarizing or paraphrasing what the subject said. Do the quotes reveal emotion? Do they create credibility? Do they demonstrate character? Do they break up the article, creating a more pleasing music? Is the speaker being clever or witty or colorful?

Think about it.

What Dialogue Is

Dialogue, according to my dictionary, is "a conversation between two or more people." But in fiction writing, the term is used more generally to mean the words a character speaks, whether he is with one or more people or alone.

Dialogue is the chocolate-covered munchies of fiction reading. Well-written dialogue is just a little more fun than the rest of reading. Dialogue, like nonfiction quotes, brings the people front and center.

What Dialogue Isn't

"Sorry I'm late. Any calls?" Bill said.

"Yes, the Dutch Flower Shop called," Andrea told him. "They sent you a bill and haven't got a check yet."

"For the roses?"

"I guess."

"I sent that check last week."

"It must have gotten lost in the mail," Andrea said.

"What's for supper?"

"Kielbasa."

"With the onions and the peppers, the way you usually make it, in those Syrian bread pouches?" Bill asked.

"Yes."

Does this dialogue sound real?

It should. It's a transcript of a real conversation.

Is it good dialogue?

No. It provides very little information, tells you nothing about the characters, is as tension-free as an empty hammock, and is about as exciting as an evening on the town with Jerry Falwell.

Why?

Because dialogue that simply duplicates real speech doesn't work. When real people get together they say real dull things like, "Hi, how are you?" and "I'm fine, how's yourself?" and "See you later, I'm on my way to the store to pick up some cat food." Zzz.

Good dialogue only appears to be real speech. It is real speech distilled until only the most interesting, most exciting, most emotional, or most dramatic words are left. Dialogue is real speech's greatest hits.

When Should You Use Dialogue?

With nonfiction, dialogue is sometimes useful, but with fiction it is essential for a pleasing pace. Your short stories will sail with dialogue, and often sink without it. And if you write a novel with little or no dialogue, chances are no editor will ever get anywhere near the end of it. Well-written dialogue used in the right places is, for many readers, the best part of the reading experience.

Many writers are not comfortable writing dialogue, so they never use it. Other writers are too comfortable writing dialogue, so they use it when they shouldn't. I can't give you a precise formula for when to use dialogue and when not to, but I can give you a pretty good guideline.

As you begin any sentence, or any paragraph, there is a job you are trying to get done. Think about what that job is and ask yourself, "Who can do that job best: dialogue or narrative?"

Here are some examples of jobs you might need done, and how your two workers might do them.

1. Provide Information.

Narrative: It had been a month since Nushka had seen Major Garonovitch.

Dialogue: "I haven't seen Major Garonovitch for a month," Nushka said to Muffin the Third, the major's cat.

2. Reveal Character.

Narrative: Randy was in a bad mood when he came home from work.

Dialogue: "Customers!" Randy practically shrieked as he came through the door. "They're incredibly rude. They're obnoxious. I hate them all. I don't care if I ever see that store again."

3. Move the Story Forward.

Narrative: When Talbot got to the warehouse he realized that Vinnie had murdered Markowitz.

Dialogue: "Freeze, Talbot, or I'll give you what you gave your sleazy friend, Markowitz."

4. Create a Sense of Place.

Narrative: Beauregard invited his friends to return.

Dialogue: "Y'all come back real soon, you heah."

Here are some other jobs you might want done. See if you can come up with examples of how dialogue and narrative might do them:

5. Create a Sense of Time, Such as the Middle Ages.

6. Describe a Place.

7. Summarize Much of What Has Already Happened.

"Okay, Gary, that's great," you're thinking. "I'll just use whatever does the best job in any situation. But how do you define 'best job,' bozo?"

You can't define it exactly. But you can get a pretty good idea by asking yourself several questions.

Which way will accomplish the most work for the number of words spent? Which way will excite my reader? Which way is in contrast to what has been going on for the last several paragraphs? (If you've just written two pages of dialogue, then the answer is narrative.) Which way is most pleasing to the reader's eye? Is this material I want to focus on or is it just transitional material getting me from one point in my story to another?

After you have asked yourself these questions, go with your instincts. But remember, you're looking for the *best* way, not the *easiest* way. So ask yourself one more question: "Am I writing it this way because I don't have confidence in my ability to write it the other way?"

Exercise

I've given you seven reasons why you might use dialogue, and four examples of how dialogue could do a better job than narrative.

Now you do it. I'll give you the reason you might want to use dialogue and the narrative sentence. You write the dialogue.

1. Provide Information
Narrative: It had been snowing all day.
2. Reveal Character
Narrative: Gail was fed up with all the boring chitchat she was hearing.
3. Move the Story Forward
Narrative: The missing diamonds were found in the totem pole.
4. Create a Sense of Place
Narrative: The Kentucky Derby was about to begin.
5. Create a Sense of Time
Narrative: It had been more than a million years since the earth had vanished.
6. Describe a Place
Narrative: Jamey's mother had taken him to the Ohio State Fair.
7. Summarize Much of What Has Already Happened
Narrative: Major Garonovitch explained how the thief had gotten away with three hundred pounds of frozen mashed potatoes.

Pace Nonfiction with Dialogue

We usually think of dialogue as something we put into our short stories and novels, but if quotes can quicken the pace of nonfiction, dialogue should be able to do the same thing. And it can. My last few books were nonfiction and they have as much dialogue as the average novel. Without dialogue they would have been boring.

Here's an example of how I used dialogue in *Without Mercy* (Pocket, 1990), a true story about Dee Casteel, a pancake house waitress who was sentenced to death for helping to arrange two murders.

In this scene, which is based on interviews with the murderers, Dee, and Allen Bryant, who asked her to arrange the murder, have just gone to the victim's house to dispose of the body.

> They discussed dumping the body in the Everglades, less than an hour away, or possibly dropping it in the Miami Canal, but finally they decided that the safest bet was not to move it far at all.
>
> "I've got five acres here," Allen said. "I could just take it out back and dump it."
>
> "It will smell," Dee said. "Animals will find it. Somebody might wonder why animals are feasting on a corpse in your backyard. Don't you think the best thing is to bury it? You don't intend to get rid of the property, do you?"
>
> "No. I'm going to keep it no matter what happens. Henry and I will probably move out here."
>
> "Fine, then bury Art here."
>
> "When?"
>
> "Well, not in broad daylight," Dee said. "Later."
>
> "Okay, good," Allen said. He seemed to be calming down now that they had decided what to do with the body. "Now, I've got to tell Mrs. Fischer."
>
> "Mrs. Fischer? Who's Mrs. Fischer?"
>
> "Art's mother."
>
> "What are you going to tell her?"
>
> "I'll tell her that Art went to North Carolina on business."
>
> "Won't she think it's a little strange that Art didn't say good-bye?" Dee asked.
>
> "She's practically senile. We'll tell her that Art did say good-bye and she just doesn't remember."
>
> "We" again, Dee thought. "Where does she live?"
>
> "Here."
>
> Dee couldn't believe what she was hearing. She felt an alarm go off inside her.
>
> "What do you mean, here?"

"Right out front, in the little trailer."

"His mother lives here, on the property?" Dee was shouting. She bolted up from the table, knocking her glass of Scotch to the floor. "Right here? You murdered Art right here, twenty feet away from his mother?"

"I didn't murder him."

"Oh, no. You just stood by while somebody else slit his throat with a razor."

Now, fuming with fear and sobbing uncontrollably, she was standing over him, waving her arms wildly.

"Will you calm down, you're getting hysterical," Allen said.

"Hysterical? Jesus, Allen, I can't imagine why I'd be hysterical just because you've got me involved in a murder and the man's mother lives twenty feet away."

"We'll take care of it. We'll take care of it."

"Take care of it? For God's sake, you can't take care of it. The man is dead. Dead. Art is dead. You killed him and you've got me involved. This is not a dream, Allen, we're not going to wake up from it."

"You have to get hold of your friend, Irvine."

"For what?"

"Well, isn't it obvious?" Allen said. "For Mrs. Fischer. She has to be killed, too."

"Oh, my God," Dee said. She had spent her rage, her fear, even her sympathy for the dead man, and now she was empty. She collapsed into her chair, reached blindly for the glass that wasn't there, and finally pushed her face into her hands. The sound that came out of her was like the wail of a wounded animal. "This can't be happening," she said, "this can't be happening."

"Well, it is happening," Allen said. "We've got to finish it."

"No!" Dee shouted. "No, no, no." She pounded on the table. "I didn't sign on for a killing spree. We're not going to kill some old lady."

Allen looked as if he'd been slapped.

"Well, dear, what do you propose we do with her?"

"We let her live," Dee snapped. "How's that for a novel idea?"

"She's old. She's senile. She can't even cook her own meals. We had to shut off her gas because she kept turning on the stove and forgetting to light it."

"I'll feed her," Dee said.

"You'll feed her?"

"Yes, from the restaurant. I'll bring her meals over. Whatever has to be done, I'll do it. Anything, Allen, just don't kill her, okay? I'll take care of her."

"What if she finds out about Art? I could end up in jail. So could you."

"She won't find out anything, I promise."

Allen stared at Dee for a long time. "Okay," he finally said, "but if she starts asking too many questions, we call Mike Irvine. I'm not going to jail because of some old lady."

Of course the events in *Without Mercy* are easy to relate in traditional storytelling fashion, so the material cries out for dialogue. But a magazine or newspaper article is usually not a narrative with a beginning and an ending. Because of this, and because you must economize on words, you can't use a lot of dialogue in most articles. But in many articles you will find that a small amount of dialogue can be used and it can improve the pace of the story by giving life to people on the page, breaking up the page visually, and creating a new sound for the reader to listen to. That's what Stanley Bing did in his article about good management techniques (*Esquire,* April 1986).

> "I'm wondering how such a dumb thing could happen to such a smart bunch of people," Don mused at the meeting dedicated to sorting out the crisis. He smoothed his translucent pate for a fearful moment, then chortled. "I'll tell you what," he said. "Let's forget about pointing fingers and try to see how the best staff in the business can make sure this kind of thing doesn't happen again. Okay, gang?"

Coming Up with Original Dialogue

While many writers tend to repeat the clichés of description or the stereotypes of characterization, there is no such bugaboo common in dialogue. Certainly there are clichés of dialogue, usually lines from old movies, like, "Stop or I'll shoot," but they are not used often and they are not big contributors to the problem of unoriginality in dialogue.

The writer who is unoriginal in his dialogue is not usually repeating specific lines that he has heard a thousand times, but rather, types of lines that he hears every day. Common conversation, such as the kielbasa dialogue we heard earlier, or like this:

> "I've got to go to the post office," she said. She had a stack of letters in her hand.

"Are you going to your doctor's appointment now?" Richard asked.

"No," she said. "I'll stop back here first. I know how you like to see the mail. And I'll take Buster with me when I go. He's supposed to get a shot at the vet."

"Would you pick up some stamps while you're at the post office?" he asked, remembering the stack of unanswered letters on his desk.

This is ordinary everyday conversation, but it is not good dialogue. The problem with the dialogue above is that the writer is just playing back an old tape recording in his mind, instead of creating a new conversation. To come up with original dialogue, do the same thing I said to do for original description. STOP and THINK.

Here are some of the things you should think about.

When you write dialogue do what an actor does. Get inside the character. Ask yourself, "What am I feeling at this moment in the scene?" Your dialogue will be much better if you stop to think about what the character is feeling before you write it. Is he angry? Is he sad? Is he hiding something? Is he happy?

Maybe when you stop to think about the above dialogue you decide that Richard is feeling deadline pressure from whatever work he is doing at his desk. Because he senses that time is short, he speaks no unnecessary words. You might change the dialogue:

"I've got to go to the post office," she said. She had a stack of letters in her hand.

"Doctor, too?" he asked.

"No," she said, "I'll stop back here first. I know how you like to see the mail. And I'll take Buster with me when I go. He's supposed to get a shot at the vet."

"Stamps, please," Richard said, remembering the stack of unanswered letters on his desk.

Or maybe you decide that it is the woman who is feeling harried. She's a little overwhelmed by all the things she's got to get done today.

"I suppose I'll have to go to the post office," she said. She held a stack of letters tightly in her hand.

"Are you going to your doctor's appointment now?" Richard asked.

"Oh God, the doctor! No, no, let me see, no, I'll come back here first. I can't let everything hold up the mail; you need it. Maybe I can save time by taking Buster with me when I go. I can't believe he needs another shot at the vet already."

Obviously you could do a lot more than I have done in those examples, but I wanted to stay close to my first passage to make the point about originality. Think about what your characters are feeling and you will create words that will come from *their particular situation*, not from similar situations in general.

Another thing to think about is the overall tone of the dialogue scene. Sometimes the writer makes the assumptions about the mood of a scene, and he can often come up with original dialogue by questioning and changing those assumptions.

For example, when your cop brings a murder suspect in for interrogation, do you automatically assume that the cop is hostile and domineering, and the suspect is resistant, that there is an adversarial relationship between them? What if you recast the scene with the idea that these two are businessmen negotiating? The cop wants information, the suspect wants freedom. Maybe they could be very civil to each other, either in a phony way or in a sincere way. That new premise doesn't have to change the outcome of the scene. The cop still finds out that the victim was a loan shark, or whatever. But the new premise creates a whole smorgasbord of original dialogue possibilities.

When I wrote *Finder* I had to write a dialogue scene in which Marilyn Greene announces at the dinner table that she has quit her job in order to pursue a career as a private investigator. As I originally wrote the scene the mood is one of antagonism. Chip, her husband, is angry with her for quitting. She gets angry with him. He gets angrier with her, and so forth. After I reread the dialogue I realized that it conveyed the same mood as several other scenes in which Marilyn and Chip had argued. To the reader it would feel like a scene he had read before, and because of that, the dialogue would sound unoriginal. So, to make the dialogue original, I reconsidered the mood of the scene. Instead of letting the dialogue build up to an argument with someone walking out or slamming a door, as they had in previous scenes, I decided I could accomplish the same work, but with fresher dialogue, if I introduced a humorous tone to the dialogue. Here's what I came up with.

"You can't just quit your job," Chip said.

"Sure I can."

"It's irresponsible," he said. "We need the money. What makes you think it will be so easy to get another job?"

"I've already got one."

"Oh, you're not going to start that stuff again about raising kids being a job. I know it's work, for God's sake, I do my share of it. But it doesn't pay."

"I'm a private investigator, remember?"

"Oh, Jesus!"

"Oh Jesus, yourself," I said. "I can do it. I got my license, didn't I? I can specialize in finding missing persons."

"Oh, great," Chip said. "I'm sure there's a big call for that. I bet there's millions of missing persons right here in Albany, huh? Marilyn, get realistic. How many cases do you think you can get out of Albany, Schenectady, and Troy? Or did you think million-aires were going to call you from Palm Springs and say 'My wife's missing, can you get down here right away?' "

Chip liked to laugh at his own jokes, and now he was more amused by himself than he was angry with me. Soon the kids started giggling, and even though I knew I was the butt of the joke, I smiled. It was nice to see everyone happy.

"I called Benjamin Bragonier today," I said when the laughter died down. "He's the lawyer who advertises in the paper. He told me he gets plenty of business just in Albany and all he does is immigration cases."

"Ben Bragonier is a lawyer, for God's sake," Chip said. "You can't charge what lawyers charge."

"I suppose you're right," I said. "Gee, now that I think of it, I wonder what I should charge."

"Oh Jesus!" Chip said.

Put Tension in Dialogue

Good dialogue between characters has tension.

The tension I'm talking about is not just the obvious tension that is present when two people are arguing and you're wondering who's going to punch whom in the face. I'm talking about the tension that arises when the speakers are on the same side, but one is in conflict with himself, such as a young man trying to get up the nerve to ask for a kiss. There is tension in dialogue between two people who love each other, but one doesn't know how to say it. The speakers don't have to be adversaries; there just needs to be some issue, some question, some sort of space between them that keeps the reader asking, "What's he going to say now that she's said that?"

In dialogue, an unfinished sentence, an unanswered question, or a cutting remark can create reader tension. But tension in dialogue is too important to be left to those occasional devices. Tension is the heart of successful dialogue, and all of your dialogue should have it.

The following dialogue is believable, but it is not exciting. It would not hold a reader's interest for long because it lacks tension.

> "I'm glad you made it," Ellen said when her mother arrived at the door. "I was getting worried."
>
> Hazel came in and dropped her bags on the floor. "I got tied up in traffic on the Connecticut Turnpike. It's a real mess today."
>
> "Did you stop to eat?"
>
> "Yes, I stopped at Burger King for one of those, what do you call them?"
>
> "Whoppers," Ellen said. "They call them Whoppers."

Good dialogue creates questions in the reader's mind. It makes him wonder what will be said next. It makes the reader tense.

Tension could be added to that dialogue in several ways. You could put tension directly into the spoken words.

> "Well, you finally made it," Ellen said when her mother arrived at the door. "I was getting worried. I hope you at least had enough sense to stop and eat. You know how your blood sugar is."
>
> "I ate, I ate."
>
> "Where, Ma, where did ya eat?"
>
> "I stopped at Burger King. I had one of those Big Macs."
>
> "Whoppers, Ma. Whoppers, that's what they call them. Big Macs are at McDonald's."
>
> "Okay, so I had a Whopper."

In that example, the tension is between the characters and it comes out in the words they speak. However, tension in a dialogue scene doesn't have to be in the spoken lines. It can be between the lines.

In this next example I will leave the dialogue just as it was originally, but I will increase reader interest by adding tension between the lines of dialogue. Also, I will change the source of the tension to show you that the two characters don't have to be antagonistic toward each other.

"I'm glad you made it," Ellen said when her mother arrived at the door. "I was getting worried."

Hazel came in and dropped her bags on the floor. She stood by the counter as if she needed it to hold herself up and she struggled to take deep breaths. For the first time Ellen saw her mother as old, frail. The light had gone from her eyes. Ellen's heart pounded.

"I got tied up in traffic on the Connecticut Turnpike. It's a real mess today." Hazel said when she finally caught her breath.

"Did you stop to eat?"

"Yes, I stopped at Burger King for one of those, what do you call them?"

"Whoppers," Ellen said impatiently. "They call them Whoppers."

Tonight I'll cook, she thought. Yes, she would cook a good healthful meal for her mother and then everything would be all right.

So tension is that quality of "something else going on" during the dialogue. It's what makes the reader concerned enough or curious enough to keep reading even when the spoken words are mundane.

Now maybe you're saying, "That's great, Gary, I get the point. But what if it's just Ma arriving for a visit, and I don't want any tension between her and Ellen and I don't want her looking old and frail? What if I don't want something else going on?"

If that's the case, then there's no reason to write the scene with dialogue. You'll just bore the reader. Simply write, "Ma arrived," and get on with your story. Remember, if the reader doesn't care what happens next, then the dialogue isn't working.

The reader should never have the sense that the speaker knew a half hour ago what he was going to say. Dialogue works best when it appears to be created at the moment, in response to the last words spoken. When you have two people speaking to each other, visualize each line of dialogue as having a hook on it that yanks out the next line of dialogue from the other character.

Exercise

Here's an exercise I use at my Writers Retreat Workshops.

Below is an example of what good, tense dialogue might look like without the spoken words. I'll provide you with a series of events and feelings. You replace them with spoken words. In the future, when you are having a hard time coming up with compelling dialogue, imagine it this way first, as waves of feeling being exchanged between two or more people.

Hank wishes his son was more athletic.

Martin, the son, thinks Hank should stop harping on that point.

Hank thinks Martin should try harder.

Martin thinks Hank should accept him the way he is.

Hank is hurt by that comment.

Martin is sorry he hurt his father's feelings.

Hank thinks Martin should go out for the basketball team.

Martin is feeling that his father doesn't love him.

Hank thinks sports would be good for Martin.

Martin thinks sports are stupid.

Hank thinks Martin just doesn't understand.

Martin thinks Hank makes a fool of himself at football games.

Hank's afraid that people will think his son is a sissy.

Martin is feeling pressured.

Hank is wishing he had a kid like Joel Prescott, who lives down the street and is captain of the hockey team.

Martin is wishing he had a father who would be prouder of his academic achievements.

Hank is proud of his son's high marks.

Martin wishes he would show it.

Milk the Dialogue

Tension works only if its end is delayed. You have to get the reader on edge and hold him there. So when your dialogue has grabbed him, got him wondering what's going to be said next, don't let him go too quickly. Hold that interest by milking the dialogue. Remember, I'm not talking just about life and death situations, or arguments and fights. I'm talking about all the dialogue you write, conversations between people who might get along fine but have a "tension gap" between them because of a misunderstanding, a difference in viewpoint, a competitive spirit, an insult, any number of less-than-earthshaking things.

In the example below from my novel-in-progress *Dear So And So,*

Wayne and Scotty, the narrator, are friends. Scotty has written a letter, entering himself in a contest to replace an advice columnist. Wayne is suggesting that since Scotty has no counseling credentials, he lied about it. This is how it would look if I didn't milk the dialogue.

> "Scotty, I know you can do this job because I've heard you give people advice. But the *Boston Post Dispatch* doesn't know that. They think you're just some failure from Clinton, Massachusetts, who's looking to make an easy buck."
>
> "Well what can I do?" I said. "I can't just make up counseling credits."
>
> Wayne closed his eyes and for a few peaceful seconds kissed the rim of his wine bottle. I thought I had lost him. "Now that," he said, opening his eyes and pointing the mouth of the bottle at me, "is a very good idea."
>
> "You're right," I said. "I'll lie."

Can you hear what happens when Scotty agrees to lie? All the tension is drained out of the dialogue because Scotty and Wayne agree. They are going in the same direction. They are not in conflict.

In order to keep the dialogue tense, I need to have them in conflict on this point, going in different directions for a while. This is how I milked the dialogue.

> Wayne closed his eyes and, for a few peaceful seconds, kissed the rim of his wine bottle. I thought I had lost him. "Now that," he said, opening his eyes and pointing the mouth of the bottle at me, "is a very good idea."
>
> "Just make up credentials?" I said. "That's lying."
>
> Wayne stared at me. His eyes were getting real wet-looking now. "Have you seen the paper today?" he said.
>
> "No. What about it?"
>
> "Six terrified tourists were sucked into the sky by a UFO. A baboon girl married a wolf boy. And in Oklahoma there's a pickup truck with the power to heal people."
>
> He smiled again, closed his eyes briefly, and nodded his head, as if to say "So there!"
>
> "Is there a point," I asked, "or have you finally flipped out?"
>
> "The point is that newspapers lie all the time, so why shouldn't you lie to them."
>
> "You're talking about some rag at the Food World checkout counter," I said.
>
> "Hey, it's a newspaper, isn't it? Have you seen the *Post Dis-*

patch recently? Ever since Raul Kingsley took over, Lawrence Dracut has had a free hand. He's turning it into a rag."

Kingsley, the New Zealand communications magnate, had taken over the paper in January. Arnold Sack was out, and Lawrence Dracut was now the top dog.

"How about the *New York Post*?" Wayne went on. They're all liars. It's just a matter of degree."

"So you're saying I should lie to them because they lie to me."

"Absolutely," Wayne said. "It's either that or work for a living. Besides, if the publishing world played fair with people you wouldn't be in this mess. All you're doing is playing them at their own game."

"Deceit and treachery?"

"You got it, pal. Deceit and treachery. It worked fine for three of our last six presidents."

"Maybe you've got a point," I said.

"Of course I've got a point," Wayne said. He sat up now. His eyes were wild and he shook his hands in the air as if they were in flames. "Look, I'm not saying that lying is always good. All I'm saying is that this is one of those cases where lying makes sense. You have certain counseling abilities, but there are small-minded people out there who aren't interested in ability; they're interested in pieces of paper that say you have ability. College degrees, that sort of thing. You're never going to convince them that they are idiots, so it makes sense to lie. It won't change your qualifications and you'll still have to survive on your own merit."

"If I beat the six thousand to one odds," I said.

"You'll beat them. Besides, if you don't get the job then lies won't matter one way or the other."

Wayne was right, I knew. The lying wouldn't really change anything. It would just give me the fair chance that I had a right to. Without some counseling credits I didn't have a prayer of becoming the next Molly Collins.

Exercise

Using one of the following situations write six paragraphs of dialogue. That is, each speaker speaks three times. (That probably sounds like a lot, but a paragraph of dialogue is usually just one line.)

Read what you have written. How can you milk the dialogue? How can you hold on to some of the tension and continue with dialogue that is compelling for the reader and is working for you?

Think about it. Then rewrite the dialogue so that you have twenty paragraphs, each speaker speaking ten times.

1. A husband and wife are discussing whether or not they should give up having a telephone.
2. A teenager is trying to buy Milli Vanilli tickets from his friend.
3. A pair of elves can't decide which road to take through Fairyland.
4. Diana and her friend, Laurie, each think the other is fooling around with the local postmaster.
5. A wolf has offered to escort a little girl to her grandmother's house.

Movement

Dialogue is an integral part of your story, not an addition to it. Characters don't step forward and make speeches. Their words and actions are all part of the continuing flow of the story.

Your dialogue works when it doesn't look like a chunk of writing that you jammed in between two paragraphs. To create this sense of movement, of a continuous flow of action, you inject movement into the dialogue itself. Just as actors on a stage rarely sit still and talk to each other, your characters should have some "business" to do when they talk, something to keep the story visually interesting. But because dialogue must be fast-paced to work well, the action within it should move quickly. Include bits of description and action, but always get back to the words people are speaking.

In this scene from my book *The Pie-In-The-Face Murders,* you'll see that none of the action is necessary to provide the information I want to get across, but the little bits of business make the dialogue more interesting. That, of course, is not the only job they do. These bits of business also reveal character, increase conflict, and make entire scenes more memorable to the reader. But they are especially efficient at improving dialogue. One reason is that they heighten the tension a little by making the reader wait an extra few seconds to hear "what he's going to say, now that the other fellow said that."

> I left my truck parked in front of Frances Parang's house and walked to the service station. People get a little skeptical about

my being a big-time magazine writer when they see me pull up in a laundry truck.

I found Galdetto in mortal combat with a soda machine that had screwed him out of a quarter. He was a big fellow, bright with sweat and bent like a bow because an enormous ball of flab hung from his middle like a sack of something heavy. He looked like the kind of guy who would throw a beer bottle at an umpire.

"Jerry Galdetto?" I asked.

"Yeah, yeah, who you picking?"

He didn't look at me. He looked straight at the soda machine as if it might jump him if he took his eyes off it.

"Nobody," I said. "Just want to ask you something."

"Yeah, well let me ask you something, what do you know about soccer, huh?" He pounded one of his beefy hands into the machine and waited for it to take a swing at him.

"Kyle Rote, Jr.," I said.

"What about him?"

"Nothing. I've heard of him, that's all. And that's all I know about soccer. Why?"

"Some guy wanted to place a soccer bet with me today. What do I know from soccer? Ain't that the game where they kick each other?"

"Something like that," I said. "They play it a lot in Europe, who do you think killed Parang?"

"Shit, man, is that what you're here about?"

He turned and looked at me, then turned back quickly before the machine could find an opening. He jabbed it with his left hand. "Come on you animal," he screamed.

"You ain't a cop," he said. "You must be a reporter."

"Right."

"Well, I ain't saying nothing. I mean I know who killed Ace, there ain't no question about it. You think I don't know? I know all right. But I ain't saying nothing. When the time comes I'll take care of it for Ace, but other than that I ain't saying nothing about it. Come on, you motherfucking machine!"

"How about why?"

"How about why, what?"

"How about telling me why somebody had Parang killed?"

"You think I don't know, huh? I'll tell you why. Ace was black-mailing the guy, that's why. The guy come into some money and Ace figured he should get some."

"I see," I said. "It's all very clear now. Just some stranger Ace heard had money, some guy off the street, or maybe some guy he met at a Knights of Columbus meeting."

"No pal, I ain't saying that. Don't you get what I'm saying? Ace was into something with the guy. The guy was supplying Ace with grass for a while, but he quit Ace awhile back."

"Why?"

"He just finked out and said he wasn't interested no more. Only Ace found out the guy was coming into some money and was trying to protect himself. So Ace figured he was entitled to some of it. In return, he wasn't going to tell the police that this guy was supplying half the city with grass. Now that makes sense, don't it?"

"Sure. What was the guy's name?"

"You think I don't know?" He punched the machine one last time, then said, "Aw the hell with it!" He shoved another quarter into the slot and pressed the button. This time the soda came out.

"To tell the truth," Galdetto said, "I don't actually know the guy's name. I never met him or nothing. But there's ways of finding out, you know."

"I wish I knew some," I said.

If I had taken out that soda machine and just left in the words people spoke you would know a lot less about Galdetto, and the dialogue would not have worked as well. You'd find it hard to believe that Galdetto would stand around answering questions if he didn't have to stay in one place to get his soda. Also, the soda machine was something to "look at." Just as most people prefer television drama to radio drama, readers like to have something to "watch" while they're listening to dialogue.

Exercise

I'm going to show you one more dialogue scene, but before I do, I'm going to set it up for you and give you only the dialogue. You write it your way before you look to see how I did it.

The scene is a typical scene from the opening of a romance novel. A woman meets a man and they have a conversation. But there must be something going on to keep them in the conversation, such as the soda machine in the previous example. Certainly they could stay in conversation simply because they were attracted to each other, but it gets kind of boring if all your scenes are two people just talking. It is better to create a situation that forces them together for a brief time.

In this scene I use a flat tire. Jill, our heroine, is driving along a country road in a town she has just moved to. She gets a flat. She noticed that there is a man working nearby in a ditch on a farm. She looks in the trunk.

She lifted the jack, put it back. Then she pressed a firm thumb against the spare tire to be certain it was good. She grabbed the tire iron, hefted it, tossed it on the ground. She was having a tough time admitting to herself that at twenty-six years of age she didn't know exactly how to change a flat tire. She looked again toward the man in the ditch. Should she call him? He'll probably think I'm an idiot, she thought, and she couldn't bring any words to her mouth.

Anyhow, the man notices Jill and he walks over to her. The dialogue begins and the situation of the flat tire holds them there. Here is the dialogue. You make up the rest.

"What seems to be the problem?"

"I've got a flat tire."

"You're right. You've got a flat."

"Very observant," she said.

"Why don't you fix it?" he asked.

"Don't know how."

"Now there's two ways we can do this," he said. "One is that I can stand here and supervise while you crouch down and change the tire. That way you don't have to feel like a helpless female and I can be a truly liberated male. Or, I could do the neighborly thing and change the tire for you. And if you watch me carefully you'll know how to do it next time."

"Well I don't know," she said. "I hate to put you out."

"If I were you, I'd put me out," he said, "seeing as how you're wearing a clean skirt and blouse and I'm wearing enough dirt to bury a cow."

"Okay, you talked me into it," Jill said. "Just tell me how I can help."

"Parker Lane."

"What about it?"

"That's my name. Parker Lane."

"Oh, I'm sorry. I thought it was the name of a street. I'm Jill Trahan."

"Nice to meet you. What part of New York are you from?"

"New York?"

"Yes. You're from New York, aren't you? The license plate on your car says New York. Hey, you didn't steal this car, did you?"

"No. I did live in New York until last week. I've moved up here. Haven't had a chance to change my registration yet."

"What tempted you away from New York?"

"Well, my mother died a month ago, so I moved here to help my dad run his business."

"Trahan, did you say? Ruth must have been your mother."

"Yes. Did you know her?"

"Sure, I get all my printing done at your mom and dad's shop. I liked your mother a lot, she was a nice lady."

"So I guess I'll be seeing you at the store from time to time," Jill said.

"Yes. And if it suits your taste you might frequent my place of business."

"What do you do?" she asked.

"Your dad's shop printed these, so you might as well have one," he said.

"A minister?" she said.

"Services are Sundays at ten," he said. "Perhaps we'll see you there."

Here is how I wrote that dialogue scene.

Jill opened the trunk of her car and fussed around with some tools for a bit. She lifted the jack, put it back. Then she pressed a firm thumb against the spare tire to be certain it was good. She grabbed at a tire iron, hefted it, tossed it on the ground. She was having a tough time admitting to herself that at twenty-six years of age she didn't know exactly how to change a flat tire. She looked again toward the man in the ditch. Should she call him? He'll probably think I'm an idiot, she thought, and she couldn't bring any words to her mouth.

But the man looked up then and saw her predicament. He climbed out of the ditch and began walking toward her. He walked slowly . . . ambled was the word that came to Jill's mind . . . and at first she thought he must be old. But as he got closer she could see that he was young, mid-thirties, and his slow gait was intentional, perhaps a cultivated style of walking that reminded him to be calm about all things in life.

"What seems to be the problem?" he said when he got close to her, on the other side of the fence. He seemed to be amused. He leaned on a fence post, offered a welcome smile. His blue work shirt was covered with ditch dust. His dungarees were almost black with dirt, and even his face was thoroughly smudged. He looked like a little boy who had slipped into a mud puddle and stayed there just for the fun of it.

"I've got a flat tire," Jill said. She gazed down the road one way, then the other, as if help were on the way.

The man straddled the lower fence pole, ducked under the upper one, and came through to meet her on the other side by the car. He was slender and agile and she liked the way his dungarees snuggled against his legs and waist. Jill imagined that he was pretty nice to look at under all that dirt, but all that she could be certain of was that his intelligent greenish eyes were captivating.

The man walked around to the road side of the car, stared down at the tire and said, "You're right. You've got a flat."

He wasn't being nasty. Her impression of him was that he'd had a hard morning working in the ditch and now he was going to have a little fun teasing the stranger.

"Very observant," she said.

The man smiled, looked again at the flat tire.

"Why don't you fix it?" he asked.

"Don't know how," she finally admitted.

The man glanced once more at the tire, as if it were a clock and he was keeping very careful track of the time. Then he ambled to the back of the car and peered into the open trunk. He pulled out the jack and the spare tire and laid them on the ground behind the car.

"Now, there's two ways we can do this," he said. "One is that I can stand here and supervise while you crouch down and change the tire. That way you don't have to feel like a helpless female and I can be a truly liberated male."

He paused, as if he were giving an audience time to absorb point number one of his speech.

"Or," he said, "I could do the neighborly thing and change the tire for you. And if you watch me carefully you'll know how to do it the next time."

Jill was perplexed. She wasn't sure what was the right thing to say.

"Well, I don't know," she said. "I hate to put you out."

The man studied her carefully. His bright green eyes swept from her face to her feet and back again. Clearly, his gaze was flirtatious, almost sexual, but it was done with such good humor and such a delighted boyish grin that Jill was not offended. The appreciation in his face made her feel pretty.

"If I were you, I'd put me out," he said, "seeing as how you're wearing a clean skirt and blouse and I'm wearing enough dirt to bury a cow."

"Okay, you talked me into it," Jill said. "Just tell me how I can help."

The man picked up the jack. He shoved it under the car, placed it properly, and started pumping. Jill kept looking between him and the road, to be sure no cars were coming.

"Parker Lane," the man said without turning from his work.

"What about it?"

"That's my name. Parker Lane."

"Oh, I'm sorry," she said, "I thought it was the name of a street." Then, realizing that he was waiting for her to announce her name, she added, "I'm Jill Trahan."

"Nice to meet you," he said. From his crouched position by the car he extended one mud-crusted hand, and with a devilish look straight into her eyes he dared her to shake it. He seemed delighted when she did.

He fastened the tire iron onto a lug nut and twisted hard. The muscles in his arms strained against the fabric of his filthy shirt. Then the nut loosened and he began twirling the tire iron on it like a toy until it came off easily.

"What part of New York are you from?" he asked.

"New York?"

"Yes. You're from New York, aren't you? The license plate on your car says New York." He kind of peeked over his shoulder at her. "Hey, you didn't steal this car, did you?"

"No," she laughed. "I did live in New York until last week. I've moved up here. Haven't had a chance to change my registration yet."

"What tempted you away from New York?"

"Well, my mother died a month ago, so I moved here to help my dad run his business."

"Trahan, did you say? Ruth must have been your mother."

"Yes. Did you know her?"

"Sure," he said. "I get all my printing done at your mom and dad's shop. I liked your mother a lot, she was a nice lady."

They talked for a few minutes about Jill's mother. Parker told her how he liked to flirt and joke with Ruth Trahan whenever he stopped to pick up an order at Trahan Press, the downtown printing and copy center where Jill had now gone to work with her father. The talk of her mother crystallized the sorrow which had hung over her ever since the funeral. For a long time Jill could not speak. Parker seemed to understand this, and he said nothing.

When the tire was changed Parker threw the tools back in the trunk and slammed it shut.

"So, I guess I'll be seeing you at the store from time to time," Jill said, pushing thoughts of her mother into the background.

"Yes," he said. "And if it suits your taste you might frequent my place of business."

"What do you do?" she asked.

Parker searched his pockets. Finally out of one deep dungaree pocket he pulled a long leather wallet that was surprisingly slim and elegant, considering the way he was dressed. He poked his dirty fingers in it and gingerly removed one of his clean white business cards. He handed it to Jill.

"Your dad's shop printed these, so you might as well have one," he said.

In the middle of the card was a drawing of a church steeple. And below that, the words, "The Rev. Parker Lane," and on the sides the church address and home and office phone numbers.

"A minister?" she said.

"Services are Sundays at ten," he said. "Perhaps we'll see you there." Then he gave her a cute little hip-high wave, as if he were sweeping dust off a table. He climbed back through the fence, and Jill watched him amble back to his ditch.

Don't Describe Dialogue

"I've got to go," she insisted.

"Then go," I responded, "but don't blame me if the ping-pong table gets warped."

"Warped?" she questioned. "But you promised. . . ."

"Promised?" I challenged. "Promised, indeed! Men like me don't make promises."

"Men like you!" she exclaimed. "All men are like you: beastly!"

"Beastly?" I sniffed. "You dare to call me beastly?"

"Yes, beastly," she intoned.

"Then go," I cautioned, "but don't walk down any dark alleys if you value your life."

The problem with that dialogue, aside from the fact that it's just some silly stuff I made up for fun, is that people are insisting, intoning, cautioning, responding, questioning, and challenging, but nobody seems to be *saying* anything.

Many beginning writers seem to cherish these synonyms for *say* or *said,* and they avoid "he said" and "she said" as if the phrases were carrying a fatal disease.

I think there are two reasons for this.

One is that the new writer is afraid of repeating the same word over and over. And well he should be. A word too often repeated reminds the reader that a writer is at work. But phrases like "he said," "she said," and Hermonodo said" are an exception. Coming as they do on the coattails of dialogue, where the reader already knows that words are being said, the words *say* and *said* slip by unnoticed, while *sniffed, exclaimed,* and *orated* attract attention. The important thing is the noun or pronoun, the *he* or *she* or *Hermonodo* that lets the reader know who is speaking, and in good dialogue even most of those words are unnecessary. So limit the sniffs and the exclamations to those times when they really improve the writing in exchange for the small disturbance they cause. Use "he said" and "she said" and "the potato farmer said" to establish who is speaking, and return to them not with every exchange, but whenever there is a chance of the reader being uncertain about who is speaking.

Another reason many new writers use so many synonyms for *said* is that they don't think the words within the quotation marks convey the emotion or attitude they are trying to get across, so they try to bolster the statement by adding "he screamed" or "she persisted."

For the same reason, many also form the habit of tacking on adverbs to describe how something was said. Consider this:

"Go to hell!" he said angrily.

"I don't want to go to hell. I thought Miami Beach was too hot," he replied humorously.

"You know, you're really getting on my nerves," he shot back impatiently.

"I'm sorry. I'm usually more cheerful when people tell me I'm out on the street after forty years with a company," he said sarcastically.

"Okay, okay. Look, Dan, it's over. There's nothing more we can say to each other. Let's just end it," he sighed resignedly.

Now reread that dialogue and see if you can comprehend the tones and attitudes without any of the *-ly* adverbs. I'll bet you can.

There are exceptions, but generally dialogue that works is dialogue that clearly communicates the feelings and intentions of the speaker without being boosted by synonyms for *said* or adverbs such as *angrily* or *sadly*.

Don't underestimate the ability of the reader to catch the subtleties of speech. If you work hard at the dialogue and it sounds right to you, have faith that the reader, given the overall situation and the nature of the characters, will hear it as he should.

Another sign for over your desk: DIALOGUE SHOULD CONTAIN ITS OWN TONE OF VOICE.

Exercise

Below is a list of emotions, attitudes, and intentions that a character could have. For each, write a line of dialogue. Don't describe the dialogue in any way. The dialogue should reveal the character's feelings.

1. Anger
2. Love
3. Jealousy
4. Regret
5. Concern
6. Despair
7. Sarcasm
8. Desire

9. Joy
10. Annoyance
11. Rage
12. Satisfaction
13. Uncertainty
14. Curiosity
15. Determination

Avoid Heavy-Handed Dialogue

The reader gets many facts from dialogue, either because only the speaker knows the facts, or because the writer has concluded that dialogue is the most readable way to provide those facts.

But writing dialogue to provide information must be done with care. If it's obvious to the reader that dialogue is there only to provide information, he will feel as if he's been accosted in the middle of reading and told, "Just a minute, I've got to tell you some stuff you need to know before you read any further." This sort of dialogue is called *heavy-handed dialogue,* and it doesn't work. Heavy-handed dialogue results from characters speaking for the reader when they should be speaking for each other. George tells Joyce things that Joyce obviously already knows, and the reader loses the illusion that the conversation would take place even if he were not there to hear it.

Here are some facts that a writer needs to get across to the reader through dialogue:

A couple is waiting for a new car to be delivered. The car is a Mustang. The day is Saturday. It's raining out. Carolyn is the couple's daughter. Carolyn was recently in an automobile accident. The husband has to leave for Cincinnati the next day.

What these facts have in common is that the husband and wife already know them and would not ordinarily tell them to each other. But you want to inform the reader of these facts through dialogue, so you have to work them in somehow.

Heavy-handed dialogue would go something like this:

> "Gee, Joyce, do you suppose our brand-new red Mustang will be here soon? It's two o'clock, the time they promised delivery."
> "Yes, George, today is Saturday. Another rainy Saturday!"
> "I hope it gets here soon."

"Yes, it would be a shame if you didn't get to drive it today, since you've got to go to Cincinnati on business tomorrow."

"Well, if it doesn't show up until Monday, you make sure our daughter Carolyn doesn't drive it. I mean, after all, she had an automobile accident just last week."

Dialogue sounds phony when people tell each other things they already know. But dialogue that delivers information already known by the characters *will* work if you push the information into the background. Focus the sentences on something else.

"Well, it's two o'clock. Where's the car?"

"It will be here, George, just settle down. Today's Saturday—they're probably shorthanded."

"Shorthanded, hah! Probably joyriding in my car. They'd just better watch the cornering in this rain; I don't want to see a scratch on that car."

"Cornering? For God's sake, it's only a Mustang, it's not a Maserati."

"Yeah, well, it's *my* Mustang, and it looks like I'm not even going to get to drive it."

"You'll drive it, George, you'll drive it. Unless you're planning to stay in Cincinnati forever. Besides, you're not even leaving until tomorrow."

"They're probably picking up broads in it, that's what they're doing, picking up broads in my car. Look, if it doesn't show up until Monday, you guard it with your life. I don't want Carolyn near it, you understand. She is not to drive that car ever."

"Joanie Davis lets her daughter drive their new car."

"Joanie Davis's daughter didn't rack up our station wagon last Friday night."

"Oh, for crying out loud! Carolyn hit the ice and skidded. Could have happened to anybody."

Heavy-handed dialogue also occurs when one character tells another all kinds of things he didn't ask for, for no apparent reason except that the writer couldn't find a better place to provide the reader with the information. Consider this:

She responded just the way the women in his dreams had, pressing her body against his, clutching him with wild need, her heart pounding against his chest. Her lips turned to fire against his and he knew she wanted him more than she'd ever wanted anything.

"It's been so long," Don said. "Too long."

"Oh, it's been a long time for me, too," she murmured. "Ever since my husband drowned three years ago in a vat of chocolate syrup. He'd forgotten his life jacket. He was already dead when I got there. All this time I've wanted a man so badly, but I didn't dare. Even when I took that three-week vacation in Elgin, Illinois, I didn't fool around, though I had offers, believe me, lots of them. And at the rope factory, where I worked with my brother Dwight, there were lots of nice guys, but. . . ."

Et cetera.

If you find yourself writing dialogue where people answer questions that weren't asked, then find some way of getting the question asked.

"How long's it been?"

"Five years. Ever since my husband died."

"Died? Aren't you a little young to be a widow?"

"He drowned. A vat of syrup and one careless step. That's all it took, and Hubie was gone. He was dead when I got there."

"Five years, and you've never been tempted?"

"Oh, I've been tempted all right. Couple of years back I spent three weeks in Elgin, Illinois. Quite a town, I'll tell you. Came close there, came real close."

"What stopped you?"

"Oh, I don't know. I was afraid I'd get a rep at the rope factory. Used to work there with my brother Dwight. There were a lot of nice guys there, too, and they weren't shy about asking, if you know what I mean. But. . . ."

Exercise

Here are several situations. Using dialogue only, and no more than six exchanges, try to communicate to the reader what is going on. You can use "he said," or "she said," but nothing else besides the words spoken by the characters. Your goal is to make the dialogue believable and to avoid heavy-handed dialogue like, "Imagine me, the director of this movie, trying to talk a big star like you out of stage fright."

1. A major rock star is trying to talk a too-young groupie into going home.

2. A writer is interviewing a condemned prisoner.
3. A man and woman are on a stagecoach. He's going to meet his mail order bride. She's going to meet her mail order husband. They are unaware that they have been matched with each other.
4. A bookie is trying to bribe a Ping-Pong player into throwing a match.
5. Two unhappy wives are planning to murder each other's husband and to arrange alibis for themselves.

Avoid Direct Address

Most beginning writers have a bad habit of inserting names into every line of dialogue. It's awkward, it's artificial, and it marks the writer with a scarlet "A" for amateur. If you read this example out loud, you should be quickly cured of the habit.

"Well, Melanie, did you go to Gary's workshop?"

"Yes, James."

"How was it, Melanie?"

"Pretty good, James, but he said one thing I didn't quite understand."

"What's that, Melanie?"

"James, he said that in dialogue, you shouldn't always be writing the name of the person being spoken to. In fact, James, he said to almost never do it."

"Why Melanie, I can't believe he said that. Why would he?"

"According to him, James, we almost never use a person's name when we speak to him in real life."

"That's ridiculous, Melanie. You and I do it with every exchange, don't we?"

"Yes, James."

Don't Write Unnecessary Dialogue

While good dialogue can improve the pace of your story, keep in mind that unnecessary dialogue is just a bunch of unnecessary words with quote marks around them.

Dialogue should never be used to fill up space on the page, to create scenes when a simple transition will do, or to cover ground that could be covered more quickly or effectively with narrative.

Just because something can be put in dialogue doesn't mean it should be. If it has no story value, character value, or information value, it won't improve the pace of your story, so don't put it in dialogue.

One of the mistakes I see often in manuscripts is the creation of dialogue for introductions.

> "Jeff, I'd like you to meet Mrs. Heffner," Angie said. I reached out and shook Mrs. Heffner's hand.
>
> "Hi, Jeff," she said, smiling.
>
> "And this young lady is Mrs. Heffner's secretary, Deanna Frost," Angie said. "Deanna, this is Jeff Conti."
>
> We shook hands. "Hi, Deanna."
>
> "Hi," she said. "Nice to meet you."

Some writers do this every time one character is introduced to another. It's boring. It makes the story crawl. It frustrates the reader. Just write: "Angie introduced me to Mrs. Heffner and Deanna Frost, her secretary."

Then get on with it.

There is no unsinkable rule about when you should use dialogue and when you shouldn't. But here's a good generalization: Look at the dialogue you have written and ask yourself, "If a stranger were nearby would she try to eavesdrop on this conversation?" If the answer is no, don't use dialogue. If the answer is yes, use it.

Chapter Eight
Characterization

Write About Real People

It has always seemed to me that the reason many science fiction television shows and movies and stories are so dismally dull is that the writers imagine people will be different in a mere thousand years or so. They load up their scenarios with deadly laser guns and metallic panels that go burp-burp-burp, and they strip their characters of jealousy, lust, glee, love, confusion—in other words, all that is human. Planets where there is no passion and galaxies where no one laughs glut the universes these writers create. Armies of clones and government by machine, cold and loveless, all ignore the basic reason that people go to the movies, watch television, and read.

People.

That's what it's all about. We read to touch other people. To identify with other people. To compare ourselves with other people. To laugh at other people. To see, to hear, to feel other people.

Imagine this: You are in a room with a stack of books, a pinball machine, a cheeseburger, a pile of nice new clothes, and a tub of warm water. And you are lonely. Which comfort source would you turn to? Which can give you that human contact, that people fix you need to take the edge off your loneliness?

What *good* science fiction writers know (and good writers in general know) is that people have been made out of the same stuff for years and they will continue to be made out of that stuff for a long time.

Whether you intend to write science fiction or not, you can learn a lot from reading some of the works of good science fiction writers. You will notice that while technology erupts and erases all the environments familiar to you, recognizable human qualities continue. People are still people, whether they're in Detroit, Afghanistan, or on planet Zip-3.

So good writing is about people. There are exceptions, but fewer than you might think.

The Universal and the Specific

A girl I once dated told me that when her mother nagged her to eat everything on her plate by saying, "Millions of people are starving to death in China," she would reply, "Name one."

If her mother had been able to name one, the plate might have gotten cleaned.

That's because the girl would have felt guilt, sympathy, pain—whatever her mother was trying to get across.

The reason is that each of us is one single person. Each reader is an individual who identifies with other individuals, not with masses.

When you watch the eleven o'clock news, which bad news troubles your sleep more, "Forty-two people were killed in Iowa when a westbound train derailed near Davenport," or "One of the passengers, seven-year-old Jeffrey Wells, of Waterbury, Connecticut, was found dead with his teddy bear clutched in his arms"?

Who do you *feel* something for?

It's hard to feel for the forty-two nameless, faceless people, but it is so easy to cry for the seven-year-old Jeffrey.

Usually when you write you'll be trying to make your readers feel positive things for your characters: sympathy, concern, friendship. Sometimes you'll want your readers to experience negative emotions: hate, disrespect, revulsion. In either case, you want the readers to *feel* something about the character, just as you felt something about Jeffrey that you did not feel about the forty-two passengers.

To make your readers feel something for your character, you must make your character a specific person. You must find that teddy bear so that your character emerges from forty-two passengers as an individual. You must show some *specific* characteristics.

But the *feeling* you're trying to elicit in your readers is just the opposite. You've never met your readers, so you must strike a chord you know to be *universal.*

Find the specifics of character that unlock a universal emotion.

I'm a man. How is it that as I read about a woman who is frightened as she approaches childbirth I can feel for her and care about her? I can't reach back into my experience memory and find childbirth. I can't even find a trip to the hospital. But I can reach back into my *emotional* memory and find *fear*; we have all experienced fear, if not over childbirth, then over something else. Fear is universal.

Your readers may never have lost a dog, as the boy in your story has, but they have probably lost something. They have known the universal sense of *loss*.

If you interview a congressman who is running for the Senate, find the characteristics he has that demonstrate his ambition. All of your readers won't run for the Senate, but all of them have experienced *ambition*.

If the bank president uses a lot of six-syllable words because he's insecure, then put them in the story. Your readers may not know many six-syllable words, but they understand *insecurity*.

Much of writing has a mirror-image effect. The writer has an image in his mind, which he translates into words. The reader sees the words and translates them back into an image. The writer of fiction asks, "If I felt nervous" (universal feeling) "what might I do?" (specific action). So he creates a character who wrings his hands while he talks. The reader comes along and sees a character wringing his hands and wonders, "Why is he doing that?" which is another way of asking, "How would I be feeling if I were doing that?" and concludes, "Oh, he's nervous."

Your story won't be destroyed if a character who isn't nervous wrings his hands. "Make every word count" doesn't mean load every word with significance. But every word you write *is* an opportunity to improve the whole, and writing works best when the largest number of wise, thoughtful choices are made.

Keep in mind, too, that writing is always an act of faith. You write something in the belief that the reader will understand what you're talking about. In the case of characters and their feelings, you're safe. If you once felt something basic, primal, something that wriggled in your soul, you can be sure the reader has felt it, too, and all you have to do is find the characterization that will show it to him.

Exercise

Here are some issues and events of concern to society. However, if you wanted to write about these matters in a way that would make the reader care, you would have to personalize, give the reader someone to identify with. For each of the following, think of either the fictional character or nonfiction interview subject who could best create emotions in the reader. Keep in mind, however, that you also have to be entertaining and informative, so choose carefully. If you want to write about the San Francisco earthquake, for example, a "guy whose house was destroyed by the earthquake," would not be as interesting as a seismologist who tries to warn the city that the quake is coming.

1. World hunger
2. Arson
3. Cancer
4. Nuclear war
5. The environment
6. Apartheid
7. Feminism
8. Gun control
9. Drug addiction
10. Bad manners

Identification

One of my favorite novels is Dan Wakefield's *Under the Apple Tree*. There is no resistance to Wakefield's prose, no bumps or rough spots. I hated to see the book end. I found *Under the Apple Tree* exciting, touching, and compelling, so it might surprise you to learn that the novel had virtually no sex, murders, suicides, divorces, terrorist attacks, counter-spies, or secret passageways. It's a simple story about a twelve-year-old boy on the homefront during World War II.

Why would any reader care about a twelve-year-old boy doing ordinary things?

The answer is "identification."

Artie Garber, Wakefield's twelve-year-old hero, lives in a small Illinois town. The war is on and Artie worries a lot about invasion. So he helps out. He goes up on roofs to watch for German planes.

Now, as adult readers we know that no German planes invaded any small Illinois town, and that such a thing was unlikely. We know that what Artie is doing is unimportant. So why do we climb to the roof with him?

Because it's important to him.

Why do we watch for German planes when we know they are not coming?

Because he doesn't know that.

We get Artie's feelings of exhilaration, his fears, his hopes, and his triumphs through reading, because we identify with him. We pretend that we are him.

Let's take another book I read recently, *The Bridge Across Forever* by Richard Bach. Bach is a wonderful writer who believes in soul mates and predestination, and those beliefs are integral to the book. To me they are as meaningless as tarot cards, and yet I was enthralled by the book. Why?

Identification.

It's not important that I agree with Bach about finding a soul mate. I'm not a Catholic either, but one of my favorite novels is about a priest trying to find his proper place in the church. What's important in the Bach book is what he believes in and that his beliefs fuel his writing in a way that makes me feel what he feels. I can feel like me anytime. We read so that we can feel like somebody else for a while. That's what identification is.

What does this mean to you? It means you don't have to always write about "important" things like war or politics or multinational conglomerates. You can write about a girl's wish that a certain boy will call for a date, or the thousands of people who are changing professions in midlife, or the process of making friends. The issues in your book or story don't have to be important to the world. They just have to be important to the fictional character or real person with whom the reader identifies.

Identification is important to the writer in another way, before he begins to write.

Take, for example, *The Blaspheming Moon*, a book by Christopher Hewitt.

The Blaspheming Moon is an imagined diary of the artist Achille Emperaire. Emperaire is an important and interesting artist, but let's face it, you've probably never heard of him and neither had I until I came upon the book. Which leads us to the question, "Why would anybody want to write a book about an artist that few people have heard of?"

Christopher Hewitt suffers from a congenital bone condition called osteogenesis imperfecta. He has bones that can fracture, he writes, "like the snapping of green bamboo or a stick of celery." As a result, Hewitt views life from a wheelchair. Achille Emperaire also suffered from osteogenesis imperfecta, though, unlike Hewitt, he could walk with a cane. When Hewitt first saw a portrait of Emperaire, he was, he says, "shocked by the striking resemblance between Emperaire and myself." That's when Hewitt began to research and learned about the disability.

So Christopher Hewitt wrote a book about a little-known artist because he identifies with him. And it's a pretty good reason. The men lived in different centuries, in different countries, but they have a bond, a shared experience, the experience of living with a specific disability.

In his introduction Hewitt writes, "The physical similarity between Emperaire and myself is merely the pretext for my writing the book and has little to do with the subject matter." This is true. It is the inner similarity that has everything to do with the book.

So if you want to write about anybody, whether he is a real person or a fictitious character, search for that level on which you identify with your subject. Find the shared experience, whether it is suffering, jubilation, or anything in between and write from there, because your understanding of the character springs from that shared experience.

Characterization in Nonfiction

Character is "the combination of qualities or features that distinguishes one person, group, or thing from another," says my dictionary. And *characterization* is "a description or representation of a person's qualities or peculiarities."

Characterization is a word generally associated with the writing of fiction. Short stories and novels, teleplays, movie scripts—all depend heavily on believable, interesting characters to attract an audience. In fiction you *have* to characterize. Your story succeeds only if the people in it fascinate, anger, please, tickle, or otherwise affect the reader.

In nonfiction that's not necessarily true. Your writing can work because you educate, entertain, instruct, or enrage the reader. A story about installing CB radios could work perfectly well without any characterization.

But people show up in almost everything you write, so characterization is an important part of writing nonfiction that works. Putting flesh-and-bones people into your articles gives those articles a life and a movement that sets them apart from articles in which no one's heart is beating.

Characters in your nonfiction fall into two categories. Some characters have to be there because your story is about them, as in interviews with Nobel Prize winners and profiles of famous jugglers. Other characters don't have to be there, but you add them to give your article greater dimension and color; for example, you might spend three hours with a hypnotist and describe her workday for your article on hypnotism.

The newspaper and magazine profiles you remember are the ones in which the writer used characterization, "a description or representation of a person's qualities or peculiarities." Often it is characterization that makes the difference between a dull piece and one that sticks a lasting image on the reader's brain.

My slant on a local politician was that he was loved or hated; few people were neutral about him. One of the paragraphs I used to build this image was:

> Sitting on a board where some torture the English language without mercy every Monday night, Dyer speaks clearly, coolly, and as precisely as a professor. A singer and actor in high school, Dyer polishes off each syllable before he delivers it, and if his rhetoric is often critical, haughty, and downright nasty, it is at least interesting. Things are rarely good or bad when Dyer describes them. Charges made against him have been "dilatory," some committee recommendations have been "abhorrent," and local merchants have often been "munificent" in their service to the town.

Obviously, in an article about Mr. Dyer I had to characterize him at least to some extent. But in most articles you aren't writing about a person. Still it is the presence of people that will bring your piece to life. Do you recall the piece about the train ride in the pace section? Do you remember the boys tossing footballs and the old men drinking coffee in smoky diners?

What to Look For

Everybody you meet is a potential character. If you write nonfiction, you will interview hundreds of people for articles and books. If you write fiction, you will conduct fewer formal interviews, but you should regard *all* conversations as interviews because many of the people you meet — at parties and churches, hospitals and supermarkets — will become characters in your stories. You will want to remember what they said and how they said it. You should approach each encounter with a keen eye and a cocked ear. Keep a checklist in your mind. Everyone has a particular way of talking, dressing, moving, so watch and listen carefully.

Pick out only the useful characteristics, the ones that will work. But first, you must observe *everything*, so that you'll have something to choose from.

Here's a checklist to keep in mind when listening.

Vocabulary. Does she use a lot of long words? Does she use a lot of professional jargon? Does she use certain words often?

Style of speech. Does he speak with authority, or does he sound as if he's not sure? Is he controlling the conversation or are you? Is he trying to manipulate you into asking the right questions? Does he water down all his statements with mitigating phrases like "generally" or "much of the time"?

Tone. What does her voice sound like? Is it melodious? Is it harsh? Is it the same voice she used to talk to the secretary when she was interrupted, or is she putting on a voice for you?

Diction. Does he speak clearly or mumble into his beard? Does she have an accent?

If I anticipate a particularly long interview, I will bring a tape recorder. But I also bring a notebook. The tape can only record sound. My notebook records everything else on my mental checklist. Here is the kind of checklist you should have in your head whenever you interview someone, or even meet someone who might become a character in your fiction.

Clothing. Do the person's clothes tell how rich or poor he is? Does her manner of dress show that she is careless or careful about detail? Does she dress in good taste? Does he look comfortable in the clothes he is wearing, or is he really a poor boy dressed up like he's a rich boy?

Jewelry. Does she wear a watch, or is time not important? Is the jewelry expensive, ostentatious, sentimental? Is it religious? Does it indicate some other belief, like a pendant that's an astrological sign, or perhaps membership in some organization? Is he forty-two years old and still wearing his high school class ring?

Grooming. Does she wear too much makeup? Or does she glow with good health without makeup? Are her nails long and alluring or short and functional? Are they bitten down? Does he dye his hair? Does he care about his figure?

General appearance. What about posture? Does she slump in the chair or sit up straight? Does he smile a lot when he speaks? Does he gesture with his hands? Is she saying "come closer" or "go away" with her stance? Does he have a big nose, or an intractable pimple that might affect his feelings about himself? Does she reach out and touch you when she speaks?

These are all attributes that would not show up on your tape recording. You can observe them without asking a single question. When sprinkled throughout an article they give it a life that spoken words, no matter how revealing, cannot provide.

Beyond these more or less objective observations you make while your subject is talking, there is, of course, the whole range of *what* he said, and what it discloses: The words people speak reveal more about their character than anything else.

The one major area from which character emerges is, of course, the subject's history. Was he abandoned as a child, and how does that affect him now? Was she the queen of the prom and the star of the girls' basketball team? What character traits have resulted from these experiences? The answer to the question "Where do I look to find clues to character?" is "Everywhere."

Exercise

Take a notebook and pen and go someplace public, a park, a train station, whatever. Pick out a few characters and go through the checklist I have given you. Then add your own items to the checklist. See how much you can find out about a person just by watching her. Observe the ways in which she reveals character. Then think about the many ways you can reveal the characters, either real or invented, that you write about.

Stereotypes

A stereotype is to characterization what a cliché is to description. A stereotype character is one that your editor has seen almost as many times as he's seen his mother, and that character is another enemy of originality. When an editor tells you that your character is a stereotype, he means that instead of creating a living, breathing person, you have wheeled in a dummy from the stereotype warehouse, which is just two long blocks away from the cliché warehouse.

In the manuscripts that were sent to me last year I saw these stereotypes several times each:

The wisecracking private detective who is hardboiled and cynical.

The sweet old schoolteacher who bakes cookies for everybody.

The innocent young girl in the big city who falls in love with Mr. Wonderful the first time she sees him.

The wise, handsome, and successful hero who falls in love with the innocent young girl in the big city the first time he sees her.

You get the idea. Perhaps you've hired a few of these mannequins to do work you were supposed to do.

Stereotypes are not confined to fiction. Even though the people in your nonfiction are real human beings, they are stereotypes if they don't show up on the page that way. Hollywood publicity was filled with stereotypes for years. The starlets all seemed to be the same virgin from a small town in Kansas. The handsome new leading man always seemed to share the same manly values as the last handsome new leading man. Today many of our less original sports writers always portray the hard-working, unsung utility infielder as if that's all there was to him. The nonfiction stereotype results when the writer takes a one-dimensional view of his subject, either because the writer hasn't really looked at that person, or because he's afraid to take chances.

An editor I know (who, incidentally, is not gruff, harried, or cynical) once told me that the most common problem with the profile articles he rejects is that the writer seems to have fallen in love with his subject. The person comes off as perfect, and that makes for a pretty boring article.

In fiction and nonfiction the stereotypical characters are always too something. The girls are too pretty, the men too handsome, the villains too cruel, the heroes too heroic, the politicians too corrupt, the vine-covered cottages too cozy, the director too talented, the children too adorable (as are the puppies), the little old ladies and ministers always too sweet.

Here is an example from one of my old manuscripts. It was to be a novel called *Spring Was Never Waiting*.

> Clay was a tall, good-looking guy who never left a female head unturned. He had lustrous dark hair, thick eyebrows, perfect teeth, and a friendly smile. He had the body of an Olympic gymnast and the quick, agile movements of a cat. His complexion was flawless and so were his manners. He moved with the confidence of a king. Clearly he was a man who was totally in control of his life, and perhaps the lives of many others.

Anytime you create a character who has "perfect" something, "flawless" something else, and is "totally" anything, go back and rethink it. Chances are you are creating a robot, not a person.

As we will see in the next section, there's nothing wrong with these stereotypes as a starting point. You have to start somewhere. But look at a stereotype as the granite into which you chisel your individual and atypical character.

The character who emerges should be not quite like anybody else. He should be inconsistent, he should have good points and bad, strengths and weaknesses. There should be some surprises in his makeup.

Typecasting

For several months now I have been having an affair with a woman whose husband is a linebacker for the Denver Broncos.

What do you think? Do you think my wife knows about the affair? Do you think the woman's husband is a big, mean guy who will squash my head like a grape if he finds out? Do you think there is something wrong with my marriage and the woman's marriage? Do you think the whole thing is conducted in secret while he's off cracking heads with the Los Angeles Rams?

How would your answers change if I told you I was having an affair with a woman whose husband is a bookkeeper for a small-town bank? Or if I told you I was having a friendship with the woman?

It's possible that my wife thinks the affair is a great hobby for me.

It's possible that my lover's football-playing husband is the unjealous sort who thinks I'm great fun to have around.

It's possible, but not likely.

Most likely when you read the original sentence you assumed the affair was secret, and you assumed that the football player would resort to violence if he found out. You made those assumptions not because you necessarily believed they would be true in every case, but because you knew those were the prevailing images: affairs are secret, football players are violent; and you also knew that I was trying to tell you something. So your response is based on the attitudes of society, which you assume you share with me, and you will hold on to them until I start adding facts that tell you this instance is different.

It doesn't matter if I think affairs among the married are not improper or if this particular football player is a meek sort who wouldn't step on a cockroach. If I'm proposing something that contradicts the accepted social image, I have to tell you. If I'm not, then I don't.

The reader will assume that your billionaire oil baron is a conservative who votes Republican until you explicitly state that the guy is actually pouring all his money into the Socialist party.

The reader will assume that your unescorted woman, wearing a tight red dress and high heels, sitting in a sleazy bar, is a cheap pickup or a prostitute, until you explicitly state that the woman is a happily married local librarian who just stepped out for a drink.

Whether you agree or disagree with the reader's sexist stereotypes, racial prejudices, class assumptions, etc., you still have to take them into account.

The images in the reader's mind are the only images you have to work with. If he thinks that your unescorted woman in the bar is a cheap pickup, then that's what you're going to convey when you present such a situation, whether you like it or not. What's worse, even if the reader doesn't feel that way, he thinks that *you* think he does, so when he asks himself the question, "What is the writer trying to tell me?" he comes up with the same answer until you tell him more.

You can't call up the reader and say, "Gee, you shouldn't feel that way." The point is he *does* feel that way, and you have to write accordingly. If you don't want your reader to see the woman in the bar as a cheap pickup, then you must use more words to explain that such is not the case, or avoid characterizing her that way in the first place. Don't call her "unescorted." Don't say the bar is "sleazy." Don't describe the dress as "tight." Ignore the high heels.

Instead, mention the librarian's horn-rimmed glasses, her wedding ring, the delicate way she sips her drink, and her constant use of five-syllable words.

The choice is yours.

There is no such thing as objective characterization.

My definition of *objective* here is the third in my dictionary: "uninfluenced by emotion, surmise, or personal prejudice."

The reason is simple. Every time you write something, a word, a phrase, a sentence, you *could* have written something else . . . and the reader knows it. You said the woman was unescorted when you could have said she was overweight. You said the woman was married to a football player when you could have said she was blind in one eye. The reader assumes, quite logically, that you chose to tell this fact instead of another for a reason. He assumes you had an *intention.*

Until you tell the reader otherwise, he assumes you want him to typecast. That is, he thinks you've chosen to tell him characteristics that are "typical of people like this" so that he can go searching through his mental "types of people" file that has been established by real life, other books, neighbors' comments, television, and movies.

Since the reader assumes you write with his stereotypes in mind, since he is going to act *as if* you do, you have no choice but to comply, or your writing simply won't work. The reader is running the show. The communication takes place in his head.

Your writing would become pretty dull if you tried to make all your characters conform to the types the reader carries around in his brain (that is, if you made all your ministers compassionate, your interior decorators prissy, and your female truck drivers mannish). The reader's first image is usually the stereotype; you can use that as a springboard to your own twists of characterization. If you write "Edna took in stray kittens, and she often baked cookies for the neighborhood children," you show the reader that Edna is a type: nice, sweet, gentle. If you write "Edna loved children and kittens, but she liked to go out late at night and slash the tires of cars that burn too much gasoline," you're still using that nice, sweet, gentle type as the standard from which Edna deviates. In other words, you use the type as a way of showing how your character is different.

So give your characters traits that you think readers find typical of the kind of person you want them to see. If your character is like the type, then you've characterized well. If the character is not like the type, then write about the traits that make him different.

Exercise

Here is an exercise that will help you to come up with original characters.

1. Imagine a character you want to write about. She can be a fictional character or a real person for a work of nonfiction. Give me a three-word description of that character, such as "a war hero" or "a retired schoolteacher."

2. Write three adjectives that would support a stereotype of that character — that is, three adjectives that the reader would assume if he knew nothing else about the character. For example, if you used "war hero," three adjectives in the stereotype would be "male, brave, patriotic" (even though she could be a cowardly anarchist.)

3. Now tell me one thing that would shatter my assumptions. Tell me something true of your character that is not true of the stereotype. Perhaps your war hero *is* male, brave, and patriotic, but if you tell me that he also collects ceramic pigs I will begin to see him as an individual. When you do this, choose a trait that really is true of your character, not one you've thrown in just for the sake of making her different. The deliberate contrast, such as the homosexual football player, is itself a stereotype.

4. Think about how this quality might have gotten your character in trouble once, or gotten her out of it. How did it win her praise or bring her condemnation? How does she use it to manipulate people, or how do people use it to manipulate her?

5. Describe a scene in which you would reveal character through this trait.

6. Write the scene.

Now let's see how this sort of exercise might enrich a book. The book we will work with is Edwin O'Connor's famous novel, *The Last Hurrah*. The book's main character is Frank Skeffington, an aging,

Irish-Catholic, Boston politician, a man who might easily have filled a stereotyper's mold. But in the hands of a fine writer, Skeffington came to life. He outgrew the book and stepped out of the pages and into the public consciousness, so that today he is known to many people who never read the book.

By the time I read page four of *The Last Hurrah*, O'Connor had convinced me that I was in the room with a flesh-and-blood Skeffington and that I knew the man well. Naturally, I went back to see how he had done it.

I found that O'Connor had created an eminently believable Frank Skeffington in the first chapter by working largely with one trait that was in the character, but not in the stereotype. That trait was Skeffington's love of reading.

On page one Skeffington is thinking about retirement, "far from the madding crowd," he says, using a literary allusion. When the reporters ask him what he would do in retirement, he answers, "Read."

And in the next few pages O'Connor shows us:

1. What Skeffington reads:

The reporter had been persistent. "Which great books?"

Skeffington's eyes had opened, the silver head had lifted, and once more the reporters met the deadpan look. "I don't know whether you'd know them or not," he had said thoughtfully. "The Bible, which is a book composed of two parts, commonly called the Old and the New Testaments. The poems and plays of Shakespeare, an Englishman."

2. How Skeffington feels about reading:

After breakfast he picked up a book and settled down by the long front bedroom window to read; this had been his morning custom for nearly fifty years. When his wife was alive, much of the time he had read aloud to her; for the last ten years he had read silently to himself. He read poetry for the most part, and he read chiefly for sound, taking pleasure in the patterns of words as they formed and echoed deep within his brain.

3. How reading has influenced Skeffington's career:

It was an incongruous picture: the aging political boss, up shortly after dawn, preparing for the daily war of the wards by reading a volume of verse; it was a picture from which Skeffington — who was capable, at times, of great detachment — derived considerable amusement. He knew that the widely publicized habit had given rise to indignation, even fury, among his opponents; in several campaigns it had cropped up as a major issue.

4. How Skeffington's reading affected some other people:

"Here we are in this grand city of ours, payin' the highest tax rate we've ever paid, and the garbage hasn't been collected for weeks," he would cry. "Our back yards are bein' turned into veritable *bedlams* of nauseous perfumes and where is the mayor while all this is goin' on? I'll tell you where he is; he's up in his mansion on the avenue, readin' *pomes*! The city smells to high heaven and Frank Skeffington's got his nose in a book!"

All of this emerges because perhaps one afternoon Edwin O'Connor placed a sheet of paper on his desk and labeled it "Skeffington's Character Traits." And then, pausing to think of just the right thing, he wrote, "Skeffington reads."

Description as Indirect Characterization

Everything you write delivers a message to the reader, whether you intend it to or not. This doesn't mean that every word is a problem. It means that you should ask yourself if a word or phrase you write is going to deliver a message you don't want delivered. Sometimes when you say things "just because they are true," you accidentally deliver messages that contradict what you really want to say. If you interview a successful Baptist evangelist one morning and there just happens to be an empty whiskey bottle on his desk because the janitor left it there, you can't write it into your description and expect the reader to accept it at face value as just part of the scenery.

If you write, "A maroon curtain hangs behind the Reverend Wilson, and the surface of his desk is cluttered with papers and prayer books, an empty whiskey bottle, copies of his new record album, and a Bible signed by the President," the reader will assume that you're trying to send a message with that whiskey bottle. The reader doesn't think you mentioned it "just because it happened to be there." The reader thinks you mean it to say the Reverend Wilson is a drunk, or a hypocrite, or something.

Physical characteristics can deliver messages as quickly as empty whiskey bottles, so be careful in deciding which ones to include.

Earlier I said that if you mention a woman's tight red dress and her high heels, the reader will picture her one way, but if you mention instead her horn-rimmed glasses, he will picture her a different way. The reader asks himself, "What kind of a person would *choose* to wear this?" (do this, say this, etc.), and his answer derives, logically, from the prevailing societal attitude.

At first you might think that when you include a descriptive detail that doesn't result from a *choice* the character made, then no characterization takes place. For example, if you tell your reader a girl got hit by a car, he can't find a character type file in his brain for "girls who get hit by cars," because anybody can get hit by a car, regardless of personality. He doesn't make assumptions about this girl until you tell him more.

Logically, then, if you write that a woman has a scar on her face because she got hit by a car when she was twelve, your reader wouldn't draw any conclusions about her character because he knows that anybody can get a scar on his face, regardless of personality.

But our physical appearance, whether we choose it or not, has such an influence on our personality and our motivations that you cannot help but characterize when you describe. The reader has a thin file marked "girls with scars on their faces," and it says that such girls felt ugly in high school so they didn't get asked for dates, and they're still shy with men. It says that they were ridiculed by the other kids, and it made them insecure. So if your character with the scar is sought-after and secure, don't mention the scar "just because it is there," unless you're prepared to provide information that will dispel the reader's "girl with a scar on her face" type.

This is a serious problem in both fiction and nonfiction. In nonfiction the reader has to find an answer to the question, "Why did the writer mention the scar?"; in fiction the question is "Why did the writer *put* the scar on the girl's face?" In either case, the reader assumes there is a reason. Many a fiction writer makes the mistake of adding the scar just because he's basing the character on somebody he used to know who just happened to have a scar.

This whole process applies in varying degrees to all physical description. If you say a woman is fat, the reader assumes she is gluttonous and perhaps jolly. If you say a kid has pimples all over his face, the reader assumes he is shy. If you say a man is tall and broad shouldered, the reader assumes he is aggressive and confident.

If you must employ physical description that will lead to faulty assumptions, try to erase the false image as quickly as possible:

"Though her face resembles a recently sighted asteroid, she has more men chasing her than Farrah Fawcett."

Credible Characters

A character has credibility if the reader believes that the character could do, and would do, what you say she does. The character lacks credibility when the reader says, "Oh, she couldn't do that," or "She wouldn't do that."

I talked to my friend Chris Keane about this. Keane is a screenwriter, a novelist, and a writing teacher.

Like all writing teachers Chris sees a lot of manuscripts in which the characters and the writer seem to have, at best, a passing acquaintance.

"Too many writers just don't know their characters," he said, "and so they have characters acting in ways that are incredible to the reader."

"For example?" I said.

"Well, one guy gave me a story in which his heroine, Lana, is a somewhat mousey young lady, meek, mild mannered, sweet. In one scene she's walking home from the theatre and she is assaulted. She was in danger. How did she get out of the situation? Simple. She unleashed a series of vicious karate chops and sent the assailant to the hospital. The writer thought this was a pretty good scene, a lot of flying limbs, and the like."

"But?"

"But it was totally without credibility. There were two credibility problems that had to be solved. One was, *could* the character do this? All of a sudden Lana knows karate. There was never a hint of it before. So I told the writer to go back and plant some karate training, and also show us Lana's motivation for taking the training in the first place. It doesn't do us any good to plant the training if we still believe that Lana would never go to karate school.

"But there was a much more serious credibility problem with the scene. Lana was merciless in her attack. Yet she had been portrayed as meek, mild mannered, and so forth, the kind of girl who would probably strike one blow and then run off into the night. Even if we believed she could do it, because of her training, we still didn't believe she *would* do it, because of her character as we had learned it. The girl doing the karate was just not Lana, but somebody that the writer needed at the moment. This is not a credibility problem you can solve simply by going back and planting something. The problem is that the writer didn't know his character well enough."

I asked Chris for a solution to the problem.

"Simple," he said. "Before you write a word, sit down and write a three- to five-page biography for every significant character. That's what I do. It is essential for the writer to know where his character was born, what his goals are, what his fears are, how does he feel about his mother, his father, and so forth. This may seem like a lot of extra work, but it's necessary and it actually saves a lot of time. If you do the biography you will never get writer's block. You will create real flesh-and-blood characters and you will know who they are, what they are capable of, and how they would react in any given situation."

Exercise

This exercise is for fiction writers only, and you can probably guess what it is. Yes, write a three-page biography for one of the characters you want to put into a novel or story. Put in when he was born, where, how many sisters and brothers he has, his fears, his ambitions, his hobbies, his likes and dislikes, anything you can think of.

What Does Your Character Feel and Want?

My friend Crosby Holden lives in Dallas, Texas, and his manuscripts were the best ones I got. One was *The Great Chili Cookoff Caper*, a novel.

"Dear Crosby," I wrote, "You have a good workable story. It's orderly, it's logical, it is not confusing. You have believable characters, an exciting background, and good local color. Reading the book made me hungry for Mexican food, and that's always a good sign. But there are some problems."

Of course there were some problems. That's why he sent me the book.

The Great Chili Cookoff Caper is a story about two boys, Kevin and Juan Pablo, who get involved with bank robbers during the festive chili cookoff weekend in a small Southwestern town.

Because plot emerges from character, it is important for characters to have strong, believable motivations in order for those motivations to fuel the forward movement of the story. Putting it another way, readers can't care that much unless they believe that the character cares that much. As Crosby's story went along, we saw that Kevin, the main character, wanted to solve the bank robbery, but we didn't really see why.

I wrote to Crosby, "As you get back into the book I think you have to give a lot more thought to motivation. What is it that keeps Kevin going? As it is, he often talks about being a hero, but that doesn't seem strong enough by itself. After all, he is putting his life in danger. Why does he want to be a hero? Is he trying to make up for some bad behavior? Does he desperately need to impress somebody? Is he trying to prove to himself that he's brave, smart, whatever? Think about this. Right now there's nothing at stake. If Kevin fails to figure out who robbed the bank and bring them to justice, it doesn't matter; he suffers no great consequence. And if he figures it out, there's no great gain. Solving it and not solving it have just about the same emotional result, and so the reader takes just a passing interest. Make the whole thing urgent. Make Kevin passionate about his need to solve this, so that we can care more. Make us really worry."

Here are some possible motivations that come to mind:

1. Kevin made a fool of himself once before on something like this.
2. Kevin acted like a coward recently and needs to redeem himself.
3. Someone Kevin cares about was victimized by the robbery.

So, credible plots emerge from credible characters having credible motivations. Can you think of three more reasons why Kevin might want to solve a bank robbery?

When you think about character motivation, think about it in a very broad way. When I write a novel I have index cards taped to my word processor. On one I have printed "What Does He Want?" Another says, "What Does He Feel?" All through the writing of the book I am reminded to ask those questions of my characters.

These questions are not just important for overall motivation as it affects plot. They determine how a character acts in every scene. Be like an actor. Get into the skin of every character and ask yourself, "What is my character feeling right now? Scared, happy, nervous, lonely?" Do this for all your characters before you have them act.

Crosby's other major credibility mistake was the most damaging one that writers make in this realm.

At one point in the story Kevin is on the roof of the bank robbers' van when they drive away. Juan Pablo, Kevin's friend, witnesses this. From everything we know about Juan Pablo up to this point, it is clear that his solution to the problem would be to go to the police. But he doesn't. Juan Pablo remains rather casual about the whole thing and he tells no one.

Why?

Because if Juan Pablo went to the police, that would change all the future action of the story as the author envisioned it. He didn't have Juan Pablo go to the police because that would not have worked well for the plot of the story.

This is a fatal mistake.

I wrote to Crosby, "It is just not believable that Juan Pablo would see his friend carried off on the roof of a van driven by dangerous men, and then not tell anyone. It's a case of a character acting in an unbelievable manner simply to solve one of the author's plot problems. Characters have to act out of their own nature, not the author's needs, or the story won't work. Maybe the only way to solve this is to take Juan Pablo out of the van scene and have Kevin tell him about it later."

Write this on a piece of paper and hang it over your desk:

CREDIBLE CHARACTERS ACT OUT OF THEIR OWN NATURE, NOT THE AUTHOR'S PLOT NEEDS.

Sometimes the character who is acting in an unbelievable fashion is so minor that you can't make the necessary changes. You have to change somebody or something else.

For example, a Louisiana writer sent me a novel set in the 1800s. His main character, Calvin, is seventeen years old, a pimply, gangly, sexually inexperienced youth. One night Calvin goes to a tavern where he meets Dolly—beautiful, voluptuous, twenty-one years old . . . a hot little number. Dolly takes Calvin to her room, where, between tankards of ale, she makes mad love to him all night. As he's reeling his way home at sunrise, Calvin is assaulted by sailors, who have no trouble capturing him and impressing him into duty on a ship that is sailing for England.

In this case Calvin did act out of his own nature. Any seventeen-year-old boy in his right mind would have gone to Dolly's room, especially one like Calvin who probably doesn't get many golden opportunities. The person who didn't act out of her own nature was Dolly. Why would a gorgeous and much-experienced twenty-one-year-old woman want to spend the night was a callow, seventeen-year-old, acne-plagued lad she had never met before?

Dolly had acted out of the needs of the plot. But since she was such an incidental character it would be awkwardly out of proportion to try to build some foundation for her behavior, such as: When Dolly was sixteen her seventeen-year-old boyfriend died in a button factory accident and ever since that time she has tried to recapture the feelings of being with him by seducing every seventeen-year-old boy she can get her hands on, no matter how pimply and gawky he happens to be.

The sensible way to handle this, if the Dolly scene is necessary, would be to go back and somehow convince the reader that Calvin is attractive to older women. Reconstruct his face, or his body, or his personality; do something to make us believe a woman like Dolly would get excited about Calvin and invite him to her room ten minutes after meeting him.

Give Your Characters a Life

There is one more point I want to make about credible characters, because it concerns a mistake I made often (even after I was getting published) and which I see in most of the manuscripts I read.

It is very important that your characters have a life beyond the confines of the story. Too many characters come across as actors who were hired to play a role. They seem to have no history, no future, and nothing on their minds except the business of the story. These characters lack credibility. You must create characters who seem to have a full life, who seem to go places and do things even when we are not reading about them. You can do this with a few well-placed details. When your character goes to a movie, maybe "it reminded him of a movie he had seen two years ago when he and Janet were going steady." If he pulls a jack-knife out of his pocket, maybe "it was a gift from his cousin." These details say that your character was alive two years ago and going to movies, that he had girlfriends, that he has a cousin and family, and they probably have family gatherings with cakes and balloons and everything, all of which has nothing to do with your story, but a lot to do with your character.

Chapter Nine
Viewpoint

What Is Viewpoint?

Think about a house. It could be a house you once lived in, or one you've visited often, or one you've always wanted to own.

Now think about where you are in relation to that house. Are you in front of it? Behind it? Are you in the yard looking at the side of the house? Are you floating above it, looking down at the roof? Where are you?

Now imagine that you are not in front of the house. You are not behind it. You are not beside it or below it or above it. You are no place in relation to the house. Can you do it? Can you be no place in relation to the house and still see the house?

Of course not. You have to be someplace in relation to a thing in order to see it.

And your reader always has to be somewhere in relation to your writing in order to see it. That's his viewpoint.

Viewpoint is the place from which the reader views your story. If you imagine your story as a movie, then viewpoint is where you place the camera. Usually the camera is inside a character's head, looking out through his eyes. He is the viewpoint character and the camera records what he sees, smells, hears, and tastes. But the viewpoint is an emotional camera, not a mechanical one, and when you choose a viewpoint you are also choosing what the viewpoint character feels, thinks and believes.

Viewpoint is generally discussed in the context of fiction because fiction presents far more opportunities for the writer to use different viewpoints and also far more chances to make viewpoint mistakes. For that reason most of this chapter will deal with fiction.

However, while viewpoint in nonfiction is relatively less important, it is still important, and we will discuss it. Also, keep in mind that when you write narrative nonfiction—that is, nonfiction that tells a story about characters, such as Truman Capote's *In Cold Blood,* all of the points about viewpoint in fiction apply to you.

Before we go into some of the types of viewpoint, I want to show you what happens when viewpoint is not well handled.

> George Miga stood outside of the old Victorian house in Connecticut holding his three iron and eyeing the plastic golf ball. This time, he thought, this time I will hit it to the tree with one stroke. Ruth McCarty, standing at her window in the living room, wondered what on earth George was doing. George glanced at his watch. Where was Keith? Keith was supposed to join him for this game of golf on the lawn. And what about Ernie Wallace, he thought suddenly. His heart started racing as he realized what might have happened to Ernie.
>
> Keith was upstairs. He and Strunk had finally persuaded the college girls to come to their room, and now they had to do some fast talking to impress the young ladies.
>
> "You see, the solution to mankind's ills . . . ," Strunk was saying.
>
> Keith gave him a look, as if to say, "Jesus, don't start them off with mankind's ills; you'll bore them to death."
>
> Strunk thought it over, decided to change his approach slightly. Talk some politics with them, he thought, then maybe get out the guitar. They sure were sweet young ladies.
>
> "Well, actually," Strunk said, "there is no solution to mankind's ills. But let me tell you my plan for the revitalization of society."
>
> No, Keith thought, this is not the way to impress college girls, telling them about the revitalization of society. But Keith had something that he knew would impress them.
>
> "You girls want to see something incredible?" he said. They smiled. The one in the short skirt said, "Sure." Her name was Cindy and she was thinking that this Keith guy was pretty sensitive for a man.
>
> Keith went to the dresser. How would they react when they saw it, he wondered. He opened the top drawer slowly, dramatically.
>
> Right around this time Ernie Wallace was knee deep in a vat of chocolate syrup. The plant had closed down for the weekend and there was no one to hear his cries for help. He could feel

himself sinking, sinking, just the way Hubie had. The phone, he thought, if only I could reach the phone. Cameron, the night watchman was just outside of the warehouse, but Ernie didn't know that.

Meanwhile, George was getting ready to swing at the plastic golf ball.

Do you see what's happening here? You're being yanked around and you don't like it. This is what happens when you switch viewpoint at the wrong times. The reader gets settled in, involved in a scene from a particular viewpoint and suddenly is made to look at it from another direction or at another scene altogether. It's as if you took him to the movie and as soon as he got comfortable you said, "Let's sit over there," then he got comfortable over there and you said, "Hey, there's some great seats up back."

Your writing won't work if you don't have a clear concept of where your reader is standing in relation to the action of your story. Try to keep the reader in one place as much as possible, and when you do move him, do it smoothly, at appropriate times and for good reasons.

There are many types of viewpoint, but a discussion of four of them should be enough to make the point.

Single Major Character Viewpoint

In this viewpoint the main character in a story is the only one who shares his thoughts with the reader. The reader knows what the main character sees, hears, smells, tastes, thinks, and feels, and at the same time that the main character sees, hears, smells, tastes, thinks, and feels it. The reader has exactly the same access to information as the character, no more and no less, no sooner and no later.

This is the most commonly used viewpoint. It is the easiest to handle and it is the one that is closest to the reader's real-life experience.

The single major character viewpoint can be written in the third person:

> Most of the time David called his grandfather Max Levene. Some people might have thought that it was disrespectful, but his grandfather never did and David never meant it to be.
>
> Max used to call David on the telephone and he'd say, "Hello, Duvid—that's how he pronounced David—"this is Max Levene, your grandfather."

David always thought that was the biggest riot. After all, it wasn't as if he knew fifteen other guys named Max Levene. David liked to tease Max and he would say, "Levene? Levene? That does sound familiar," and Max would say, "Duvid, it's me, Max Levene, your grandfather."

Or the first person, which is how my wife Gail and I actually wrote that opening to our novel, *David and Max.*

Most of the time I called my grandfather Max Levene. Some people might have thought it was disrespectful, but Grampa never did, and I never meant it to be.

He used to call me on the telephone and he'd say, "Hello, Duvid"—that's how he pronounced David—"this is Max Levene, your grandfather." I always thought that was the biggest riot. I mean, it wasn't as if I knew fifteen other guys named Max Levene. I liked to tease Max and I would say, "Levene? Levene? That does sound familiar," and Max would say, "Duvid, it's me, Max Levene, your grandfather. Me, Max Levene."

Those are main character viewpoints because all of the information is available to the main character. We would have violated viewpoint if we had written something like this:

Though David didn't know it, it wasn't Max at all who made the phone calls. It was Morty, Max's older brother whom Max had never even mentioned to David. If David had known, he would have been shocked.

In that passage I have stepped out of David's point of view and shown information not available to him. The reason this can happen in fiction is that you have an "author," a person who has all the information, and a "character," a person who only has as much information as the author says he has. The break in viewpoint occurs when the character's viewpoint reveals something that only the author knows.

If you haven't got a tight grasp on what I just said, don't worry. I'll give you more examples later. I only mention it now to enhance a point about viewpoint in nonfiction.

The point is that in nonfiction you would almost never make that mistake, because in nonfiction there is usually only the writer-narrator, and no other character. So there is no "information gap." The author can only tell you what he knows.

Minor Character Viewpoint

In this viewpoint the camera is in the head of a minor character of the story. The rules are the same. The reader is entitled to no less and no more information than is available to the minor viewpoint character. This also can be written in the first or third person, but is more likely to be in the first person, as in *The Great Gatsby*, which is told by the minor character, Nick Carraway.

> There was music from my neighbor's house through the summer nights. In his blue gardens men and girls came and went like moths among the whisperings and the champagne and the stars. At high tide in the afternoon I watched his guests diving from the tower of his raft, or taking the sun on the hot sand of his beach while his two motor boats slit the waters of the Sound, drawing aquaplanes over cataracts of foam. On weekends his Rolls Royce became an omnibus, bearing parties to and from the city between nine in the morning and long past midnight, while his station wagon scampered like a brisk yellow bug to meet all trains. And on Mondays eight servants, including an extra gardener, toiled all day with mops and scrubbing-brushes and hammers and garden-shears, repairing the ravages of the night before.

Carraway, the minor character, is telling the story, though he is not deeply involved in the events he describes.

If you read *The Great Gatsby* you come up with a lot of reasons why Fitzgerald might have chosen the minor character viewpoint. But one obvious one should suffice. By the end of the novel the main character, Gatsby, is dead. In fact, he was dead before Carraway began his narrative.

Omniscient Viewpoint

The omniscient viewpoint is like ABC TV's coverage of the Olympics. There are cameras everywhere. There are cameras in every character's mind, there are cameras that have X-ray lenses and can tell you what's going on on the other side of a wall or the other side of the world. There are even cameras that can look into the future.

With the omniscient viewpoint you can write things like:

> Unbeknownst to Michael he would in ten years time marry this girl he now treated so ungallantly. Not only that, but they would have two children, one of whom would grow up to be a lawyer

in the prestigious firm of Discuillio and Piscitelli. In fact at that very moment, in a small town in Italy, Guido Discuillio, age ten, was playing with his Yo Yo in his room while his mother cooked pasta in the kitchen, and Guido thought, "When I grow up I will be a lawyer, and I will have my own office." Michael smiled at the girl, wondering if he would ever see her again.

As I say, in the omniscient viewpoint you can write something like that. I don't know why you would want to, but you could.

The omniscient viewpoint was more successful in fiction years ago when writers didn't have to compete with TV miniseries, movies, and major league baseball for attention. These days readers demand a tightly focused, compelling story, and with fiction they can rarely get that from the omniscient viewpoint.

I recommend that you avoid using the omniscient viewpoint in fiction, for two reasons.

One is that it is very difficult to master. There are too many options. Let's say you have your lovers, Jack and Jill, climbing a hill to fetch a pail of water. Well, what if Jack falls down and breaks his crown and goes tumbling down the hill? Do you stay in Jack's point of view and describe the nausea and the growing sense of terror he feels as he tumbles down the hill? Or do you stay in Jill's point of view and describe her sense of frustration over not knowing how she is going to get the pail of water down the hill by herself? And what if Jill goes tumbling after? Then what? Do you stay in her head and write about her feelings of self-loathing for making the same mistake Jack made? Or do you switch to Jack's viewpoint and describe the sight of Jill tumbling toward him as he lies injured at the bottom of the hill?

You could go crazy with all the options offered by omniscient viewpoint. And every time you make the wrong choice you will make the reader angry, because he will feel entitled to some other body of information which he would prefer to see.

The other reason that it is difficult to make omniscient viewpoint work successfully in fiction is that it is so different from the reader's real-life experience. In real life he can't see what's going on in Italy, or what will happen ten years from now, so it is more difficult to believe that it is possible in your story.

The reader of nonfiction will accept an omniscient viewpoint much more easily than the fiction reader, because he is not identifying with the narrator; he is listening to her. Also, a piece of nonfiction begins with the premise that the writer knows a lot about the subject at hand and will share whatever she thinks is important, no matter how much time or space it covers. Though the following passage would be extremely disturbing in fiction, the reader of nonfiction would accept it easily.

> In the early 1890s Jesse W. Reno invented the first crude version of the escalator. By the 1930s the descendents of his device would be carrying people in banks, department stores, and subway stations all over the world. By the 1980s some escalators would be made with treads more than five feet wide, able to carry three persons standing side by side and move as many as 10,000 passengers per hour.
>
> At about the same time that Reno was working on his invention, another inventor, Charles D. Seeberger, was developing a similar device, but it would be twenty years before the Otis elevator company would combine the best features of the Reno and Seeberger inventions to produce an escalator of the type we know today.

While the nonfiction reader will travel more easily through time and space, there is a limit to this sort of thing. You are still moving the reader around, and you have got to do it as seldom as possible.

Dual or Multiple Viewpoint

Years ago I read a novel called *John and Mary* in which half the chapters were written in John's viewpoint and half in Mary's. Though the author did switch from one mind to the other it is important to note that this is not omniscient viewpoint. It is single character viewpoint here, and another single character viewpoint there. It is not omniscient because at any given time in the story there is an implicit rule that says we can only see, hear, and feel what one character is seeing, hearing, feeling. With omniscient viewpoint the rule is we can see anything at any time. With *John and Mary* the author alternated between two different single character viewpoints. That is called dual viewpoint. It could have been three or four different characters and that would be multiple viewpoint. Books have been written in which every chapter is a new character's viewpoint. And the viewpoint change doesn't have to occur at the beginning of the chapter, either. It can occur within a chapter, or within a short story. So you can see that avoiding the omniscient viewpoint is not all that limiting. By creatively using the single character viewpoint with different characters at different times, you can cover a good deal of ground. But beware. It is when writers indiscriminately use the multiple viewpoint unknowingly, unnecessarily, or ineffectively that they make a mess of things.

If you use the dual viewpoint, balance the two viewpoints. If you write Chapter 1 in Jack's viewpoint and Chapter 2 in Jill's viewpoint and then Chapters 3 through 17 in Jack's viewpoint, the reader will be disturbed by the question, "Why isn't he writing in Jill's viewpoint?" since you've already told her that such a thing is possible. Any time you announce a rule of the game, such as, "We are allowed to see into two different minds," you are obliged to use it from time to time. Otherwise you leave the impression that the rule was not made for the good of the story, but simply to solve some technical problem you had in Chapter 2. This, of course, applies to multiple viewpoint as well as dual viewpoint.

Viewpoint Mistakes

Making a viewpoint mistake, as we discussed earlier, means that you have yanked the reader out of her comfortable position without giving her something in return that's worth the disturbance you've caused. Sometimes you switch viewpoint without knowing it, and sometimes you know you've done it but you don't realize how much trouble you've caused.

Just remember that every time you change viewpoint you disturb the reader.

The viewpoint change is not so jarring when it occurs at the end of a scene. The reader is not expecting to be moved, but at least she's expecting to see something different. And when the viewpoint change occurs at the start of a new chapter there is even less disturbance, because the reader believes she has seen all there is to see from her particular angle, and so she is ready to look elsewhere.

But when you change viewpoints in the middle of a scene, while the reader is entranced by what she is watching, you disturb her greatly and if you do it often she will forsake you. So viewpoint rule number one is: Never change viewpoints when you don't have to. And rule number two is: If you change viewpoint make sure you reward the reader for her troubles, with an exciting new scene or chapter, or some compelling new information. (This, incidentally, applies to every aspect of your writing. Never disturb the reader without giving something in return. There must always be a payoff.) The example I gave earlier was extreme, to make the point obvious. What follows is more typical.

My friend Bonnie Ireland in Dallas is a good fiction writer. She sent me one book, which I think is close to being publishable. Then she sent me *The Quality of Mercy,* which I have just begun. Though I've only read a few pages I can see that the greatest problem with the book is going to be viewpoint. So let's get to work on it. Here is the first page and a half.

> The Reverend Guntree's fist punctuated the last words of his sermon with a magnificent wallop. Vibrations resounded back and forth across the heavy wooden beams above, even the pedestal platform on which the Reverend stood, shook and rattled so that the metal parasol over his head made strange jangling sounds. Everyone in the congregration jumped. Those who had momentarily closed their eyes opened them in frantic haste, fearing the anger of God had fallen upon them. No one, but no one, slept while the Reverend was delivering his Sunday morning message to the little town of Penance.

At this point Bonnie has not yet committed herself to a viewpoint. We know that we are somewhere in the church, but all of the information in the first paragraph is available to anybody in the church.

> Suddenly all sounds came to an end. The pulpit righted itself with a final lurch, and in the silence Reverend Guntree's dark piercing eyes swept across every pew and connected his congregation.

Okay, now we have eliminated Reverend Guntree as the viewpoint character. By showing us his dark piercing eyes, Bonnie has put us in the audience looking toward Reverend Guntree. But where exactly in the audience are we?

> Ellie Quinceblossom saw the Reverend's eyes light on her. She gave a slight cough and blinked her eyelids fast. Lifting a plump arm encased in black lace, she fiddled with the grey curls at the nape of her neck and giggled nervously. Then she looked hard at the back of Willie Neff who sat in front of her.

Now the viewpoint has been established. The camera is inside Ellie

Quinceblossom's head. From here we can see the back of Willie Neff's head, the Reverend, the pulpit, etc. This is fine. No viewpoint mistakes yet. We should not be told anything about what's behind Ellie, unless the author tells us that Ellie turned around.

> Willie was beginning to think the Reverend was looking at him. He twitched his unruly moustache and could feel the red glow coming higher and higher up his neck until his cheeks bloomed like one of the red roses in his garden.

There it is, the first change in viewpoint, and it's jarring. We had just gotten settled inside Ellie's head, when we were yanked out of it and pushed one row forward into the head of Willie Neff, where we were given information that was unavailable to Ellie.

> But the Reverend was wondering how he could get Ellie to pay another penance because the Altar Cloth was almost worn out and no one in his congregation could tat or crochet like Miss Ellie Quinceblossom.

Just as we are catching our breath from the first movement we are yanked out of Willie's head, brought all the way up to the pulpit, and spun around so that we are now facing the congregation, looking out through the eyes of the Reverend. This is very disturbing.

> Suddenly, out of the silence, the huge wooden doors at the front of the church opened with a series of squeaks. Who would dare come in at the end of his sermon? All in Penance were accounted for . . . he had seen to that with his own eyes.

Okay, we are still in the Reverend's point of view, looking toward the front of the church. Maybe we can get comfortable now and watch the story unfold.

> The Reverend's face turned ashen. There was shock and utter bewilderment expressed on his rugged features as he looked beyond the congregation. With one accord all eyes watched and wondered.

By showing us the Reverend's face, the author has yanked us out of the Reverend's point of view and back into the audience looking up toward him. How else could we see his rugged features? This is the third viewpoint change and we are still in the first scene. As readers we are getting yanked all over the place, and we're getting dizzy.

Bonnie's mistakes here are typical. She's writing her scene from up in the sky, instead of grounding herself someplace and describing what she sees. She should imagine herself as a big heavy movie camera someplace in that church and then she will notice how often she is moving the camera.

So how can she fix this? Does she have to get rid of most of the information because she can't switch viewpoints? No. She just has to decide who the viewpoint character is, and then reveal that information in a way that would be available to that character.

We'll talk later about how you decide who should be the viewpoint character, but let's assume for a moment that Bonnie decides that Ellie Quinceblossom should be her viewpoint character. With only Ellie's perceptions available to her, Bonnie could rewrite like this:

Ellie Quinceblossom sat quietly in her pew and listened as the Reverend Guntree's fist punctuated the last words of his sermon with a magnificent wallop. Vibrations resounded back and forth across the heavy wooden beams above; even the pedestal platform on which the Reverend stood, shook and rattled so that the metal parasol over his head made strange jangling sounds. It seemed to Ellie that everyone in the congregation jumped. Even those who had momentarily closed their eyes opened them in frantic haste, perhaps fearing the anger of God had fallen upon them. No one, but no one, slept while the Reverend was delivering his Sunday morning message to the little town of Penance.

Suddenly all sounds came to an end. The pulpit righted itself with a final lurch, and in the silence Reverend Guntree's dark piercing eyes swept across every pew and connected his congregation.

When the Reverend's eyes lighted on her, Ellie gave a slight cough and blinked her eyelids fast. Lifting a plump arm encased in black lace, she fiddled with the curls at the back of her neck. She imagined them as the blonde they used to be, rather than the grey they had become. She giggled nervously. Then she looked hard at the back of Willie Neff, who sat in front of her.

Willie was twitching at his moustache the way he always did whenever he thought the Reverend was looking at him. A red glow of embarrassment rose along the back of his neck and flooded his cheeks. By God, he's blooming like one of the roses in his garden, Ellie thought.

Glancing away from Willie and back to the pulpit, Ellie noticed that the Altar Cloth was worn and tattered. Perhaps she could make another, Ellie thought. She sat up a little straighter in her pew, thinking there was still no one in the congregation who could tat or crochet as well as she could.

Again her thoughts wandered to Willie Neff, and she was invaded by that sense of sadness that often came with thoughts of Willie. There was a time when she thought Willie would ask her to marry, but he never had and she never knew why. It would have been a beautiful wedding right here in this church. She began to sketch the details in her mind, when suddenly the silence of the church was broken by a series of squeaks. Ellie turned and stared at the huge wooden doors at the front of the church. They were opening. Who would dare come in at the end of Reverend Guntree's sermon? Ellie looked around. It seemed that every member of the congregation was already in church.

She looked at the pulpit. The Reverend's face had turned ashen. There was shock and utter bewilderment expressed on his rugged features as he looked out at the congregation.

Choosing Viewpoint

Remember the Jack and Jill story? Who would you choose for the viewpoint character? Would you use dual viewpoint? Would you use omniscient viewpoint and write something like, "Poor Jack did not know it, but soon he would fall down and break his crown." Would you use a minor character viewpoint? "I saw Jack and Jill going up the hill that fateful day. They had a pail with them. Apparently they were going to fetch some water."

The number of choices can paralyze you at the typewriter. I have a novel-in-progress called *Local References* which I have been dragging out of my closet once a year since 1967. The reason the book has never been finished is that I have never been able to stick to a decision about its viewpoint.

The viewpoint decision can be maddening because as soon as you choose a viewpoint you have to make sacrifices. Some clever piece of description has got to go because it describes something your viewpoint character has never seen. A witty bit of dialogue has got to bite the dust because nobody ever said it to your viewpoint character, and he would never say something like that himself. And so forth. But that's the way it goes in the writing game. You've got to put your ego aside and make decisions that are best for your readers.

One thing always to keep in mind is that you want to keep things as uncomplicated as possible. In a short story, for example, always use a single character viewpoint unless you have an extremely compelling reason for doing something else. The scope of a short story is rarely wide enough to support anything else.

A careful analysis of what your story is really about will help you to choose a point of view. Ask yourself, which character has the problem that must be solved in this story? Who will be changed the most by the events of this story? Who has the ability to solve the problems of the story? Whose behavior best demonstrates the message of your story? If you are writing a mystery, then choose a viewpoint character who can't have all the facts until the end of the story.

Also, in choosing a viewpoint, consider the reader. Usually when we write a short story for a magazine we write the story first and then figure out what magazine we want to send it to. But if you know what magazine you want to sell to before you've decided on viewpoint, then ask yourself who the magazine reader will identify with. If you are writing the Jack and Jill story for *Redbook,* then Jill should probably be the viewpoint character. If you are writing it for *Playboy* then Jack will make a better viewpoint character. If you are writing a novel for men and women then you may want to have at least one male and one female viewpoint character. If your story is about two brothers and one of them is a psycho murderer, your reader will probably identify more easily with the other brother as the viewpoint character.

If you've done all this and it is still not obvious what viewpoint you should use, or who the viewpoint character should be, begin the story in different viewpoints and see which one feels right.

Choosing a Viewpoint Character in Nonfiction

I said earlier that the reason there were few viewpoint switches in nonfiction was that nonfiction usually does not have a writer-narrator and a character. However, the concept of character viewpoint is still valid in nonfiction for a couple of reasons.

One reason is that sometimes you relate anecdotes within your article, little stories that illustrate some point, and in writing the anecdote you have to wisely choose the viewpoint character just as you would with any other story.

If you are writing an article about how employees at nuclear power plants can take some responsibility for their own safety and you have an anecdote about the time there was almost a catastrophe because an employee refused to take orders from a government inspector, you will probably tell the anecdote from the point of view of the employee. If your article is about how difficult it is for government inspectors to enforce regulations you would probably write the anecdote from the point of view of the inspector.

The other reason that you have to think about character viewpoint in your nonfiction is that, even though nonfiction doesn't have a writer *and* a character, it has a writer who *is* a character. Remember that viewpoint is an emotional camera, and it has an attitude as well as a placement. At first glance the "attitude" of the nonfiction narrator might seem to be a totally different meaning of the word "viewpoint" from the one that we have been discussing. But it's not. "Attitude toward material" is another way of saying "viewpoint character." Even though you are almost always the narrator of your nonfiction you take on a specific personality for each article or book. If you regard that personality as the viewpoint character then you will not make the mistake of violating viewpoint by switching from a humorous character to a solemn one or an impartial character to a biased one. You will stick to the viewpoint character, the personality you've created.

Here are excerpts from two different articles. After you've read each, try to describe the narrator. Is he hip? Is he cynical? Is he funny? Is he serious? How old is he? Describe the way you see him.

> I'll never trust Michael Douglas again. For a week before I went to the beautiful city of Cartagena, in the northwest corner of Colombia, I was poking the television screen every time *Romancing the Stone* came on HBO and boring people with the line, "That's where I'm going." Only it turns out that though much of the movie's story takes place in Cartagena, not one frame of it was shot there. It was filmed in Mexico.
>
> So forget *Romancing the Stone*. And while you're at it, forget a slanderous piece of swill called "Smuggler's Blues," an episode of *Miami Vice* that portrayed Cartagena about as well as *Dynasty* portrays the average American family. Although the show was actually taped in Cartagena, that friendly, peaceful city came off looking like Al Capone's Chicago — exactly the kind of exposure Colombia didn't need. It's no secret that Colombia has an image problem, second only to Richard Nixon's.

We say the name Robert Goddard and we envision a bespectacled man with a mustache, standing in an Auburn field shooting rockets up to heights considered shallow by today's standards. We know that what he did was important, but like most great men of science, Goddard's image has become mechanized, screwed onto our imaginations like a cog in the technology he pioneered. We forget that behind the calculations and the experiments there breathed a flesh-and-blood man with other interests, with hopes and feelings. We forget that the man grew from a wistful Worcester lad who liked to fly kites and could gaze for hours at the flight of birds, and that it was those feelings that inspired his scientific achievements.

In the case of Robert Hutchings Goddard, the achievements are numerous. His work laid the foundation on which today's space adventures are built. He tested the first rocket engines to use liquid fuel. In 1929 he sent up the first instrument-carrying rocket. He accumulated more than two hundred rocketry-related patents and though his work was largely ignored here in America, it was basic to the weaponry developed by Germany in the 1930s and during World War II.

Have you described the two narrators? Are they somewhat different?

I am the narrator in both, and I wrote both articles during the same month. But because of differences in the material and the audience I have brought different parts of myself to each story. My attitude in each story has become my viewpoint character.

Describing the Viewpoint Character

Do you remember Reverend Guntree's dark, piercing eyes? Do you remember where you were when you saw them? In a pew looking toward the Reverend Guntree, of course. If you were inside his head—his point of view—you would not be able to see the color of his eyes, or the shape of his nose, or anything else about his face or hair. This is a problem with character viewpoint. In order to describe a character, it seems you have to violate viewpoint by yanking the reader out of the character's head, and turning her around so that she can stare back at the character and see what he looks like. Or, of course, you could always do something like this:

> As she strolled along main street that morning Beatrice caught a glimpse of herself in the wide window of Lincoln Drugs. She saw that her hips had widened slightly, no doubt from the rich

food she had been wolfing down all through her California vacation. As usual, the mannish turn of her shoulders made her look
not as feminine as she would like. But the sparkle was still there
in her blue eyes, which coruscated like distant lakes in the sunshine, and her long blonde hair, freshly washed, seemed especially lustrous today. What about my nose, she wondered, poking
at it as she stared at her reflection. Is it as crooked as I think?
She smiled to study her teeth. They were her best feature. People
said she had teeth like Farrah Fawcett. As Beatrice stood looking
forlornly at her forgettable figure she wished she had a lot of
other things like Farrah Fawcett.

You could do that. But don't. And don't have your viewpoint character looking in mirrors, the placid surfaces of crystal clear ponds, or
the shiny fenders of recently waxed Oldsmobiles to see what she
looks like. The only good thing that can be said about that sort of
thing is that it shows that the writer is sensitive to point of view, and
is trying not to violate it. The problem with this reflection business is
that it is overused and it has the same effect as a cliché, a stereotyped
character, or a predictable plot. The reader recognizes what is going
on. He sees the writer at work, and the writer comes off looking like
an amateur.

So what can you do? Well, I talked to my friend Gary Goshgarian
about that. Goshgarian is a novelist, and he is also a professor at
Northeastern University where he teaches creative writing. Gary, I
said, what about describing the viewpoint character?

"Well," he said, "of course there's always the old mirror trick, or
the reflection in the store window. But no writer with any sense
should try those. I see a lot of that sort of thing and it never works
well; it's always awkward. But there are a number of effective ways.
One is to show other people's reactions. If women glance back at a
guy when he's walking down the street, then we can surmise that he
is handsome, sexy, whatever. If people look up at him, he's tall. If
they look down, he's short. So the reaction of other characters tells
us a lot. And there are the character's own little activities. If he gets
food on his moustache then we know he has a moustache.

"But even better, I think, is to find a way to make the reader
believe that the character is thinking about his appearance. You can't
just say, 'As Dan walked past the Arlington Street subway station he
thought about his red hair and the fact that he was only five foot six.'
That's too heavy-handed. But if you can find an emotional connection

you can get the information across without disturbing the reader. Let's say the story is about Sam's relationship with his father, and his trying to live up to his father's image. You might write something like, 'Sam's hair was not as red as his father's and at five foot six, he was not even as tall as his dad. God, he thought, I haven't 'measured up to the old man in any way.' This, to me, would not be a break in viewpoint, because we haven't seen Sam by jumping outside and looking at him. We have seen him by listening to thoughts that we believe he would have.''

Follow Goshgarian's advice and also keep in mind that a precise visual description of your main character is not as important as you might think, and often is detrimental. After all, your reader is identifying with this person, and doesn't want to be reminded too much of the differences. The reader's strongest image of your character does not come from what you say he looks like. It comes from the character's actions in the story. If Donald has a hard time opening a jar of pickles in the first scene, can't seem to get his belt tight enough in the second scene, and gets tossed around by a gust of wind in the third scene, the reader will have a much more vivid image of him than if you had spent fifty words telling her how skinny and frail Donald is.

The Deeper Meaning of Viewpoint

In this chapter I have talked mostly about viewpoint as camera placement. From where is the reader seeing the story? But when you choose a character's viewpoint you are choosing his entire view of the world, and that includes his prejudices, his ignorance, his fears, and so on. Character viewpoint is not objective. It is constantly influenced by the nature of the character.

"Viewpoint is slippery," Gary Goshgarian said. "It's a hard concept to get hold of. But the writer has to, because it is all tied up in the contracts he makes with the reader. The writer has to remember that viewpoint includes the character's perception of the world, and the writer must write out of that perception, not his own."

Here, for example, is what the inner city neighborhood looks like when ten-year-old Tommy goes to visit his cousin Cliffy for a month in the summer.

> It made his neighborhood in Lancaster seem pretty dull by comparison. In Lancaster there was nothing to do in the summer,

but here there were hundreds of things. People left things right out on the sidewalk and after just one walk around the block with Cliffy, Tommy had collected an old faucet, half of a comic book, and the knob from a car's gearshift.

There weren't just a few houses, like in Lancaster. There were dozens of them on every block, and in one of the back yards Tommy saw an old tub that would make a great ship when he and Cliffy played pirates. The houses were tall and close together and between them were secret passageways where Tommy could hide when he and Cliffy's friends had water pistol wars. The back yards were small squares of dirt surrounded by wooden fences, but almost every fence had a slat missing, so you could take a shortcut to the construction field two blocks away.

A lot of kids had scooters and Tommy was going to learn how to make one out of wooden crates, planks from torn-down houses, and broken roller skates. This place was fantastic.

That passage is written in Tommy's viewpoint and we can imagine that it is from a story about a boy who spends a month at his cousin's in the city. But what if it's really a story about a woman who sends her son to live in the city for a month? What if her name is Ellen and she's the viewpoint character? What would the camera see then?

After her goodbyes to Tommy, Ellen stood out on the sidewalk in front of her sister's house. She wanted Tommy to experience new things, new people, but she wasn't at all sure that she wanted her son living in a place like this for a whole month. Things were not green and spacious here the way they were in Lancaster. The houses were crowded close together, with squalid little alleys between them, and the streets were littered with junk. A breeze tossed a torn old comic book across her feet. A few feet away, just lying on the sidewalk, was a discarded faucet with a jagged edge that could quickly cut a child's finger, and beyond that a piece from an abandoned car, debris dropped anywhere by people so impoverished that they no longer took pride in their surroundings.

In one back yard an abandoned tub sat rusting in the summer heat. Ellen could just imagine how easily it might tip and fall if kids played in it. "Watch out, I got no brakes," someone shouted, and a little boy zoomed past her on a homemade wooden scooter. The people here were too poor even to buy bicycles for their children. What a dreadful place to have to raise a kid.

Exercise

You have been invited to a Saturday night party at the home of Warren and Marilyn Fierst. I want you to go to the party and write a 400- to 500-word scene describing it.

The following statements are true:

1. On Saturday afternoon Warren Fierst was told by his doctor that he has only six months to live.
2. He has not told anyone yet.
3. There is an attractive young man by the name of Randolph Lehman at the party. He and Marilyn Fierst have been carrying on a secret love affair for a year.
4. Also at the party is Mrs. Dolores Garnet, a woman of about sixty. She has embezzled $100,000 from her employer, and is planning to fly to Argentina in the morning.
5. There is also at the party a fat middle-aged man, Roy Burg, a private detective. He was hired by Dolores Garnet's employer, who knows she stole the money and wants Burg to follow her until she leads him to the cash.

Here's the catch. You don't know any of these facts. All you know is what you see, hear, feel, smell, or taste. But try to write the scene from your viewpoint, hinting at these facts from things that, realistically, you might observe. For example you wouldn't write, "As soon as Warren came to the door it was clear to me that he only had six months to live."

But you might write, "Warren came to the door. He looked pale and worried. I had to introduce my date twice. Obviously, his thoughts were somewhere else."

COFFEE BREAK

This coffee break is for writers of magazine and newspaper articles. If you write only fiction, you are free to move on to the next section.

One terrifying aspect of being a writer is that objectively viewing what you have written is impossible. Sure the article you've just finished looks well written, but you know that your file cabinet is filled with atrocious manuscripts that you thought were fabulous when you wrote them. So how can you tell if a particular article should be mailed or flushed?

Well, you can't, not completely. There's no perfect tuning fork to tell you when your writing has changed tone, for example. You know it when you hear it, but what if you don't hear it? And what about fairness? If your article presents two sides to an issue, who is going to tell you if it does so fairly? There's no Solomon for writers.

But don't despair. There are a few solid things you can grab on to in this cloud of confusion. Some components of good article writing do have weight and size and you can measure them and say, "Yup, that's big enough."

There are tests you can run, and nothing is ambiguous about their results. If you score high on the tests, chances are that your article is in excellent shape.

One thing you can test is the lead. After you've written your article look at the lead and ask yourself if you have kept the implied promise that it makes.

Let's say your lead is:

"Before we settle down to wait for spring, let's brew some magic memories—Bill Rohr, 1967, the no-hitter that wasn't, and the impossible dream that came true."

Now read your article with that lead in mind. Were the memories you wrote about worthy of the adjective, *magic*? Did you explain the "no-hitter that wasn't" and did that dream really come true against odds that made it seem impossible?

Be careful that you don't overstate the lead just to grab the reader. Remember, the more you promise, the more you must deliver.

And what about your slant? Of each paragraph that you've written, don't ask only, "Is it a good paragraph?" Ask, "Is it a good paragraph relating to my particular slant?"

Maybe your article is supposed to be about handicapped skiers, but when you look it over you see that you wrote several paragraphs that refer to handicapped bowlers, marathon runners, and ice skaters. You have to get rid of them, or broaden your slant and write an article about handicapped athletes.

Look also for quotes. Nobody can tell you the exact number of quotes you should have in an article, but if you have none, your article is going in with one strike against it.

Anecdotes are another ingredient found in most successful articles. An anecdote is a little story, usually one paragraph, that illuminates a point of your article.

To test your article for anecdotes just count the number of anecdotes in it. Three is a nice number in an average-sized article, but it's not mandatory. The important thing is to discover whether or not you have developed the habit of using anecdotes. If you haven't, it can be costing you sales. If your article has no anecdotes, go back through it and look for an opportunity to use one.

And what about service value in a service article? A service article is one that serves the reader with *useful* information. That is, after they read the article they can do something. "How to Bake a Cake" is a service article because readers learn to bake a cake. "The Nutritional Value of Cakes" is also a service article because the reader can now choose which cake to buy based on information in the article. But an article like "The History of Cakes" is not a service article.

To test your article for service value, ask yourself what readers should be able to do after reading it. If it's "How to See Europe for the Price of America," readers should be able to go to Europe and spend no more money than they would have spent on a domestic trip of the same length. So did you tell them about the best airline deals, the least expensive hotels, the lowest prices on everything?

If you wrote about bed-and-breakfast weekends, did you give the reader the prices, the addresses, the directions, the schedules, and the information about tipping? In your "Trip to the Museum" piece, did you give the reader the hours of operation, did you tell him whether it was appropriate for kids, whether dogs are allowed, whether or not there is a ramp for the handicapped? Service value is not glamorous, but like a good lead, a strong slant, a variety of quotes, and a few anecdotes, it will help you sell your article.

Chapter Ten

Unity

Why Is Unity Important?

Unity, that quality of oneness in your writing, means that everything you write should look as if it were written at one time, by one person, with one purpose, using one language.

It's important because life is a mess. Well, maybe not a mess exactly, but life is just a bunch of stuff. It's random. You could slip on the ice and break your leg, or you could land safely and find a hundred dollar bill. Life isn't thinking, "This is a story about a guy who has good luck" or "This is a story about a guy who has bad luck." Life just sort of happens and we look at events later to figure out if they mean anything.

The fact that life just sprawls all over the place is kind of scary, and so human beings look to artists like you and me to organize life, to make sense out of it. Artists don't just paint a bunch of stuff; they paint pictures of things. Even the painter of abstracts seeks a unity which is called composition. Composers don't sit down at the piano and say "Gee, I think I'll write a bunch of notes." They choose notes carefully to create an overall effect. In fact, to my mind, unity is as good a criterion as any for determining what is art and what is not.

Where there is no unity there is no sense of satisfaction. As a writer, you must aim for unity in everything that you write or you will not satisfy your readers. Don't just write a bunch of words. Write words that have something to do with each other.

The Reader Assumes Unity

In 1980 I spent three days in West Dennis, Massachusetts, on Cape Cod. When I got home I found in my mail several sets of writer's guidelines from a publisher of romance novels. The publisher wanted me to hand them out to my writing students, which I did. But I kept one set and I said to myself, "Heh, heh, I could write one of these things."

At this time I owned a 1969, mustard-colored Ford Mustang, which had a broken headlight. So I studied the writer's guidelines and I wrote a book proposal of two chapters and an outline and I sent it to the publisher. About a month later an editor telephoned me and offered me a contract to write a novel.

Is anything bothering you? The Mustang perhaps, with the broken headlight? Of course it is. Because it doesn't seem to have anything to do with my story. When you read it you assumed it was part of the unity of my story. It didn't occur to you that the Mustang business popped out of the typewriter when I wasn't looking, or that I just put it in there for the hell of it. You figured it had something to do with everything else. And you politely waited to find out what. But after a few sentences went by, and I didn't mention the Mustang again, a voice in your mind began to nag you with the question, "What's the Mustang got to do with this?" If I had continued longer you might have forgotten about the specifics but you would know there was "something" that didn't make sense. You would be disturbed. The writing would be unsatisfying.

So that's my story. Now let's talk about Mona Erickson's story, and how she violated unity.

Mona, who lives in Cleveland, Ohio, sent me a story about a seventeen-year-old girl from Cleveland who takes a summer job at the New York World's Fair in 1964, meets a boy, and falls for him. It's a pleasant story about young love. But there is one scene in it where the girl's aunt, who lives in New York, comes to the girl's apartment and gives her a new typewriter, because the girl will be going off to college in the fall. There's a lot of material about how attractive the typewriter is and as I read the manuscript I just assumed that the typewriter scene had something to do with the story. Maybe the girl would write love letters on the typewriter. Maybe she would write a story about her New York experience. Maybe she would give the typewriter to her new boyfriend because he needs to write a ransom note. Something. But by the time the story ended and the sweethearts parted, the typewriter had not served any story purpose. It just sat there in the girl's room.

When I asked Mona why the typewriter was in the story she said,

"Oh, no reason. But when I was in New York in 1964 that really happened. I've always remembered that day, and I thought it was such a touching, lovely thing for my aunt to do that I wanted to put that scene in for her."

Hmmm. Well, I'm sure Mona's aunt was a lovely lady, and I'm sure your aunt is equally wonderful, but don't put anything in to please her if it's not part of your story. The fact that something happens to be true is not a good reason to write about it. The fact that it's relevant is.

Unity of Slant

In writing nonfiction, you can never write everything about a subject, so instead you write some things about a subject. What unifies those things is the slant. You can't write an article about volunteers. That's too broad. So you write an article about the shortage of volunteers for charitable organizations. To be part of your unity, every sentence you write must have something to do with the shortage of volunteers in charitable organizations.

It is easy to drift away from your unity. If you've learned interesting things in your research you tend to share them, even if they are irrelevant. But those paragraphs which violate the unity of your article will disturb your reader, so you must go back and remove them.

Let's say you've written the article about the shortage of volunteers in charitable organizations.

You wrote about the fact that traditionally the volunteers have been women and, with more women working outside the home, the pool of potential volunteers has become shallow.

You wrote about the fact that many charities have had to hire paid staff, and that has reduced the amount of money they can distribute to the needy.

You wrote about the fact that the new tax law will have an adverse effect on charities because only people who are itemizing can deduct for charitable contributions.

You wrote about the fact that charitable groups have become more aggressive in recruiting volunteers through phone calls and house calls.

Reread your article. With each paragraph don't ask only, "Is it a good paragraph?" And don't ask, "Is it a good paragraph about my subject?" Ask, "Is it a good paragraph relating to my particular slant on my subject?" You'll see that you wrote a paragraph or two about the new tax law. That material belongs in an article about tax deductions or charity fundraising, but not in one about the shortage of volunteers in charitable organizations. It violates the unity of your slant. Take it out.

Unity of Theme

For me "theme" was always one of those intimidating literary terms that made me afraid to be a writer. When I was twenty years old and had begun to write short stories, I lay awake nights, stricken with the fear that some creative writing teacher would say, "Gary, would you tell the class what the theme of your story is?" And, I, suddenly realizing that I had nothing original to say, would mumble some moronic cliché like "Virtue is its own reward." The class, of course, would howl with laughter, and I would spend part of the next day lugging my Remington typewriter to the edge of a deep river. This never happened, but the reason I was tortured by such visions was that my high school English teachers, and probably yours, had made theme sound like some really big deal, and they had told me that my theme had to deliver some sort of message or moral.

Forget all that foolishness. Your theme is not a message or a moral. The theme of your story is whatever you answer when somebody says, "Hey, Marian, what's your story about?" That is not an unreasonable question. After all, if you saw a newspaper notice that said, "There will be a discussion at Hudson town hall tonight at eight p.m.," you would be perplexed. But if the notice also said, "The theme of tonight's discussion is 'Should beach balls be outlawed in Hudson?' " you would have enough information to decide whether or not you wanted to go to the discussion. So if all you can say about your story is, "It's about a town that outlawed beach balls," that's enough. Keep in mind, however, that not all themes are good themes. A bad theme is one that imposes no limits on the writer. "Growing old," for example, is so vague that it is worthless. A good theme has walls around it; it has limits. "Growing old is better than the alternative," "A man grows old in a single moment," or "Three old men plan a bank robbery" would all be good themes.

You must know the theme of your story so that you will know when you have violated its unity.

Unity applies to theme in fiction in the same way that it applies to slant in nonfiction. Theme, like slant, is a junk detector. It tells you what to leave in and what to leave out. Leave in the stuff that relates to your theme. Take out everything else.

My wife Gail and I wrote a short story called "Streams" which, in another form, is Chapter 4 in our book, *Good If It Goes*. If someone were to ask me what "Streams" is about, I would say, "It's about a boy named David who would rather play basketball than go to Hebrew school, and who is trying to enlist his grandfather's help in the disagreement with the boy's parents."

Having said that, I now know the theme of the story and can look at every scene in the story and ask myself, "Does this relate to a boy who would rather play basketball, etc.?"

In scene one the family goes to Newton, where the grandfather lives. (Yes, this relates to our theme because David is going to see his grandfather and he's thinking about his persuasion strategy.)

In scene two the family goes to temple. (Yes, because the whole weight of the parents' argument is that David must keep his Jewish tradition. If the family had gone to a truck pull we would have a hard time defending that as part of our unity.)

In scene three the boy and his grandfather walk down to a stream where the boy brings up the problem. (Yes. This is the heart of the story.)

In scene four the boy and his grandfather walk back to the house where they celebrate Rosh Hashanah. (Is this part of the unity of the theme? Yes, because the grandfather has taken the parents' side, but he has also taught David the importance of tradition. If they had come back and celebrated a birthday, or someone's promotion at the umbrella factory, we would have violated our unity, and we would take the scene out.)

Unity of Tone

Your writing won't work if the reader doesn't know how he's supposed to feel.

Memorial services don't work if people giggle.

Comic monologues don't work if the audience weeps.

Your writing won't work if the reader doesn't react emotionally the way he "should."

By *tone* I mean a consistent attitude about the material, an attitude that the writer weaves into his work. He expects the reader to maintain the same attitude for as long as the story lasts. That is unity of tone.

In effect, the writer starts off by saying, "Please listen to this. It's very serious," or "I don't want to overdramatize this, but it *is* important," or "Hey, let's have a few laughs over this subject."

The writer sets the tone at the beginning of the piece, and if he does anything to contradict that tone, the writing doesn't work.

Don't send your reader mixed messages.

Here are three different leads for an article on photography. Each establishes a different tone, a different attitude.

The writer announces, "Let's take photography seriously."

> If you've ever stood quietly in a darkroom, peaceful in the amber glow of a safelight, and watched the varied shades of gray stain the surface of photographic paper to re-create a moment that once was . . . then you know something of the alchemy that lures one to the photographer's craft.

The writer announces, "Photography is interesting, but let's not take it too seriously."

> From the snapping of the shutter to the drying and mounting of the print, photography is an enchanting mixture of science, art, and magic. And while we might speculate for hours on why Cousin Lloyd would want to become a chiropodist, no such wonderments perplex us when we meet a man or woman who takes pictures for a living. We've all peered through a lens from time to time and with the push of a button brought the inexorable rush of time to a grinding halt. We understand.

The writer announces, "Let's smile indulgently at photographers."

> Photographers are a queer lot. They stand for hours in the dark, dipping overpriced paper into little tubs of smelly chemicals, all for another glimpse of Amy's first birthday cake. And when the phone rings downstairs they cannot answer it. They've got this thing about letting light into their world.

Once you've set the tone, the trick is to stay with it. Read the third lead and then pretend that the first lead is the second paragraph in the same article.

Can you feel yourself being yanked around? You don't know how you're supposed to feel.

My friend Jan, the one who's a facilitator, is becoming quite a good writer. So I'm sure she won't mind if I use one of her little mistakes as an example of the importance of maintaining a consistent tone.

I gave her a class assignment to write about a blind person. In the piece that Jan wrote, the blind man is tapping his way down an alley, when he is surrounded by four thugs. Jan had created an ominous mood or tone, one of terror, the blind man's sense of helplessness. A hand reaches out and pushes the blind man to the ground. Someone kicks his walking stick away. The thugs move in. And as the tension grows, Jan wrote, "One of the thugs suggested that they beat him up."

That word "suggested" rang a bell in my head. It didn't work. I knew I was reading. I saw the writer at work.

Why?

Because it clashed with the tone of the piece. *Suggesting* is something done by people who are a little short of power, not by thugs who have a blind man on the ground. When people in power "suggest" things, the word becomes humorous, even ludicrous.

Remember this: The reader is always aware of the words you use and of the fact that you chose to use them. He takes your mistakes seriously. It doesn't occur to him that a word slipped by you or that it jumped onto the page when you weren't looking. If your words are funny, the reader assumes you put them there to make him laugh. If your words are provocative, he assumes you put them there to provoke. He expects your individual words and phrases to be consistent with the overall mood you have created, and if you put in words that make him laugh when you're not trying to be funny, or words that make him sad when you are, you'll create a discrepancy in tone, and the writing won't work.

Another of my students, Claire Volk, a writer from Nashville, Tennessee, violated the unity of her tone in a different way.

Her story was based on a real incident in her life. She had been assaulted by a handyman, who apparently intended to rape her but was scared off by her screams.

The early passages of the story are filled with the fear, the indignation, the sense of vulnerability being felt by the character based on Claire.

> She could feel the wall pressing against her back. There was nowhere to go. As he moved toward her she tried to scream but nothing came out.

So the tone is set. The writer is saying to the reader, this is a deadly serious situation. And yet when we get to the end of the story we read:

> I learned later that Fred had tried this with other women. I guess he had his work day set up just the way he wanted it: a little work, a little sex, a little work, a little sex.

That humorous ending violates the tone. It jars the reader. The reader feels confused. "You told me to feel this way, now you're telling me to feel completely different," he thinks.

When I explained this to Claire she told me that she had written most of the story shortly after the real incident, and the ending much later. That's what I had guessed. It's not uncommon for us to joke about serious, even frightening, matters when they are safely behind us. It's probably even healthy. But Claire's readers didn't have that six months. They got the serious tone followed immediately by the humorous tone, and they were in no mood to joke about what had just happened.

Exercise

In the following paragraph the writer violates the unity of his tone. Read the paragraph. Before you read any further, write in your notebook the sentence that you think begins the violation of the tone. Then think about why.

> Oscar Curvels ran like hell. He heard the police behind him. "Stop the bastard!" one shouted. "Shoot him!" Curvels kept running. The pain in his feet grew sharper now, like rods of steel being shoved through the bone. He slammed into the fence before he could stop himself. Then he crawled up, and with aching arms pulled himself over it. He landed with a thud on the other side. As he started running again he heard the first gunshot. He imagined a bullet crashing into the back of his skull. Better a quick death now than ten more years in a cell, he thought. His lungs felt like fire. His heart pounded. His legs were swollen with pain. "Kill him," someone shouted, and he waited again for the explosion in his head. Off to his left a gorgeous amber sunset hung like a lantern in the peaceful azure sky, tossing strands of golden light through clouds of cotton that crouched above the purple peaks of distant mountains. He heard the gunshot. He ran

faster. Sweat poured down over his eyes. The wail of a siren grew closer.

Did you catch it? If you didn't, read it out loud and listen for it.

That whole sunset business is a discrepancy in tone. It clashes. All along I'm telling the reader to feel tense, feel rushed, feel sore. Then suddenly I change my tone, saying, "Oh, don't worry; there's no rush. Take a minute and relax. Look at that pretty sunset; isn't that something?"

It's a mixed message. The reader doesn't know how he should react. The writing doesn't work.

There's no end to the examples I could give you. But all I can really do is give you the concept of tone, and stress the importance of establishing it clearly and adhering to it faithfully. You'll develop your own ear and eye for this. Just remember that the reader is always reading two things: the individual words and the overall story. Your job is to keep these two in harmony by not contradicting on the word level the tone you set on the story level.

Unity of Viewpoint

I've written a chapter on viewpoint so I won't belabor the subject here. Briefly, unity of viewpoint doesn't mean that you can use only one viewpoint in a story. It means that your use of viewpoint should appear to have some overall pattern. If you wrote a book in which odd-numbered chapters were written in the omniscient viewpoint, and even-numbered chapters were in character viewpoint, the reader would get a sense of unity. But if you wrote fifteen chapters in the omniscient viewpoint and then switched to character viewpoint for the last two chapters, the reader would be disturbed by the questions, "How come the writer is doing this differently now? Is this the same book, or what?"

In viewpoint, as in other aspects of your writing, several changes can create a unity of their own, but a single change will be unsettling.

Unity of Premise

If an article has a slant, and a short story has a theme, what does a column have? It has a premise, a basic statement that the author wants to communicate. The premise gives the column unity. When the premise is abandoned the unity is broken and the reader is lost.

Sometimes the premise is stated right at the beginning of the column, as when Andy Rooney says something like, "Did you ever wonder how vegetables got their names?" Just as often the premise is implicit.

Most of the writers who sent me column manuscripts to critique made the mistake of forgetting the premise. Typically, the writer began a column with a definite idea in mind, but her mind wandered. She thought of something clever or profound to say, and she wrote it in, even if it had nothing to do with the premise of her column.

This mistake is particularly rampant among writers of humor columns. They can't pass up a good joke even when it destroys the unity of their column.

One of the funniest people to send me pages was Lou Burnett, from Warner Robins, Georgia. Lou is a humorist, and he was regularly getting his columns published in a few smaller-town newspapers. But he wanted advice that would help him improve his columns so that he could take a shot at bigger markets and maybe syndication. Lou wrote in a nice personable style. He created the same voice in every column, which is essential for a regular column. He was consistent in the length of his pieces, the style, and the format of short paragraphs. All of this was important, because the reader of a regular column looks for the familiar. She wants this week's column to look a lot like last week's column.

The major weakness in Lou's column was his inability to remain focused all the way to the end, to maintain that unity of premise.

"Dear Lou," I wrote. "You're a very funny guy, but a lot of people can write ten funny things. The trick is to write ten funny things on one subject. The reader will lose interest if he feels that you are reaching. Who's more interesting, the guy who tells three funny jokes, or the guy who can tell three funny jokes on any subject you name?"

Lou had sent three columns to me. The first was called "The Gooney Birds," and the implicit premise of the column was, "Everything here relates to the DC-3 and I'm writing about that plane now because this is its fiftieth anniversary."

The first paragraphs were fine. They all related to the airplane. But when Burnett finished an anecdote about parachuting out of the airplane, he wrote another anecdote about parachuting, which could have applied to any airplane. The anecdote sounded like something that Lou just happened to remember while writing, and it seemed unrelated to the DC-3. The unity of the premise had been broken, the focus lost, and the reader left without bearings.

The second column was called "Weather or Not," and the premise of it was, "What if government committees chose the weather?" Like the first, it was quite funny, but again when Lou ran out of material to support his premise, he started reaching. Toward the end of the column he began writing about "What if we were granted supreme power for weather?" but everything before that had been based on the joke of government committees trying to choose weather. His tightly focused joke was "government committees" and now he had switched to "people in general."

My advice to Lou, and my advice to you, is to have a strong sense of limits for each column. What exactly is your column about? Write it down on a piece of paper. After you've drafted your column go back through the manuscript. Look at each paragraph. Ask, is it funny, strong, pointed? Then ask, "Does it fit with the premise that I have written on the piece of paper?" Don't cling to any material just because it's funny or sounds clever. Be sure that it belongs in that particular column. You'll have to take out many lines that you are fond of. That's okay. You don't have to cremate them. File them and use them in a column where they do belong.

By the way, violating the unity of your premise is not the same as expanding the premise. Expanding the premise is perfectly okay, as long as you don't do it halfway through your column. Let's say you're writing a column about funny things that happen to teenaged boys. Then in paragraph three you break your premise by writing about a funny thing that happens to teenaged girls. And then you think of another funny thing that happens to teenaged girls, and then another. Instead of taking out all the girl material you can expand your premise to "funny things that happen to teenagers." But when you rewrite, make that your premise from the beginning.

Unity of premise also applies to the longer essays, such as the "Chronicle" section of *Writer's Digest* or the "My Turn" section in *Newsweek*. These pieces often cover broader ground, but they still require unity.

In one "My Turn" essay, "Trials of an Expert Witness," Elizabeth Loftus, a Jewish psychologist who specializes in memory, writes about being asked to help in the defense of John Demjanjuk, a man accused of killing millions of Jews in Poland during World War II.

Early in the piece she writes:

"Given my own Jewish heritage and strong feelings about the crime, could I possibly testify on Demjanjuk's behalf?

"I spent two months thinking about it. What of the presumption of innocence? And what of my own obligations to my science and of my science to the community at large?"

Here she has set down the premise: People are uncomfortable when they find inconsistency in themselves.

If Loftus had drifted into a discussion of inconsistency in public policy, or started writing other things that make people uncomfortable, she would have violated her premise.

In the end, she chose not to defend the man accused of the war crimes. She writes:

"Not to act consistently feels intellectually dishonest. But what about Uncle Joe and Jeremy's mother and the five survivors who would feel so terribly betrayed? It's as if I were being asked to testify for the man accused of killing my brother. My friend, quoting Emerson, reminded me that, 'A foolish consistency is the hobgoblin of little minds.'

"Emerson was comforting. I decided to leave this case to my colleagues. The cost of testifying as a defense witness would have been too great for the people I love most."

Here she is telling us how she dealt with the inconsistency, but she has not changed the premise. At the end she is saying the same thing she said at the beginning: Inconsistency is uncomfortable.

Unity of Material

When Marie Melville of Wilmington, North Carolina, became a widow she learned that she was not equipped to deal with banking, car repairs, dating, and a variety of other issues which either never arose during her married life or had been taken care of by her husband. As she learned to cope with these matters she kept notes, so that she could communicate her new knowledge to readers in the same situation. She wrote a book about how to adjust to widowhood and she sent the manuscript to me for evaluation.

This was a good book idea. There was an identifiable audience for the book, and Marie had accumulated a lot of good service information — that is, information that the reader could use.

The reason that the book was not publishable when I got it was that Marie, understandably inspired to write it by her own tragedy, included a great deal of autobiographical material concerning her husband and her own widowhood. A small amount of this material would have been okay, even valuable, because it would give the book a personal tone. But approximately half the book was Marie's personal story material, which had no service value to the reader. It violated the unity which said, "This is a nuts and bolts service book of material which is useful to the reader."

I told Marie to write her own experience only in those places where her problem could be used to demonstrate a solution to the reader's problem. I told her to take out all the rest of her personal material and try to harness its power for another book, perhaps a novel.

For a book to get published and sell well it has got to be either fish or fowl, not a fish with wings or a bird with fins. There are successful exceptions to this rule, but they are rare.

In writing the proposal for this book, if I had included a few chapters on how to sell what you write, the publishers would have said, "Well, what exactly is it, Gary, a marketing book or a technique book?" I would have to decide between the two. (That's if I were given the opportunity. Usually if an author seems unclear as to what exactly his book is, the publisher will simply reject it.) Certs can be a breath mint and a candy mint at the same time, but most books cannot.

A few years ago I wrote a proposal for a book called *You Can Play.* It was a book for all the people who felt as if they were picked last for baseball when they were kids (which is just about everybody, even though that would require a dramatic new theory of arithmetic). Each of the twenty-two chapters in my book would cover a participant sport. In each chapter I would 1) Give the reader a short history of the sport; 2) Assure her that she could play the sport even if she was an overweight, undernourished, insecure klutz, and 3) Provide her with the nuts and bolts information about how to get involved with the sport, what to wear, etc. I thought of *You Can Play* as a self-help, how-to sports book.

I sent it to an editor at William Morrow and Co. He telephoned me the day he got it. He loved it. I thought for sure I had a book sale. But when it went to committee for approval, which is what most books have to do these days, it got shot down.

The editor called me up.

"They liked it but they don't want to publish it," he said.

"Why?"

"Because they don't know what it is."

"Excuse me," I said, "I seem to be having some trouble with my phone. What was that, again?"

"They don't know where we would put it in the bookstore," he explained. "Does it go in the self-help section, the how-to section, or the sports section?"

Now, I have never agreed with any publisher's reason for rejecting a book of mine, but this one was particularly repugnant. Why not just put the book in all three sections and maybe sell three times as many books?

I sent the book proposal to a few other publishers and heard somewhat the same feeble excuse for not publishing it. In effect, they were saying that the book didn't have unity of material.

So if you have a book or an idea for a book that you want to publish, ask yourself what shelf it would go on in the bookstore. If you come up with more than one answer, choose a shelf, then go back into the manuscript and cut out most of the material that would land it on the other shelf. Who knows? You might come up with two books.

Creating Unity in a Book

Have you noticed that every chapter in this book is printed in the same typeface on the same kind of paper? Weird coincidence, huh? Of course not. It's just that readers are so demanding of unity that we give most of it to them without even thinking about it. We don't even consider the alternatives. Intuitively we know that the reader demands unity. We never start a story in the first person and end it in the third person.

There are dozens of these unities and most of them are easy to decide on.

But when you begin a book there is one decision that is never easy. What's going to hold the book together? What is it that will create the illusion that everything you write belongs in the book and everything you don't write doesn't belong in the book? What thread will run through the book and give the reader a sense of its unity?

When you write a novel, the choice of unity is usually not separated from the decision to write the novel. There are organizational problems, but generally speaking, the unity *is* the novel. The plot is what holds it together. Usually you have a story with a beginning, a middle, and an end. You move from birth to death, from first date to wedding, from job interview to "take this job and shove it." You usually move in a straight line through time from the first day to the last day. If you had no sense of unity you probably wouldn't consider the material as a novel in the first place.

But in nonfiction this is not usually the case. You have two decisions to make: What material am I going to use and how am I going to unify that material?

Your nonfiction material, whether you are writing a book or an article, usually comes to you as a bunch of information. The information doesn't know that you are writing a book, so it doesn't take the trouble to arrive in any organized fashion. When you interview one expert on horse racing you learn everything he can tell you. Then you interview another expert on horse racing and you learn everything she can tell you. But since you are writing a book about horse racing, not a book about experts, you can't write the information in the order that you got it.

When I wrote *Fatal Dosage*, the true story of a nurse on trial for murder, I didn't have this problem. A patient had died. A nurse had been accused of deliberately overdosing the patient with morphine. There was an investigation. The nurse was fired. The newspapers got the story. There was a grand jury inquiry. There were indictments. There was a trial. And so on. The unity was obvious: Just tell the story the way it happened, Gary. So I began with the day the nurse found out about the patient, and ended with the verdict.

But when I began to write *Finder*, the story of Marilyn Greene, a real woman who finds missing people, I had a problem.

I knew I had exciting material that would make for a successful book, but I didn't know what the unity would be. I didn't know how to tie it all together. I knew the book had to be primarily about Marilyn's investigative career, but her career was still in progress.

I could have divided *Finder* up into case histories, with each chapter being a new case, but then the book would have been episodic. A book is episodic when it seems to be a series of events or incidents that are isolated from each other, rather than combining to create a sense of forward movement. "It's too episodic," is one of the more common explanations for why a publisher is rejecting a book.

So I couldn't write the book as a series of case histories. Nobody would buy it. Instead, I did what all writers do. I stared at the material and gnashed my teeth.

Then I got lucky.

Marilyn's seventeen-year-old son, Paul, ran away from home.

While this was bad news for Marilyn, it was good news for me. The son of the finder of missing persons was now a missing person. I could use the period of his absence as a kind of bracket to hold the book together.

Here's how I used Paul's disappearance to unify the book.

Finder is written in the first person, as if Marilyn were telling the story. To get the reader immediately involved I opened with a case in progress, the Rachel Achorn case, proceeded to the start of a few other cases and then wrote:

> Local police departments have their own computers which can call up information from the NCIC. If, for example, Peter were picked up for vagrancy in Miami, the Miami police would run his name through the NCIC and find the information that the police had put in there. They would call the local police. The local police would call Peter's parents and the parents would take it from there.
>
> After I did that I started work on a few other cases. But something happened that brought everything to a halt. My own son disappeared.

Of course, as I began the book Marilyn's son was still missing. If he wasn't found by the time I finished the manuscript I would be in big trouble. But I guessed that he would show up, and so, ten paragraphs later, I used his disappearance as the door that would lead us into the body of the book: Marilyn's eighteen-year career.

> By one o'clock in the morning I was afraid that Paul was dead. That fear is not quite as hysterical as it might seem. Three people had been murdered in Albany county in the past six weeks. All of them had been hitchhiking.
>
> By two o'clock I was certain that Paul was okay, that he would come home to me a better person, that we would find out once and for all what was going on inside of him and we would straighten it out. But I couldn't get it out of my mind that I was somehow responsible. Could Paul's anguish be traced to my own career? Had I spent too much time looking for other people's kids and not enough looking after my own?

For the next 250 pages I covered Marilyn's career in somewhat chronological fashion. But the strand that held it together was the growth in her personal life, specifically scenes which showed Paul becoming the troubled child who would eventually run away.

In the last part of the book Paul is found and the last scene in the book is of Marilyn and Paul having lunch in Vermont where they have both been searching for a missing child.

> After lunch Paul walked me to the front door of the motel. I told him I'd come back to get him in a couple of days and wished him luck with the search.
>
> "When I get home can I have a dog?" he said.
>
> "Paul, we already have two dogs."
>
> "I know. But I want one that's mine. You know, to train, so I can help you in searches."
>
> "You want to go on searches?" I said. I could feel a tightness in my throat and my eyes were suddenly wet with tears. Perhaps I would never find Rachel Achorn, I thought, but I had found my son.

There were a few more paragraphs before the book ended, but I had shown the reader the other end of the unity strand that began with "my own son had disappeared." This was not a book about Marilyn's son disappearing. It was a book about her career, but his disappearance was the thing that held it all together.

Here's another example. I talked to Joe McGinniss, author of *Fatal Vision*, about this. Joe had written a book called *Going to Extremes*, about Alaska and the people who go there with their dreams. He told me that after he's taken his notes, and before he goes to the typewriter for the first draft, he has to go through the decision-making process about the unity of the book, which is, he said, "the hardest part of every book."

"The organizational problems are awful," he said. "What do you put in, what do you leave out? In the Alaska book, putting the ferry ride in was obvious, but then what? I used to get up in the morning and say, 'What should I do today? Should I go to Fairbanks? Should I go to Kodiak?' It can paralyze you. In the end I found a pattern for the book. I developed it from cold to warmth, from darkness to light, from those whose lives were screwed up by Alaska to those who were fulfilled. But to do that you sometimes have to rearrange things. For example, the Brooks Range section comes at the end of the book, but it really came at the end of my first summer there. And in between there are so many false trails. Sometimes I'd put in weeks, even months, gathering material, and then deciding I can't use it. It might be interesting but it's not part of what I'm doing."

"It's not part of what I'm doing," is another way of saying it would violate the unity of the book.

Here are some of the common ways that writers give book material a sense of unity.

Alphabetically. If you're writing a book of celebrity profiles, a consumer report on new cars, or "The Language of Beer Brewing," you could arrange your topics alphabetically and the reader would have a sense of unity. He would know why zymurgy, the science and study of fermentation in brewing, was at the back of the book.

Chronologically. If you are writing the history of computers, or an analysis of the Reagan presidency, you could start with the first event and finish with the last. The reader would have the sense of unity.

East to west, north to south, etc. If you were writing "The Twenty Most Interesting Cities of the World" or "Weather Patterns of the Western Hemisphere," you could move always in one direction.

Now stop for a moment and think about the chapter you have just read. Did it sound to you as if it were all written during one visit to the typewriter? Do I sound now like the same Gary who was speaking to you at the beginning of the chapter? Do you feel that you understood the overall point of the chapter? Does it seem to you that I am working with the same vocabulary I started with, expressing myself in the same ways, delivering pretty much the same message about the material?

If the answer to all the questions is "Yes," then I have succeeded in creating unity for this chapter. I have practiced what I preached in the beginning when I told you that everything you write should look as if it were written at one time, by one person, with one purpose, using one language.

Exercise

Describe how you would organize these books in order to create a pleasing unity.

1. Being There: The top 100 annual events in America.
2. Glitter and Green: The inside story of Hollywood today.

3. I Say to You This: Advice about life and stuff from Major Garonovitch.
4. Kathy Slade: Track Superstar.
5. Raising Buster: How to train your dog.

Chapter Eleven
Time

I was sitting on a dock in Newburyport, Massachusetts, when I opened William Goldman's fine novel, *The Color of Light*. Goldman began, "Late on a late spring afternoon, Chub, ambling across the Oberlin campus, was astonished to see the girl of his dreams break into tears."

I didn't know why Goldman had used the word "late" twice in the first sentence. But I knew that Goldman is a pro and the words didn't just sprout there. He had planted them there for a reason.

I began thinking about writers and writing problems. Time is one of them. How to express it. Particularly, flashbacks.

Of course, I'm assuming that you have done a good deal of writing by now and you know about grammatical tense. But still many writers slip into time frames that confuse readers. Here's an example:

> When I was a kid I used to visit my grandmother every Thanksgiving. There would be gravy and stuffing and cranberry sauce and big bowls of cookies after dinner. When she took the turkey out of the oven some of the juices spilled on her foot and burned her badly. We called Doctor Peterson.

That's a pretty obvious example, but it makes the point. I switched from Thanksgiving in general to one Thanksgiving in particular without cueing the reader. I should have written, "One Thanksgiving when Grandma took the turkey out of the oven. . . ." That would have smoothly transported the reader from the general time frame, which gave background information, to the specific time frame containing story information.

Here is another example that is typical of the ones I see in manuscripts:

> When Kimberly missed a behind-the-back scoop shot at the end
> of the first half, Miss Thompson had a fit. She was as emotional
> about the game as any male coach. She would whack her pro-
> gram into her hand over and over, kick the water bucket and
> scream, "Fundamentals, fundamentals, how many times do I
> have to tell you girls, stick to the basics."

In this case, the writer is taking the reader out of a scene in order to give her some general information about Miss Thompson's behavior. Again the reader has not been cued, and the effect is confusing.

There are two ways to improve this. One would be to cue the reader that we are now going into Miss Thompson's behavior. ("It was the same as always. Whenever a girl took a fancy shot Miss Thompson would have a fit," etc.) But the better way, most of the time, is not to generalize at all. Just show us Miss Thompson.

> Kimberly missed a behind-the-back scoop shot at the end of the
> half and Miss Thompson was on her feet screaming at Kimberly
> before the ball even hit the floor. She smashed her program into
> her hand. She kicked the water bucket and it went flying halfway
> across the court. "How many times do I have to tell you girls,"
> she shouted. "Stick to the basics."

Unless you've created some special circumstances that would cause Miss Thompson to behave differently tonight, the reader will assume this is typical behavior. The scene will be stronger, Miss Thompson will be better characterized, and you will avoid making a time-frame mistake.

When you go back through your manuscript give special attention to all the words that indicate time, such as "when," "whenever," "later," and "often," as well as phrases that indicate time, such as "in the future" and "during this period." Ask yourself, is this sentence taking place at a different time from the previous sentence? Have I made that clear to the reader?

Also keep in mind that these time words are relative, so you want to make it clear which time frame your words are related to. Let's say, using Miss Thompson again, you write, "Later she calmed down and praised the girls for the good things they had done on the court."

Which later? Later on the night that Kimberly missed the behind-the-back scoop shot, or later, in general, after she showed as much emotion as any male coach? If there's any room for doubt, make a specific reference. ("Later, though she still didn't understand why Kimberly would take such a reckless shot, Miss Thompson praised the girls for the good things they had done on the court.")

The time problem that seems to perplex the most writers is flashbacks. Many writers write awkward flashbacks because they are trying too hard to ease the reader into them. They try to take the reader through too many doors. Like this:

> When she left the studio that afternoon, Jennie noticed that the old man in the guard house was the same man who had greeted her on her first visit in 1979. He seemed no more impressed by her now that she was a big star, than he had been when she was a nervous extra coming in for a few days to work in anonymity.
>
> It had been summer then. She remembered that, though usually it was hard to remember seasons in L.A. where the changes were not as sharp as they were back home in Connecticut. Jennie glanced at the hills beyond the studio. L.A., she thought. What am I doing in a place like this? Back then she was driving a mustard-colored Mustang. Now she was being driven in a Mercedes. The Mustang had been a gift from her father. Dad, she thought. I'd better visit him soon. The old guard had waved her by and she had gone to Ted Donegan's office. He was the assistant director on that first film. He was a tall, red-headed man with a long red beard. "Perhaps I can get you something to say," he told her. It was her first break.

The problem here is that the writer is trying to bring the reader into the flashback through too many different doors. First there's the "same guard" door, then there's the "Mustang versus Mercedes" door, and the "star versus extra," and the "Dad who gave her the car versus the Dad she should visit soon." By presenting us with all these comparisons between then and now, the author is shouting, "Get ready. There's a flashback coming up." But instead of being helpful, he's just getting us confused. Getting into a flashback doesn't have to be a major production. The keys to a smooth flashback are 1) Use something memorable; 2) Go directly into the flashback; 3) Bring the reader out through the same door that led him in.

Something memorable can be an unusual word, an unusual combination of words, or something strongly visual.

Let's say your middle-aged couple is having a terrible fight, and they are talking about divorce. A good visual image to get you into flashback would be the wedding ring. The middle-aged husband storms out of the condominium. The wife yanks off her wedding ring and flings it on the floor.

> It wasn't always like this, she thought, staring at the bright silver ring. (This is the door you are bringing the reader through.) When they were married in 1954 (Be specific about the time zone you are entering) they were as happy as two people could be. As soon as they drove away from the church they were making plans.
>
> "I know it sounds crazy," Les said, "but I think I can make a go of this truck-pull thing. In the big cities thousands of people will come to see a truck pull."
>
> Liz smiled. It was hard to imagine anybody paying to see a truck pull, but Les was so confident. She just knew he could do it, and she would be with him every step of the way.

Now you're into the flashback, 1954, and you can proceed forward from there for as long as you want. Forget that you are in flashback. It is irrelevant until you're ready to come out of it. Then, use the same door, the ring.

> Les had been wrong about a lot of things, Liz thought, staring at the shiny silver ring she had tossed on the floor. But he had been right about those damn truck pulls. For some reason, people liked them. She picked up the ring, slipped it on her finger, and called her lawyer.

These were some of the things I thought about as I sat on the dock in Newburyport, Massachusetts. Then I got back into William Goldman's book. His second sentence begins a flashback. "He had fallen — quite literally — for B.J. Peacock twenty months before, his first day of orientation week freshman year." When I got to page eight I read this sentence. "And then late on that late spring afternoon, Chub, ambling along, spotted them in the shadows of Tappan Square."

There it was again, that double *late* pulling me out of the flashback. Goldman had wanted me to notice the "late on that late" so that when I saw it again I would be reminded that Chub and I are not in the time and place of the flashback. We are on the Oberlin campus on that late spring afternoon. The double *late* was a guidepost to remind me of when and where I was standing in relation to Goldman's material. If he had written "late on a spring afternoon" it might have been too common for me to recognize when I saw it again. But "late on a late spring afternoon," like a dock in Newburyport, Massachusetts, is something you recognize when you see it a second time.

Chapter Twelve
Subtlety

In an instructional book like this, messages must be repeated several times to be brought home. But repeating a point several times is exactly what I'm going to advise you not to do. So at the risk of not being subtle in the telling, I must tell you to be subtle in your writing.

Being subtle doesn't mean you can't say something three times or ten times. It means don't say it three times when one time is enough. Being subtle means don't shout to, or wink at, the reader to make sure he gets your meaning. Being subtle means don't tell the reader something if you are also showing it to him. And being subtle means don't tell or show the reader anything you don't have to.

Don't Overstate

In most of the manuscripts I read, the writer writes the same thing too many times in different ways. This is known as hitting the reader over the head with a sledge hammer and, not surprisingly, readers don't much care for it. When a writer does this I point it out by underlining the phrases or sentences that are repeating information. Here is an example from a manuscript I have read:

Compare

> Lately Ben had been *acting spacey*. Since the last day of school he had been *acting really weird*. He'd been sleeping all day and *doing bizarre things* at night.

with

> Since the last day of school Ben had been sleeping all day and doing bizarre things at night.

You must avoid overstatement, not just within sentences but throughout the manuscript. I'll give you an example from *Finder*'s fourth chapter.

Early in the chapter, I wanted to show that Marilyn Greene was interested in finding missing persons, even when she was a kid. In the original chapter I told a three-hundred-word story about a little girl disappearing from Marilyn's neighborhood, and how fascinated Marilyn was with the case. Then I told another story about a missing boy whose case Marilyn followed in the newspapers. And then I told a story about Marilyn, as a teenager, finding a lost little boy asleep on a bread counter at a grocery store, and how good Marilyn felt about being the one to find him.

Each story was interesting, but all three were there for the same reason, to show Marilyn's childhood interest in missing persons. When I rewrote the chapter I cut out two of the stories. The reader didn't need three stories to get the point. I showed him one, and he could imagine the rest.

This does not mean you should never use two or three anecdotes or examples to make a point. It all depends on the material at hand and the reader's knowledge. In this book, for example, I sometimes feel that I need three examples to be sure I've gotten my point across. Other times I'm certain that one example is enough. In the *Finder* chapter, I wasn't presenting new and complex information. I used an anecdote to make a general point about Marilyn. Two more anecdotes making the same point were just slowing the book down, so I got rid of them. (However, if the additional anecdotes had been so compelling that by themselves they were exciting storytelling, I would have used them. I will sacrifice subtlety if I feel that I am giving the reader a great yarn, a juicy bit of gossip, or a truly fascinating bit of relevant information in return.)

Overstatement occurs when the writer is uncertain about whether or not she has communicated her meaning. She tries to hammer it home with a few more words. She writes, "He laughed happily," because she is not sure that "He laughed" will show the happiness. She writes, "Leslie was terribly frightened and her heart pounded," because she doesn't trust the reader to see the fright in "Her heart pounded." Instead of compressing her meaning, she dilutes it.

Being subtle means having faith in the reader.

The reader will get your meaning more easily than you think, and it takes only a few well-chosen words to get your thoughts across.

Don't Shout or Wink

One common mistake that beginning writers make is calling attention to their writing with some visual cue such as exclamation points, unnecessary quotation marks, upper case letters, or italics. Don't call attention to the fact that something you just wrote is supposed to be sarcastic, funny, or whatever. If you try to cue your reader that something is supposed to be funny, for example, your cue becomes the literary equivalent of canned laughter on TV situation comedies, or those moronic cavalry charges that are played at basketball games to tell fans when they should be excited. If the reader thinks something is funny, he will laugh. If he doesn't think it's funny, you're not helping yourself by telling him that it was supposed to be.

Don't Tell If You Are Showing

In the style book you have read and in the style section of this book you have heard the advice, "Show, don't tell." Of course you can't show everything. Showing often takes more words than you can afford to spend. But when you do show something, it is often best to let the reader discover it for himself. Be subtle. Don't tell the reader what you have shown him or what you are about to show him, if the "showing" can stand on its own.

Here is an example from a student's manuscript:

Compare

> By ten o'clock my *super-organized husband* — who *never forgets anything* — has everything packed and loaded. He's put gas in the car, pillows in the back seat, and cash in my pocketbook. He *is the efficient one in the family.*

with

> By ten o'clock my husband has put gas in the car, pillows in the back seat, and cash in my pocketbook.

With the words I have italicized, the writer is telling us what the action of the sentence is showing us. But the reading experience is more pleasant for the reader who discovers for himself what an efficient guy the writer's husband is.

Keep in mind that showing can't always stand on its own. Often you have to show and tell, or tell and show. In nonfiction you will often tell the reader something, and then show him the same thing with an example. An example usually doesn't make any sense unless the reader has first been told what it is an example of.

Let the Reader Participate

Being subtle in your stories and articles means much more than just avoiding overstatement. And showing often means letting the reader look into his own life experience. Subtlety is at the heart of the relationship between the writer and the reader. The extent to which you are subtle is the extent to which you allow the reader to collaborate on your story, to fill in the blanks.

To use an obvious example, you would never write in a medical article, "After the injections small amounts of red blood remain on the tip of the needle," because you know that the reader knows the blood is red. The reader imagines the red without your help, just as he imagines the fright when you tell him that Leslie's heart was pounding.

The reader knows a good deal more than the color of blood. In fact, his store of knowledge is the most important element in your manuscript. Make him use it. Your reader lives in the same world you live in and because of that you can make some assumptions about what he does and does not know.

Take, for example, this opening from Erich Segal's *The Class:*

> My Harvard twenty-fifth reunion is next month and I am scared to death.
>
> Scared to face all my successful classmates, walking back on paths of glory, while I have nothing to show for my life except a few gray hairs.
>
> Today a heavy red-bound book arrived that chronicles all the achievements of The Class of '58. It really brought home my own sense of failure.
>
> I stayed up half the night just staring at the faces of the guys who once were undergraduates with me, and now are senators and governors, world-famous scientists and pioneering doctors. Who knows which of them will end up on a podium in Stockholm? Or the White House lawn?
>
> And what's amazing is that some are still married to their first wives.

Here Segal is making a lot of assumptions about the reader's knowledge. He's assuming that the reader knows that the Nobel Prizes are given in Stockholm, that the President of the United States lives in the White House, etc. But I particularly want you to focus on that last sentence.

> And what's amazing is that some are still married to their first wives.

Only thirteen words, but because Segal knows that the reader lives in the same divorce-riddled culture as he does, the sentence speaks volumes. It suggests the price of success that has been paid by many of the graduates along those "paths of glory." It says that most of the graduates have been through divorces. It also tells us that the narrator has probably seen many divorces among his friends. Otherwise, he wouldn't find it *amazing*.

The sentence describes a whole dimension in the lives of the narrator and his subjects, and it is based entirely on the author's faith that the reader knows that divorce is epidemic in America.

If Segal had written something less subtle, like, "And with the incredible growth in the divorce rate since 1958, it's amazing that some of them are still married to their first wives," the sentence would not have had the same effect. By letting the reader bring his knowledge of divorce into the story, Segal has allowed the reader to participate in the creation of the story.

Don't Intrude

Consider first the spell cast by reading. You're all alone as you read, yet you hear my voice. You don't know me. I don't know you. But we're both acting as if the other were a real individual composed of flesh and bones. The words that I'm addressing to you aren't being uttered now. They were recorded months ago, perhaps years ago. I might be thousands of miles away. I might be dead. (On the other hand, you might not even have been born yet as I write.)

All you are really looking at is a bunch of black lines that make noises in your head and create a presence that doesn't really exist. It's magic.

Take a moment and think about that spell, that curious suspension of reality that is *reading*. It is particularly true, of course, in fiction. Think of a character you know well from a novel you've recently read. Amaze yourself with the simple yet incredible fact that he doesn't exist, never did. You and the author made him up.

As a writer *you* must try to create and sustain this spell. You must seize the reader's attention and funnel it into your words for the length of the story, article, book, or even press release. You must hypnotize your reader with your action and your information and your style.

Writing works best when you hypnotize the reader quickly and hold him spellbound until you're through with him. You want his attention, and to keep it you must avoid the *distractions* that will cause his attention to wander and the *moments of boredom* that will make him search for more interesting material.

For now let's forget about those boring moments that result from dull writing, and concentrate on the biggest distraction of all:

The writer.

If the writer is seen at work, the writing won't work.

There are words and combinations of words which for various reasons have the effect of reminding the reader that he is reading, that there is a person making an effort to hypnotize him. Just as you sometimes awaken in the morning with the realization, "Oh, I was only dreaming," the reader awakens from his spell, saying to himself, "Oh, I was only reading." It's the writer's obtrusive presence that does this, just as if he had crept up behind the reader and tapped him on the shoulder.

"See, here I am thumbing through my thesaurus," the writer seems to be saying when he uses a word that is utterly wrong for the sentence.

"Here I am trying to impress you," when his writing gets too wordy.

"Here I am! I'm trying to fool you . . . with all these black lines on paper," when an excess of punctuation or some typographical trick breaks the reader's concentration and reminds him that he's reading.

When the writer is seen at work, the writing doesn't work.

Don't let the reader see you at work. It will shatter the spell. Imagine how you'd react if you saw the director's back as Mel Gibson goes driving off in the sunset. Any one reminder that a writer is at work won't be fatal, but each mistake you make is an interruption of that spell. We all can tolerate just so many interruptions before we abandon an endeavor. The moment you distract the reader, your writing stops working.

This doesn't mean that you can't become a character in your own work, like Hunter Thompson, or leave a distinct stylistic imprint on your writing, as Kurt Vonnegut does. It means you should avoid calling attention to what you're doing, to the effort it entails.

There are occasional exceptions to this rule, times when the writer can be seen at work and the writing will still work.

One example would be alliteration, the use of two or more words in a row that begin with the same letter. (She was slim, supple, sexy. He was husky, handsome, hunky.) Another example would be parallel construction, which we discussed in the Music chapter.

Why do they work?

I have two answers. I'm sure there are more.

I think one reason such devices work is that the writer is being clever. Working under a limited set of rules (such as "use only words beginning with the letter P"), he comes up with an expression that not only suits his purpose, but entertains as well. We forgive him his interruption and invite him in, just as we'd let a man who does card tricks in for a few minutes even though we're watching television. (But remember, the man who repeats "Pick a card, any card" can get on your nerves in a hurry when you're trying to concentrate on something else.)

Sometimes these devices work because they're hitching a ride in the direction the brain wants to go. The brain accepts some sounds and arrangements of ideas easily and resists others, just as it accepts confused frogs and struggles with "assimilatory coordination between schemata."

These devices work because they don't run against the grain of the brain. There's not room enough here to speculate why the brain accepts some word combinations easily and rejects others. The deep and ultimate answers to the question, "Why does writing work?" are imbedded in the cells of your brain and mine. But even if you don't know *why* writing works, you can learn through observation and practice *what* writing works.

The issue of writer intrusion is complex. Sometimes it works because the writer is supposed to be there, because he was a participant in the events he describes, for example, or because he is an expert in the field under discussion and his opinion would be valuable to the reader. Other times it works because the reader gets something in return for the interruption.

But generally it doesn't work. After all the exceptions are counted and we've made allowances for the grain of the brain and sleight-of-hand in the living room, we can still say, generally, "When the writer is seen at work, the writing doesn't work."

Exercise

Take your notebook and your pen or pencil. Go someplace quiet where there is sunshine and peace, the kind of place where you would not want to be disturbed. Ask yourself this question.

"Do I know what the hell Gary is talking about?"

Then make a list of as many things as you can think of that might be author intrusion, things that would break the reading spell.

Then think about it.

Putting It All Together

Now let's see how a skillful writer might take all of these points about subtlety and apply them to his work. My example is fiction, but it could just as well be nonfiction.

Jim Bellarosa's short story, "A Horse of a Different Color," serves as a good example of subtlety. The story, published in *The New England Sampler,* was nominated for the Pushcart Prize, which is given annually to the best stories published in the smaller magazines.

In the story, the narrator is a farmer named Jody. Jody tells about another farmer, Forest Logg, who steals whatever he can. Forest's main character trait, the fact that he is a thief, is subtly, but clearly, noted in the second paragraph.

> A neighbor was a fool to leave anything he valued lying in the open, because if Forest came by on a scouting cruise the object usually vanished that night. Next day, as a soft breeze combed through his sparse white hair, Forest could look you dead in the eye, and in the gentlest tone quickly fabricate the most outlandish but logical legend to account for his possession of another's property. And then in the same calm voice he'd declare God a genius for inventing the Seventh Commandment.

Bellarosa's story is charming, and it works perfectly because he also tells his outlandish tale "in the gentlest tone." It is subtle. The writer never breaks the spell of humor by calling your attention to the fact that it is supposed to be humorous. He doesn't wink at the reader.

For example, soon after Jody inherited the farm, he found a note about Forest, left by Jody's dead uncle. Instead of having the uncle overstate Forest's inclination to steal, Bellarosa has the uncle's note read:

> If neighbor Logg at the foot of the hill should outlive me, I urge you to secure every object you add to your estate. Unless you do, you may find a rapid erosion of your ownership. Good luck, Jody.

Here, Bellarosa is also doing what Erich Segal did in the earlier example. He is allowing the reader to bring his imagination into the story. Instead of describing or characterizing the long relationship between Forest Logg and Jody's uncle, Bellarosa has written two sentences that make us imagine all the thefts and recoveries over the years.

Three weeks later, a bag of fertilizer is stolen during the night. In the morning, Jody walks down to Logg's farm and while the two men are talking in the yard, Orrin Growler, a neighbor, drives up. Instead of telling us again the well-established fact that Forest Logg is a crafty old thief, Bellarosa shows us by writing simply:

> Orrin had lost a scythe a few days earlier and had come to take it back home.

There is an implication, rather than an announcement, that if anything in the county is missing, Forest Logg probably has it.

Jody buys a chestnut-colored horse that has one ear missing. The next day the entire horse is missing. Of course, Jody goes to visit Forest. While the two men are talking, Forest Logg's new horse comes out of the barn and stands between them. Forest's horse also has one ear, but the horse is black.

In the dialogue that follows, many less experienced writers would have been tempted to overstate, to wave their hands for applause, by writing like this:

> "I didn't know you had a horse," I needled. Without a second's pause, Forest spoke. "I have a black horse. This is it," he replied shamelessly.
>
> "Oh really! I don't suppose you noticed that he only had one

ear when you bought him," I said, knifing him with my sarcasm.
His lies had gotten me angry.

Instead of throwing in extra words that drain the humor from the
scene, Bellarosa used simple, understated dialogue and little else to
make the scene work. He wrote:

I said, "I cannot see you, Forest. Something has come between
us. Do you see it?"

Forest called over, "Yes. It is a horse."

"I didn't know you had a horse."

"I have a black horse. This is it."

"Did you know he only had one ear when you bought him?"

"Yes."

An odor drifted to my nostrils.

"Forest," I called, "I smell black paint."

"I painted my roof."

"You were sensible to paint something that was dead."

"I learned to do so from my father."

"Why did you merely buy a one-eared horse?"

"Because noises don't distract them half so easy when they
are working."

"I bought the one-eared type because they are cheaper," I
shouted.

"We both had good reasons."

"I would like to have a horse just like this one between us," I
said, "a one-eared black type."

"You have good taste in horses."

Chapter Thirteen
Tension

I've been mentally flipping coins to decide whether to call this chapter "Tension" or "Suspense." Since my paperback dictionary says that one definition of tension is "uneasy suspense" I've decided to go with tension. However, as we proceed, please keep that word "suspense" in mind.

Tension is not just something that you put into your dramatic last scene when the ax murderer is hiding in the closet. It is a cord, or a series of cords, that stretch across every paragraph that you write. And tension is not always a matter of life or death. "Will he kiss her?" is tension. "Will she slap his face or melt in his arms?" That is tension. Tension is a vital element in everything that you write. It is the thing that makes your reader turn pages.

Get your reader into that state of "uneasy suspense" and keep him there. That means the reader should always be uncertain about what's coming up and should always be asking questions. Tension can come from what's happening in a story, from the words and sentences you use to tell the story, and even from the fact that you're telling the story. "Why is he telling me this?" is a reader question which creates tension.

Find Tense Words

You can add tension to your story at every level, beginning with individual words.

Certain words have a sense of urgency or danger about them, and as you go back through your manuscripts you should look for opportunities to insert words that create tension.

In this scene from *Without Mercy*, I have italicized a few of the words which I think create tension that would not be present in some of their synonyms.

> With Art's body safely stashed away, Dee did what she could to prevent Mrs. Fischer from becoming body number two. Every day at noon and again at six Dee would place an order at the pancake house, set it on a tray, cover it, and carefully place it on the front seat of her Buick. Then she would drive to Art Venecia's property in The Redlands. The ten-minute drive was always *harrowing*. She was *haunted* by visions of someone's discovering the body in the hangarlike barn. Already the body was putting out a stench that could make a grown man puke, and *horrifying* body fluids leaked from the big wooden box like oil from a junked engine. A stranger coming by, looking for nursery work or whatever, might recognize the smell of death and put in a call to the local police. Dee, *bedeviled* by the smell of death even when she was far away from it, was always *edgy* until she had driven over the rise in the entrance road. From there she could see the big metal barn and know that no strangers were snooping around.

As you probe your manuscript for opportunities to put in tense words, think particularly of:

> Words of delay, such as "paused," "waited," and "froze."
> Compare: *"I have terrible news to tell you," he said. "Scully is dead."*
> *"I have terrible news to tell you." He paused. "Scully is dead," he said.*
> Words that imply fear, such as "defended," "hid," and "fled."
> *When he heard Virgil's footsteps approach he went in the closet.*
> *When he heard Virgil's footsteps approach he hid in the closet.*
> Words of danger, such as "weapon," "fatal," and "pain."
> *The sensation shot all the way up his leg.*
> *The pain shot all the way up his leg.*
> Words of urgency, such as "inevitable," "imperative," and "deadline."
> *Walker knew that if he didn't land this account his resignation would be necessary.*
> *Walker knew that if he didn't land this account his resignation would be inevitable.*

Arrange Sentences with Tension in Mind

Obviously the way to write tense sentences is to use tense words, such as we've just discussed. But there's more. Tension comes not just from what sentences you write, but from the order in which you write them. Tension comes from the way in which you reveal information.

Let's imagine that you have written a paragraph, and now you want to rewrite in order to put tension into it.

> When Tom got back to the farmhouse Sally had moved out and he was delighted. Her key to the front door lay on the kitchen table, along with a note that said she had gone to live with Sammy. Upstairs he found her dresser drawers empty and the closet door was open.

That's a nice enough little paragraph. There's nothing terribly wrong with it, but there is no tension in it because it answers all your questions before you have a chance to ask them. In the first sentence we know what happened and how Tom feels about it. There's nothing suspenseful about the key and note on the table, since we already know she's gone. And since we know she has moved out, we never ask, "Why are her dresser drawers empty?"

The way to get tension into the paragraph is to reveal the information in the opposite order.

> Tom got into the bedroom and saw that the closet door was open. (Why?) Sally's clothes were gone. (What will he do now?) He pulled open her dresser drawers. (What will this reveal?) They were empty. (How will he react?) He ran downstairs to the kitchen. (Why the kitchen?) That's where Sally always left her key when she went away on trips. (Will it be there now?) The key was on the kitchen table, along with a note. (What does it say?) The note said she had left him to live with Sammy. (How does he feel about this?) Tom smiled. He was delighted to be rid of the bitch.

You can create tension by changing the way you reveal information within individual sentences, too.

If your story is about a teenaged girl who isn't sure which twin brother has asked her to the prom, Glenn or Todd, and you wrote, "Todd was standing there when she opened the door," you can pull the tension cord a little tighter by changing it to, "When she opened the door, Todd was standing there," or you can pull the cord a lot tighter by writing, "The boy who had come to pick her up was Todd."

Milk the Tension

Sometimes you will find in your early drafts that you missed an opportunity for attention-grabbing tension, not because you put information in the wrong order, but because you gave it away too soon. Here is part of another scene from *Finder* in which I had missed a great opportunity to create reader tension.

> So I put the dog on a down-stay and I made my way gingerly across this bizarre-looking bridge in the dark. When I got to the other side I came into a clearing. I scanned the field with my flashlight and there staring back at me was a full-grown lion.

When my wife Gail read this paragraph she had a sense of dissatisfaction about it. I reread it and I could see the problem. I had told my readers there was a lion before I even gave them a chance to worry about the possibility of something dangerous lurking in the dark. I had deprived my readers of the tension. So I rewrote the material like this.

> I put Kili on a down-stay and I gingerly made my way in the dark across this bizarre-looking bridge. When I got to the other side I came to a stand of pine trees and then a clearing. There was only a fraction of a moon and the pine trees that towered over the area made the clearing darker. I stood quietly for a moment, thinking what an odd profession it was that led a lady into the Georgia woods alone at night with a dog waiting on the other side of a weird bridge. Suddenly something didn't feel right. There was a presence near me.
>   I thought I heard something move. I scanned the field with my flashlight. I didn't see anything. I felt afraid, but I didn't know why. Again I scanned with the light. Very slowly this time I swept my light across the darkness in a long arc. As I reached the end of the arc something flashed at me. It was a pair of eyes watching me in the dark. I turned the light back, and there, staring at me, was a full-grown lion.

I was able to milk this passage for a fair amount of reader tension because the payoff, a full-grown lion, was dramatic enough to justify the extending of the scene. If Marilyn's flashlight had finally revealed a full-grown chipmunk instead of a full-grown lion, the payoff would be too slight and the technique would not have worked.

Exercise

Below are five sentences. For each one, imagine the three sentences that led up to it and write them down. The sentences you write should be like a cord that is pulled tightly until the last sentence.

1. "I want a divorce," she said.
2. The telephone line had been cut.
3. Ten thousand dollars was missing.
4. Their lips touched, oh so gently.
5. "Yes," Carlin told the crowd that night in September, "I'm the one responsible."

Here's one way to do the first:

As soon as Tom walked through the door Dottie went to the liquor cabinet. Her hand was shaking as she poured more than the usual amount. With tears in her eyes she turned and faced him. "I want a divorce," she said.

Tension in Nonfiction

Even though the two examples I gave you from *Finder* are nonfiction, that book is a narrative and the style is more suggestive of fiction. Tension is just as important in magazine profiles, biographies, interview pieces, and most other forms of nonfiction. As with fiction, tension in nonfiction comes with unanswered questions and uncertain outcomes. Here's an example:

Cleveland Amory, writing about actor George C. Scott in *Parade*, begins with a title that creates questions: "The Loves and Hates of George C. Scott." The reader keeps reading to find out what George C. Scott loves, and is even more tantalized by the question, "What (or who) does George C. Scott hate?" Will it turn out to be a well-known celebrity? Will it be controversial?

Early in the article Amory notes that most interviewers had found Scott "either unavailable or so difficult as to make more than one wish that he had been." This creates more tension. The reader keeps reading to find out if Scott is going to be "difficult."

A few paragraphs later Amory writes, "I had assumed lunch might be involved and was pleased to note a large salad bowl of shrimp and cheese on the sideboard. Scott ignored this, however, and steered me into the den." More tension. There are later references to the shrimp and cheese bowl. That bowl is a tension creator. Why is it there, and why is Amory telling us it's there? We know that Amory is a pro and he's not calling our attention to the salad bowl for no reason. Tension is coming from "Who's going to get the shrimp and cheese?"

So while Amory etches a profile of George C. Scott through quotes and observations, he continually creates questions in our minds to keep us reading. That's what you should do. These are not questions that stay at the front of the reader's mind, but at some deep level the reader should always be asking, "What about that bowl of cheese and shrimp?" Remember that creating questions is only half the job. You have to answer them or you're going to have a reader who is still tense after he finishes your story, and he's going to blame you. He'll be annoyed with you just as you will be annoyed with me if I don't tell you what happened to George C. Scott's bowl of cheese and shrimp.

Scott fed it to his dog.

A tension-creating device is not just tacked on to an article. It can be something as provocative as a loaded pistol, or as innocuous as a bowl of cheese and shrimp, but it must be relevant. Amory was writing a profile of a man who is "difficult," a man who is widely portrayed as cranky, cantankerous, a highly talented curmudgeon. So when Scott served that huge bowl of expensive food to his dog it was a wonderful detail that revealed character. That is *why* Amory used it. The salad bowl as a tension-producer is *how* he used it. If Scott had not served the food to his dog, then Amory probably would never have mentioned the bowl.

Surface Tension

Just the fact that you've got action scenes in your story doesn't mean you've got enough tension. Bob Reiss, a novelist who has published several thrillers, tells me that when he was a teenager he wrote a novel called *Cauldron*, which has never been published. The book was about militants taking over Houston. Reiss's militants blocked the highways and sealed off the city. They held all the people as hostages, they made demands on the government, they did lots of nasty things. Reiss says there were all sorts of greedy and violent characters in his book. He sent the book off to Scott Meredith, the New York literary agent, and Reiss was surprised when it came back rejected with a letter that said, among other things, that the book lacked tension.

Reiss couldn't understand it. Here were hundreds of pages about violent people taking over a large American city. People were getting killed left and right, the U.S. Army was in there, and greedy politicians were all over the place. And no tension?

"These larger issues gave the book a kind of conceptual tension," Reiss says. "What Meredith was talking about was line-by-line tension."

This is known as surface tension, and everything you write should have it. Bob Reiss gives this example of surface tension:

> The cowboys are on their way to Fort Cheyenne to reinforce the ranchers. The ranchers are stuck in Fort Cheyenne, surrounded by vicious sheepherders. The sheepherders are sick of being pushed around by the cattle ranchers.
>
> This is a situation with overall tension because we want to know who will win and who will live. But what about line-by-line tension? Look at the three groups. Line-by-line tension is easy for the cattle ranchers and the sheepherders. They're in the middle of a fight. The life and death issues are there all the time.
>
> But suppose for some reason you have to write three consecutive chapters about the cowboys, the guys coming to the rescue. The cowboys have two hundred miles to ride. The readers know nothing's going to happen until they get there. So where's the tension for the next ninety pages?
>
> Well, one kind of tension is in the interplay of characters, what they want, who wants to lead the group, who advises them to go the wrong way. One of them is a saboteur. One of them has love problems back in Laredo and the farther away he gets from Laredo the worse the problems get. In action books much of the tension comes not so much from action as from the *expectation* of action, or conflict. Suppose, for instance, just as the cowboys were setting off on their two-hundred-mile ride we saw the local Sioux Indian chief instructing his men, "We'll ambush those cowboys somewhere along the way."

Well, bingo, even if those Indians never attack, there's suddenly danger offstage all through the otherwise eventless ride. Every time the camp goes to sleep and leaves only one guard, every time a lone cowboy strolls out into the plain to brood about his girlfriend in Laredo, or write poetry about rattlesnakes, he's in danger. Every time the slow-witted and otherwise boring mess sergeant falls behind the group with his chuck wagon, we are tense, wondering if he will become the first victim.

Keep tension in mind as you tend to all the other aspects of your writing. With description, remember that a tree is a lot more interesting if there might be an Indian hiding behind it. With characterization, you could give your heroine the fear of something that might occur, such as darkness. That would create a lot more tension than the fear of something that probably won't happen, such as the fear of being hit by a falling helicopter.

Pulling the Tension Cord

We have discussed tension in isolated ways, tense words, tense sentences, surface tension, and so on. Now let's see what happens when an experienced writer works that quality of tension into every aspect of her writing.

A few months ago I read an excellent novel called *In Shadow* by Trish Janeshutz (Ballantine). Janeshutz is a master at choosing the right word, and that talent goes a long way toward lifting her book above similar books. She is also expert at manipulating the tension cord, which is how I visualize tension in a story. Janeshutz knows how to gradually tighten the cord, when to let it out slightly, and when to give it a yank that will scare hell out of the reader.

Here is how she begins *In Shadow*:

> He watched as she made her way through the trees toward the parking lot, her lovely head jerking at the slightest noise. She clutched her purse to her right side and her briefcase to her left, as if to draw the air around her for protection.

In the first sentence Janeshutz suggests that this woman has something to be nervous about, and that makes us nervous. In the next sentence the words "clutched" and "protection" are carefully chosen. If she had "held" her purse and tried to draw the air around her for "comfort," the tension cord would go slack.

She knew she was being followed, he thought, and her terror thrilled him. He could imagine the adrenaline coursing wildly through her body, impelling her to look around. But she wouldn't. In the dark, dry leaves crackling underfoot, knowing would be worse than what might only be imagined.

Janeshutz is confirming our worst fears. We suspected that something dreadful was going to happen, and after she made us worry long enough, she has come right out and said it. So now what does she do to keep the tension going?

The walkway turned to damp ground, muting her footsteps. Clouds sailed in front of the quarter moon; he heard her suck in her breath. It was a sound women make when they are afraid or aroused, and it grated on his nerves. He ran his damp hands along his slacks, clenching and unclenching his fingers.

What has Janeshutz done here to pull the tension cord tighter? She has turned down the volume on the scene. Noise suggests companionship, life. Silence suggests death. Graves are silent. And so, where there had been at least the sound of leaves crackling beneath her feet, there is now "damp ground muting her footsteps." And what could be quieter than clouds sailing in front of the quarter moon? Our woman is frightened by the silence, so what does she do? She makes a noise, the sucking in of breath. But the noise grates on his nerves. More tension. How much does it grate on his nerves, we wonder. Enough to make him do "it" right now? Another writer might have our stalker do his deed now, but Janeshutz has control here and she's going to wring as much tension as she possibly can out of the scene. The trick is to loosen the cord just a bit, and she does that by breaking the frightening silence.

The only clear sound now was a train in the distance, hurtling through the warm humid night. Denise, Denise, he thought, it could have been so different. If you'd been good. He dug his hand into his pocket and his fingers closed around the knife. It seemed warm, suddenly heavy, as if imbued with consciousness, with an awareness of what it would have to do.

Will the noise of the train save her, we wonder. Is it an interruption, does it suggest that there are people around who will scare off the murderer? What will happen when the sound of the train is gone and Denise is left alone in the silence?

> When the last of the train sounds left the air, she heard him and spun around, a hand flying dramatically to her heart.

Okay, this is it, we think. The tension has been all used up. We know the intent, we know the weapon, we know there is no way out for Denise. Can the tension be milked any further?

> Then she saw him and laughed nervously. "Christ, you scared the hell out of me." An admonishing tone, he thought, one he knew well.

Janeshutz has found a way to slightly loosen the cord again, before the final yank. We can relax, right? This is a friend of Denise's. She feels safe now, so why should we worry? Well, there is that knife in his pocket, and there are those thoughts he was having. Janeshutz has got us exactly where she wants us, tense because we think something awful is going to happen, but not completely sure. Is he going to murder Denise? That's the question that holds us to the page.

The answer is yes. Thirteen paragraphs later Janeshutz yanks the cord. The stalker does Denise in with the knife.

But we're only on page three. Is that the end of the tension? No. The next paragraph begins:

> A sense of urgency nibbled now at the edges of his mind as he thought of the lights that had been on in Denise's building. Suppose the other woman was already on the way to the parking lot.

Yes, indeed, a new set of worries for the reader. Will this guy get caught? Will the other woman show up? Will he murder her? Trish Janeshutz has put down one cord of tension and immediately begun to pull another taut. That's what she does throughout the book. There should always be unanswered questions. The reader should always be a little bit worried.

COFFEE BREAK

Most of the people who read my book, *Fatal Dosage*, tell me it's a real page-turner, which is what a book ought to be. But some people have made the comment, "It starts a little slow and then it gets going."

Of course this comment disturbed me, so I reread the book. I wanted to find out if it really starts slowly, or if you just can't please all of the people all of the time. Then it occurred to me that all of the people who thought the book started a little sluggishly and then picked up speed had one thing in common: They were all men. And I'd bet that the thing shifted into fourth gear for them on page seventy-six.

Fatal Dosage is the true story of a nurse, Anne Capute, who was tried for first-degree murder for an alleged mercy killing. During the first quarter of the book, Anne is accused, she is suspended from her job, she tells her family about it, she gets fired, she has marital problems, and she is indicted. This part of the book also flashes back to Anne's girlhood dreams of becoming a nurse, and to her becoming instead a wife and mother. The women who read the book think these chapters move fast. Some of the men don't agree. (When was the last time you heard a man say, "I'd like to read a book about a woman's girlhood dream of becoming a nurse"?)

On page seventy-six we meet the other major character in the book, Attorney Pat Piscitelli. Piscitelli is a dashing, successful criminal lawyer and he takes on Anne's case. During the rest of the book we alternate between Anne's private life and the murder trial. The fact is that a defendant in a murder trial, even if she's the subject of the book, is a relatively passive participant. Center stage belongs to the prosecuting attorney and the defense attorney. In this case, they were both men. Men and women seem to agree that this part of the book is a page-turner.

The point is that one woman's "I read it in one sitting" can be another man's "Come on, Gary, let's get on with it."

This particular gender gap won't seriously damage my royalty statements. *Fatal Dosage* is primarily a "woman's book." It's about a woman in a profession dominated by women and it's got a woman on the cover. So, no problem. My male readers are a bonus.

But let's suppose for a minute that I had decided to write a book about a big-time criminal lawyer named Pat Piscitelli. And let's further suppose that I had decided to build the book around one of his most famous cases, the Anne Capute mercy killing case. Okay so far. It's a good idea with an identifiable mass-market audience. But suppose that when I sat down to write it, I thought it would be a nifty idea to lay down the background of the case first and to have my heroic attorney come galloping in on his white stallion on page seventy-six.

Now we've got a book about a male subject, and a man on the cover. We've got a book that will reach out to men in bookstores. We've got those same seventy-six pages that, men were saying, "move a little slow, Gary." We've got men putting the book down forever at page fifty or so, not recommending it to other men. We've got women not buying the book in the first place. What we've got is a disaster and no royalty checks.

The point is that when you write anything, you have to know who your reader is. Male or female? Child or adult? Layman or professional?

And once you know, you should write *every* word with that reader in mind. Don't begin a novel with ten pages of historical background. If your reader wanted history he would have bought history. He bought a novel because he wants a story and he wants it on page one. (And please don't write to tell me how James Michener begins his books. I know, I know.) Don't lead the reader up to "the stuff he'll really like." If the first ten pages aren't written for him he'll assume the book's not written for him and he might not get to the good stuff. If you've got something for him, give it to him right away.

Chapter Fourteen
Originality

Samuel Johnson, a man not known for beating around the bush, once told a writer, "Your manuscript is both good and original, but the part that is good is not original and the part that is original is not good."

As a writer you are a technician, but you are also a creative artist, and if you forget that word "creative" you will be wasting paper every time you sit down to write. In your writing, all of the parts should be good and many of them should be original. Your reader doesn't expect everything you write to be a news flash, but he does expect to find in your writing something he has never heard before.

For everything you write you should be able to answer the question, "How is this different from similar pieces of writing?" Does this mean that you can't write that diet article, or that you can't write a profile of Mary Tyler Moore, because these things have been done before? Not at all. Being original doesn't mean you have to invent a totally new idea every time you want to write an article or a chapter in a book.

Most good ideas are published hundreds of times and some, like "You Can Lose Weight by Going on a Diet," are published hundreds of times *every month*. Some romance publishers, it could be argued, publish the same book six times every month under different titles. But those books sell by the truckload because the readers find something unique in each one. Being original means you find new slants, creative leads, fresh information, unique formats, different ways of looking at old information, surprising conclusions, and imaginative solutions. Being original is an attitude that you bring to your work.

If you are writing magazine articles, you could bring originality to the piece by using a different format, such as writing the article as if it were a newscast. Or you might write it from a surprising point of view, perhaps writing about a celebrity the way his child would see him. But usually you bring originality to an article with your choice of slant, your fresh way of approaching the subject.

Let me give you an example. I've written several writer profiles for *Writer's Digest* magazine. In some ways the articles all had to be shaped by the same cookie cutter. They were roughly the same length, they all had to carry a lot of quotes, and each had to be filled with information that would be useful and entertaining to writers. If I hadn't tried to find original ways to approach each profile, they would have all looked the same. I would have gotten bored at the typewriter and the reader would have felt as if he'd read the article before.

Of course, I wasn't free to do just anything in the name of originality. Whatever I did had to be compatible with the magazine's requirements. I couldn't, for example, write, "What Janet Dailey Does in Her Spare Time," or "William Styron's Ten Favorite Recipes for Christmas Duckling." I had to be original within the requirements of the piece.

When I interviewed Ellen Goodman I observed that her great success, which had recently been rewarded with a Pulitzer Prize, came because her readers had the feeling "she thinks like me." And so I decided that an original angle for my Ellen Goodman piece would be to somehow insert one of those readers into the story. But this was for *Writer's Digest* so I wanted not just a person who thinks like Goodman, but a writer . . . someone who dreamed of becoming an Ellen Goodman. I chose my friend Linda Dolan, a rookie writer and a Goodman fan. While meeting all the requirements of the magazine, I built my story around the relationship between these two women who have never met.

> "Sometimes I think Ellen Goodman is tapping my phone," Linda once told me. "She says so many of the things in print that I'd like to say."
>
> While Linda understands that Ellen Goodman would be out of business tomorrow if millions of other fans weren't saying exactly the same thing, on another level Linda, like those others, suspects that Goodman is speaking directly to her.
>
> Later I ask Ellen Goodman about this in a tiny windowless

storeroom at the *Globe* where we have gone to tape an interview and escape from the clacking of typewriters.

"I've thought about this a lot," she says, pausing to think about it some more. At thirty-nine she is more youthful than the well-seasoned oracle one would expect to produce such wise and authoritative columns. She smiles often when she speaks, and her eyes get wide and her hands brush through the air as if to clear away all previous thoughts.

"What I think happens," she says, "is that I respond the same way they respond. I mean I look at something like the Eleanor Roosevelt letters flap, for example, and I say 'Yuk.' And they look at it and say, 'Yuk.' My job is to say why yuk. News is divided into stories that tell you what happened and stories that tell you what it means. I am paid to figure out what it means. I face the world with as much confusion as everybody else, but once in a while it's nice to figure out what I think a few things mean."

And what about Linda Dolan out in Shrewsbury, stubbornly lugging her typewriter to the kitchen table every morning? With two kids to raise and a husband who comes home hungry, can she ever hope to write in the same league as Ellen Goodman?

The article goes on like that, interweaving the accomplishments of Ellen Goodman and the aspirations of Linda Dolan. Between the lines I am expressing the view that each woman symbolizes the reason for the other's success. That's what makes the piece original.

Take Risks

When I wrote another of those author profiles, on novelist Dan Wakefield, my slant was to show the reader all the steps I was taking in writing the article. I told the reader what material I had read about Wakefield before I met him, how I contacted him, what notes I jotted down while talking to him, and so forth. I assumed the reader who was interested in writers would also be interested in how this writer went about writing the article about the writer.

When I wrote the piece I had a sickening hunch that my editor would take one look at it and say, "Just who does this bozo think he is, writing about *his* research and *his* questions and *his* notes? Who gives a damn?" The entire editorial office would have a good howl about my "original approach," ha, ha, and then the pages, stained with tears of laughter, would come back to me with a note that said, "Gary, pretend you are a normal human being and rewrite this."

That's the thing about being original. It's a lot like walking across the street at noon. It's risky. You always think you've come up with something fresh that works, but as soon as you drop the manuscript in the mail box a pixie elf lights on your shoulder and whispers in your ear, "You've just made a fool of yourself, you know that, don't you?"

But you have no choice. If you don't take chances in your writing you will perish as a writer, or you will become an alcoholic writer who can't understand why he never got anywhere with the writing.

Look at every line you write as an opportunity to embarrass yourself or to prove what a genius you are. In your early drafts, startle the reader with some shocking leads, pepper the page with powerful words that might not even mean what you think they mean, include bizarre metaphors and surprising analogies, write flowery prose that might make you blush later, mix the plaids with the stripes. Live dangerously. Later you can put on the safety belt, but don't pull it too tightly. In the second or third draft you can cut the inappropriate, the distracting; you can look up those powerful words in the dictionary and deport the ones that don't belong; you can chop out all the things that just don't work. Nobody ever has to know what a jerk you were. But if you're too cautious to begin with they'll never know what a marvelous writer you are.

Exercise

Being unoriginal is a bad habit. You can break that bad habit by exercising your mind. You are a writer. You probably have a treasure chest full of creativity just waiting to be hauled up from deep in your subconscious. Try these exercises. They will help you get that creativity up to the surface.

1. Think of three uses for a coat hanger on a golf course.
2. Think of a way to feed your dog when he's alone in the house for two days.
3. Think of five more exercises that are like the two above.
4. In 250 words, describe the inside of a Ping-Pong ball.
5. Find something that you wrote before you read this chapter and replace every adjective and verb, even if the new ones don't make sense.

Avoid Unoriginal Endings

Because this is the end of the originality chapter, it seems like a good time to discuss the lack of originality in endings. Nonfiction doesn't usually present the writer with difficulty in bringing the piece to the finish line. That's because in nonfiction, the writer has not created for himself a "problem" that must be solved. In fiction there is almost invariably a problem that must be solved, and the writer who hasn't figured out how to solve it in an original way often turns to cliché endings.

Of all the awful, unpublishable short stories ever written (and I've written several of them) probably 20 percent have something in common. The events of the story aren't really happening. It's all a dream. But the victimized reader doesn't learn that until the end of the story, and it's too late for him to change his mind about reading it. So if you've got a short story that ends with the revelation that "it was all a dream," I want you to take a match to that story immediately.

The dream ending is just one of the overused plot devices which brand the writer's manuscript as the work of an amateur. Another example is the writer's last-page announcement that the narrator of the story isn't a person at all, but is really a collie or a statue in the park or a 1952 Chevy convertible. Sometimes a beginning writer avoids resolving the crisis in a story by announcing that there really wasn't any crisis (it was all just a character playing a prank) or he settles a problem by creating an incredible coincidence such as having the two separated lovers on ships that collide, and the lovers end up on the same life raft waiting for the Coast Guard.

These devices are as common as dust mites because they solve a perplexing problem for the writer: How do I get out of this mess? The dream announcement is not an ending; it's what writers throw in when they don't have an ending. Desperation is often the thing that causes a writer to be unoriginal in his thinking. Of course the writer doesn't know he's being unoriginal. He thinks he's being terribly clever.

So, does this mean that nobody could ever write a good story that ends with a surprise narrator or a coincidence or a dream? No. *The Wizard of Oz* seems to have done well. But anything that seems to solve a major story problem so easily is rarely clever or original. It has probably been used as often as "My dog ate my homework."

The ending of a story should emerge from the nature of the story, the dynamics of the characters, and the plot. An ending is not just a headline that you shout at the end to explain what happened. ("Extra, extra, read all about it, Bernice was only dreaming, she wasn't really being attacked by crazed poodles from outer space.") A story ending is a point you have been moving toward. An ending, even when it is similar to other endings, should seem to be unique to the story at hand. It should not look like an ending that could be tacked on to a hundred other stories. Like everything you write, it should be both good and original.

Chapter Fifteen
Credibility

Credibility is believability, and everything you write, fiction or nonfiction, must have that quality. As a writer you are probably drawn to write about the unusual, the unlikely, the strange and fascinating. These are the things which are hardest to believe. They create reader resistance. "Nah," the reader thinks, "that can't be true. You're making it up." In the case of fiction, he knows on one level that you are making it up, but successful fiction makes the reader give up that knowledge and believe every word. We'll talk more about credibility in fiction soon, but first I want to discuss credibility in nonfiction. In nonfiction you might think that just telling the truth is enough. But it's not. The truth is not automatically credible. You have to make the reader believe it.

Show That It's True

Eighty percent of the nonfiction manuscripts I've read have credibility problems. That is, the writer says that certain things are true, but he doesn't "prove" it; he doesn't show that they are true.

Here's the kind of writing I see often:

> When brothers or sisters form a business partnership the fact that they are siblings compounds the tensions generated in getting a business off the ground and making decisions crucial to its own survival.
>
> In one sense, siblings have a better chance to make it as partners than people who didn't grow up together. Strangers don't have the history which could make them stick together with the partnership when faced with serious disputes.
>
> But in terms of power struggles siblings are more likely to

carry family roles into the workplace and with them, old resentments.

The problem with that writing is that it has no credibility. The writer is saying a lot of things, but the reader has no reason to believe they are true. Credibility has got to be brought to the material.

In other sections of this book I have shown you how some writer did things the wrong way, and what I advised. This time I want to show you how a writer did it the right way. I have edited the above passage out of an article sent to me by Phyllis Feurstein of Olympia Fields, Illinois. Phyllis didn't write it that way. Her article, called "My Brother/My Business Partner," didn't have any credibility problems. Let's see why.

> Two brothers who had never been able to share a bicycle go into business together. Each is so bent on getting his way, the boat-parts company nearly runs aground. A solution they settle on is: build a wall dividing the business into two parts. Each becomes chief honcho of a division and needs permission to enter the other's turf. The arrangement tempers what psychologists call "The ancient survival game of sibs."

Here Phyllis has done two things to boost credibility. She has given us an anecdote which "shows" us the problem instead of telling us about it. And she has alluded to psychologists, thus associating her subject with a respected, and familiar, field of inquiry.

> If this sounds like a pilot for yet another TV soap based on brothers fighting for control of a company, well . . . it isn't. Off screen brothers write their own scripts and, according to partners, business consultants, and specialists in human development, they look for ways to keep their enterprises from sinking and their sibling ties afloat.
>
> At the bottom line, the sib-run business exists for the same reason as does any other company, to produce goods and services at a profit. But being brothers compounds the tension generated in getting a business off the ground, and making decisions crucial to its own survival.

Here Phyllis is making statements about sibs who are partners, but she's also cueing the reader that these statements are coming from credible sources: partners, business consultants, and specialists in human development.

"A sib partnership is more complicated," says Peter Davids, director of the Wharton School Applied Research Center at the University of Pennsylvania. "It requires a balance of two kinds of relationships. In the contractual, it's adult to adult, a heads-up sort of behavior. Terms are negotiated and agreed upon. In the emotional, the whole person is involved and the needs are psychological and harder to satisfy."

Here Phyllis is doing perhaps the most important thing you can do to give your nonfiction credibility. She quotes an expert. She's not presenting her opinion. She's reporting what she's found out from other people. More than any one thing, this is what makes her piece read like an article instead of an essay. I said that many new writers forget to use quotes, and that quotes are needed for a nice flow. They are just as important for credibility.

In the next paragraph Phyllis quotes another expert, a Chicago consultant to troubled partnerships, and then the next paragraph:

Sam Capsouto, one-third owner of Capsouto Freres, a popular bistro among the truck docks in New York City, puts it this way: "My brothers and I developed the kind of trust you don't develop with outsiders. We learned each other's character by playing games together as kids. Sometimes we have direct communication without talking. They sense when I need help with a rowdy customer. I know how to appeal to them to get my way and how to keep from antagonizing them."

Here Phyllis is quoting again. But note that it's just a guy who's in a partnership, not an expert. All of your quotes don't have to come from experts. The man or woman on the street has credibility, too.

A few paragraphs later Phyllis writes:

The replay took a nasty turn when Terry, against Bill's wishes, sold 51 percent of the company to an outsider to raise capital for expansion. The new major stockholder had no emotional investment in the partnership. He had put in his money strictly as a means of making a return. Upon seeing Bill as a liability, he expelled the younger brother from the firm and handed the older brother a dilemma to anguish over.

Here Phyllis is showing us the type of thing that can happen in a sibling-owned business. Credibility comes from the fact that she's giving us a specific example. Many beginning writers would write something like, "If, for example, one of the brothers sold a majority interest in the company to raise money, the new owner, not being emotionally attached to a brother, might fire him." Hypothetical situations don't have the credibility of real ones. Give specific examples to back up your general statements.

Prove It

When you write nonfiction you need to remain aware of the reader's doubts, and his resistance. The resistance often takes the form of an unspoken, "Prove it."

You can prove you are right with some of the things we have already talked about, an anecdote that illustrates a problem, a quote from an expert, a specific example. All of those serve as proof for general statements that you make.

Not every statement you make has to have a quote or an anecdote or an example to back it up. Many statements are self-evident. If you are writing a profile of Richard Gere, the actor, and you write, "Gere emerged as a major leading man with the release of *An Officer and a Gentleman* and *Breathless*," you don't have to drag out the box office statistics to prove it. Everybody knows it. But when you write something surprising to the reader you create resistance and it's not always enough to be correct. You have to prove it. Let's say that later in the article you write, "Gere is shy with women." That's a bit surprising and you should back it up with something, such as a quote:

> Actress Nushka Resnikoff, a frequent Gere companion, says, "Richard is like a timid schoolboy. We went on five dates before he even tried to kiss me, and even then he asked me first if it was okay."

"Not Me" and "That's Me"

Readers also resist by saying, "not me." This is the reader's way of doubting that the issue he's reading about involves him. As a writer you must show the reader in what way and to what extent she might be touched by the thing you are writing about. But there is a flip side to this. If the writing lacks the credibility of quotes, examples, etc., the reader might be led to an inaccurate, "That's me." In both cases you must give the reader credible information with which to prove or disprove her assumptions. Of course none of this would apply to a profile of Richard Gere, but it would apply to articles on everything from air pollution to zinc supplements.

This next example is the lead from my article, "Wine and Sleep," which was published in *Dynamic Living,* a magazine for people over forty. In the first paragraph I cue the probable readers (over forty) that this material is relevant to them and to what degree. In the second and third paragraphs I provide the credible information and quotes to shoot down their "Not me's." And in the fourth paragraph I knock out the inaccurate "That's me's" by indicating which people (younger people) should not be concerned with the information at hand.

> If you're forty years old a glass of wine before bed might help you sleep better. If you're fifty the wine might help even more. And if you're sixty the glass of wine might make the difference between thrashing around under the sheets all night and sleeping like the proverbial log.
>
> Why? Well, there's a lot of reasons, but the biggest one is a mysterious substance called GABA, which is an acronym for Gamma-Amino-Butiric-Acid. GABA is found in wine, and it's also found in sleeping people, produced by the nervous system as sleep approaches. Human beings have a reduced ability to sleep well as they grow older, and a cutback in GABA production might be the reason.
>
> "Of course, good sleep is somewhat subjective," says Dr. Robert Kastenbaum, a pioneer in the wine-sleep field, who is Superintendent of the Cushing Hospital in Framingham, Massachusetts. Cushing is a general hospital for the elderly and an extended care facility. It was there that early wine-sleep research was done in the 1960's.
>
> "If we use the sleep of a young adult as the ideal," says Dr. Kastenbaum, "then we can say that people have more difficulty in sleeping as they grow older. They wake up more often, they sleep less overall, and they spend less time in the 'Delta Phase' which is the most restful sleep."

"What About?"

A third kind of credibility problem emerges when the reader says, "What about . . .?"

"What about?" occurs when you have written something that contradicts something the reader believes, and you can only gain your credibility by acknowledging it, explaining it, or disproving it.

For example, if you are writing about small economy cars and how they can save the reader a fortune during an oil shortage, you have to deal with the reader's "What about the fact that the oil shortage is over?" You need to show the reader that gasoline prices could double in a matter of months, that an oil crisis could occur at any time.

This is one of the reasons why the nonfiction writer must read a variety of newspapers and magazines and just generally keep up with what's going on in the world. If you are not as well informed as your readers, you will not know their "What abouts?" and your articles will lack credibility.

Plants

A "plant" is an idea you put in the reader's mind to gain credibility for something that comes up later. Plants are used in nonfiction and fiction but they are not crucial in nonfiction.

Let's say you are writing a profile of race car driver Sturge Thibedeau and at one point you write, "After winning the Elgin 400, Thibedeau reached his wife in the grandstand by executing a series of seventeen perfect cartwheels." While this is surprising material to the reader, you don't have to go back and plant it. You can acquire instant credibility by following it with, "Thibedeau was a gymnastics champion in college, and was a member of the 1984 U.S. Olympic gymnastics team. He still works out three hours a day in the gym, as part of his training for racing."

The reader will accept that easily because it's true. The credibility was planted years ago when Thibedeau was in college. You, the writer, didn't mention it before because it was not relevant.

With fiction you could never get away with that. If you've created a character and never mentioned anything about an unusual ability, such as gymnastics expertise, and then you have him suddenly execute seventeen consecutive perfect cartwheels, you have a serious credibility problem. What the reader hears you saying is, "Oh, by the way, I forgot to tell you, but Sturge is a gymnastics champion." The reader feels previously entitled to that information, and so he gets an ugly suspicion that you are just making up history to suit a present need. At some point earlier in the story when you don't appear to need it, make a reference to your character's gymnastic prowess. Then when he does his cartwheels, there will be plenty of credibility. Here are three more examples:

1. In Chapter 5 the luxury liner sinks. Go back to Chapter 1 and plant some disturbing engine sounds, or some talk about the danger of icebergs on the voyage.
2. In scene twenty the hero has his gun taken away from him, but he pulls a Derringer out from under his hat and shoots the bad guys. Go back and show him putting the Derringer under his hat or tell us that he always carries a Derringer under his hat.
3. On page twenty Gail scores ten long set shots in a row. Go back to page three and show Gail practicing her long set shots.

One of the common mistakes that writers make is putting in a premonition instead of a believable plant. Instead of putting in disturbing engine sounds or iceberg warnings, the writer writes something like this: "As Jeffrey boarded the ship he had a sense of foreboding. Something didn't feel right about this voyage. For a moment he thought of leaving the ship, but he knew that would make him look foolish to his friends. So he pushed the troubling thoughts from his mind and headed for the bar."

Usually there is no explanation of why Jeffrey would have a premonition. This is not an effective plant because it doesn't add credibility. It subtracts it. The idea of somebody having a premonition about a ship sinking is less believable than just having the ship sink. The exception to that would be a story in which Jeffrey has been established as a character who has premonitions which do come true. Don't put premonitions in your stories unless you are prepared to explain them and use them to move your plot.

Keep in mind that a plant cannot just be arbitrarily dropped in anywhere to provide credibility for something that will occur later. The planted information must merge smoothly with the story. It must be doing some work besides being a plant. Otherwise it will stand out like a big red sign that says, "Hi, I'm a plant. See ya later."

Here's an example of a plant from *Dear So and So,* the novel I'm working on.

Dear So and So, you'll recall, is the story of a man who enters a contest to replace a famous advice columnist. At the end of the book, it turns out that the contest was fixed. But if I never suggested that possibility earlier in the book, the fixed contest ending would look like a contrivance I had used to solve some of my plot problems. It would lack credibility. So, in order to create credibility for that ending, I must plant the idea that the contest could be fixed. But I must make my planted information do some other work. The successful plant contains information that could comfortably fit into the story even if it were not doing the work of a plant.

In the first chapter my character, Scotty, calls an editor, Al Jacobs, and tries to sell him an article about the contest.

> I must have sounded like a lunatic. I really was excited about the story, and I was shouting to be heard over the sound of afternoon traffic on Route 70.
> "It's in the bag," Al said.
> "Huh?"
> "It's in the bag."
> "What bag? What are you talking about?"
> "The bag, for Christ's sake. The contest is fixed."
> "How do you know?"
> "Instinct," Al said. "These things are always fixed. They already know who they want."
> "You're just cynical," I said, which struck me as ironic, considering my own current view of life. The pot calling the kettle cynical. "Of course it's not fixed. They wouldn't dare."

In addition to being a plant for the eventual fix, this passage is doing two other jobs. It is characterizing Al Jacobs as hard-nosed and cynical, and it is creating a reason for his turning down Scotty's story, which helps me move Scotty closer to the point of entering the contest.

Coincidence

Coincidence is the most common killer of credibility. Coincidence served Charles Dickens well, of course, but today's reader is just too sophisticated. If your plot depends on the most unlikely coincidence, your reader's suspension of belief will be shattered. She will say, "Oh come on, let's get serious. You expect me to believe *that*?"

The incredible coincidence is the hallmark of the amateur. A Vermont girl loses her puppy. The following summer her parents send her to Elgin, Illinois to spend a week with her aunt and uncle. One day she's walking home from an accordion concert. She's not fully awake yet, but she could swear that the doggy running toward her, wagging its cute little tail is . . . yes, yes, it is . . . it's Mugsie, the dog she lost in Vermont. Well, it turns out that some people who live near her aunt had gone skiing in Vermont several months back, but they were in New York before they realized that this dog had stowed away in their car. No identification, so they kept the pooch.

It's true that such bizarre things do occur from time to time in real life, and you can read about them in the *National Enquirer,* but that doesn't make them any more believable in your fiction. The effect of a coincidence is that you failed. You didn't know how to make the story work fairly, so you dragged in an obvious and unsatisfying device.

What's particularly scandalous is that many new writers use coincidence without even getting something in return. For example, a woman in California sent me a romance novel. Elena, the main character, is a designer in a big garment factory. She has never met Todd Delaney, the owner, but she has heard he is quite dashing. By the middle of Chapter 1, which takes place on Monday, she is scheduled to have an interview with him on Thursday. At the end of the chapter she walks out of the building, onto a crowded street. She goes several blocks and then she trips on a curb. A man reaches out and grabs her before she can fall. He is tall, handsome, and he has hypnotic green eyes. She thanks him, and they part.

Well you won't be surprised to know that when Thursday comes around and Elena goes to Todd Delaney's office for the interview, he too is tall, handsome, and has hypnotic green eyes. *It's the same man.*

Maybe this coincidence would be acceptable if there were some point to it, if the writer were getting something in return. But she's not. Elena was already scheduled to meet Todd on Thursday and the rest of the romance emerges from that first meeting. The coincidence created reader resistance, without giving something in return. It was pointless. But hundreds of writers do this. If you are one of them, stop it. The worst kind of coincidence is one that doesn't even work for a living.

This is not to say you can never use coincidence in your stories. You can. If you are crafty, you can make the reader believe anything. The trick is to make the coincidence seem to have some logic to it.

For example, a woman sent me a short story. In this story, Merrie, the heroine, goes to a large social gathering one night at a mansion in San Francisco. She walks out into the garden for a little air and is assaulted by a man who tries to rape her. About a year later Merrie is in Boston, checking into the Copley Square Hotel, and guess who's behind her in line? The man who tried to rape her in San Francisco. Hmmm.

The problem here is that we've gone from San Francisco to Boston, so we are dealing with the whole United States, and the two people we want to meet have to be drawn from a pool of well over two hundred million people. Pretty farfetched. The way to make this seem less coincidental is to reduce the size of the people pool they are being drawn from. In this story Merrie was a college administrator. I told the author to make the original San Francisco assault occur at a convention for college administrators. Then a year later, when Merrie travels to Boston for the annual convention she runs into the same guy. He's there because he's also a college administrator. Now instead of our coincidence being drawn from a pool of over two hundred million Americans, it is drawn from the much smaller pool of college administrators who go to the annual convention, and it meets all of the story's requirements.

Here's another example. Let's say there's a reindeer that none of the other reindeer like. They all make fun of him and they won't let him play any of their reindeer games. But at the end of the story you want this reindeer to be selected for the most important job of the year, leading Santa's sleigh on Christmas Eve. Seems pretty farfetched, doesn't it, that the least popular reindeer would be selected? But you could make it believable if you could establish a logical connection between those two things. What if the reason they made fun of him was the same reason that he was selected to lead the sleigh? Maybe he has a bright and shiny red nose, and it helps them see where they are going one foggy Christmas Eve? The logical connection would make the reader say, "Of course!" instead of "Incredible!"

Exercise

Can you think of ways to make these coincidences believable?
1. Two men meet in a bar and go through three hundred pages of adventure together. At the end it turns out that one is the other's long lost brother.
2. A boy, dreaming of treasure, finds a treasure chest in his cellar.

3. A brother and sister, separated in childhood, end up married to each other.
4. A bounty hunter, chasing an outlaw, learns that the outlaw is the man who saved his father's life years ago.

To gain credibility for coincidence number one, we could put the opening scene in a bar that's in the neighborhood where the young men were born. Though the two have lost touch, maybe each goes back to the old neighborhood from time to time.

Or we could have the introduction based on something the brothers might have in common. Maybe their father was a dart champion and when he abandoned them he left behind several expensive sets of darts. When the boys were put in separate foster homes each had a set of darts. Now they meet in the bar because they are both shooting darts.

The point is to set a foundation so that when the reader finds out they are really brothers, it seems to make sense.

COFFEE BREAK

Whenever editors gather they have a good laugh over the fact that almost everybody thinks the story of his life would make an interesting book. What's even funnier, I think, is that almost everybody is right. You could grab virtually any man or woman off the streets, and if you talk to her long enough and intimately enough, you will hear the heartbeat of an exciting and compelling story. We have all loved. We have all ached. We have all laughed and cried and stared into darkness and struggled and triumphed over adversity. We each have a fascinating history and within us all there resides the ingredients of a good novel.

But life, of course, does not break neatly into chapters, and it does not follow the novelistic path of ever-increasing peaks of conflict followed by pits of resolution. Life doesn't give a damn about what satisfies readers; it just sprawls all over the place. Every life is a great unwritten novel. It's just a question of pacing, arrangement, style. And that's why those editors are laughing. Because so many people don't seem to realize that good stories are as common as dandelions. It's good writing that is rare.

Does that mean you shouldn't use your life in your stories? Not at all. Much of what you write, perhaps most, will be drawn in some way from your experience and your emotions.

A few years back I read a book called *How to Write the Story of Your Life* (Writer's Digest Books, 1984) by Frank P. Thomas. The book is directed at people who want to write the story of their lives for any number of reasons: to pass along to children and grandchildren, as therapy, as a contribution to the record of daily life for future generations, as an exercise to strengthen writing muscles for other projects, or simply for the joy of it.

In his book Thomas has many "memory sparkers," which I think can be useful to writers of fiction. By remembering your own life, you can learn a lot about your characters. One memory sparker goes like this:

> Can you vividly recall your wedding day? When and where did it take place? Describe your feelings. Who attended? Were you nervous? Did all the arrangements go smoothly? Sometimes the things that went wrong become memorable. Are you still in touch with members of your wedding party? Look through your wedding album for more sparkers.

If you want to write fiction, this is the sort of thing you should do often. Come up with your own memory sparkers.

When I was twenty-five years old I did a rather naive thing. I wrote a memoir about my childhood, about growing up in the slums of Boston in the 1950s. It was one long memory sparker. It was filled with memories of the games we played, the places we lived, the battles between brothers, the pain, the warmth. It never got published. But a few years later, when I took the same material, the ingredients of my childhood, and applied the craft of the novelist — plotting, characterization, pacing, conflict, etc — I turned the material into a book called *The Pork Chop War*, and it did get published.

So yes, use your life in your writing. Use all the joy and anguish you have ever known. Write about the characters who have walked through your life, the incidents, the funny little things that happen. Drag every emotion you've ever known onto the written page. But remember, your life is not the story. It is just a deep well from which you draw elements of the story. If a life unsculpted made a good story, then we could all publish our diaries and we wouldn't need writers.

Chapter Sixteen

Form

So folks, here we go again, perplexed yet ever-so-hopeful writers diving headfirst into a morass of writing terms that rarely mean the same thing twice, terms that twitch and shiver in our mind like globules of mercury. Form and content, for heaven's sake! Who can even be sure where one picks us up and the other lets us off? A morass? No, a mirage would be more like it—yes, a mirage, from the distance looking for all the world like something we can lay our hands on, we can measure, we can weigh, we can seriously discuss ... and yet from two feet away containing no more heft than your average ball of dust. And yet, hearty searchers for truth that we are, we pounce on it enthusiastically, and once again we are no more successful than if we were wrestling with a cloud.

What's wrong with that lead?

Is the *form*, the writing, good? Yes, it's colorful, it's lively, it has strong verbs and some vivid images. Is the *content*, the subject, appropriate? Certainly; the paragraph is about form and content in writing, and this is a book about writing. So the form and the content are both good.

What's wrong is that they are not good for each other. They are not compatible.

The style of the paragraph is loose, almost zany. It has the personality of a carnival. It spreads all over the place like a puddle. It would be perfectly appropriate for your first-person account of a drunken escapade at Mardi Gras. The reader would come along for the ride and he wouldn't care much where you took him as long as it was fun.

But the content of that first paragraph is writing instruction. It is intended for a reader who cares very much, a reader who picked up this book to get specific information. Metaphorically speaking, the reader of this chapter is not going along for a ride; he is sitting quietly and listening intently. He is looking for instruction, not entertainment, and he wants definite points, not implications and vague allusions. So the form of the first paragraph is not wrong; it's just wrong for this particular book. Form and content must be compatible, and that's what this chapter is about.

After a story or an article has been written, separating form from content even long enough to define them is difficult. But that's OK. Form and content should be interwoven so that they appear to be inevitably bound for each other, like two perfect, inseparable lovers. The good story or article looks as if it could have been written no other way.

Content

When you think about the content of your story or article, think about just one thing: information. Whether it comes in the form of fiction or nonfiction, fact or opinion, description or characterization, the content of your story is information. That is the only clay you have to mold. Everything else is form.

At first glance it might seem that information is immutable and form is merely the frame you use to display it. This is a reasonable way to look at a story before you write it. But once you commit information to any form, the information and the form become the same thing.

Compare

> Wade Boggs did hit a home run, but he struck out three times.

with

> Wade Boggs did strike out three times, but he hit a home run.

By changing the form, you also slightly alter the content, the information.

Every time you change the form of your writing, even one word, you change the content, sometimes subtly, sometimes drastically. Your job as a writer is to make sure that form and content are on the same team. They should be working with each other, not against each other.

While content has only one meaning, form has several. The form of your story can mean the type of story, the length of the story, the format, the slant, or — and most important — the style in which it is written. I'll discuss them, starting with the easy ones.

Form, Meaning Story Type

By story type, I mean novel, short story, nonfiction book, magazine article, poem, whatever it is called. The wise choice of which form to use for your content is almost always obvious.

If, for example, you are trapped in an elevator for two hours with Jack Nicholson and he spends the time telling you about his life and career, it becomes immediately clear that your best shot at selling this material is in the form of a magazine article, an interview-profile of Jack Nicholson. Only the most optimistic or inexperienced writer would expect to turn it into a publishable poem, a short story, or a book about people who have gotten trapped in elevators with celebrities.

Because the decision on type of story is so obvious, you may not think of it as a decision at all, until it turns out to be the wrong decision.

One of the most common comments from editors rejecting book proposals is, "I think this would work better as a magazine article." That usually means that the material is not compelling enough to attract $15 from a book buyer (or even $3.95 for a paperback) or that there's not enough material to justify an entire book. The attempt to fatten magazine article material into a book is the most common wrong decision about type of story. Not every subject is suitable for a book. Most articles you read could not become books. (Though it's common for an article to become a chapter in a book or for a series of articles to become a book.) Few people would buy a book titled *How to Save on Heating Oil Costs This Winter* or *Elgin, Illinois: Vacation Paradise*, but those are perfectly appropriate ideas for articles.

Form, Meaning Length

Obviously, a decision to put your information in the form of a book instead of an article is a decision about length. But within the "type of story" categories, length is also an important form and content consideration.

The length of the story must be appropriate for the scope of the material. You could write a four thousand-word article, "The Boston Celtics: The Greatest Dynasty in Sports," but if your article is about "The Boston Celtics: Their Greatest Game," fifteen hundred words would probably be the most you could write without repeating yourself and putting your reader to sleep.

The length must also be appropriate for the nature of the material. A very thin book on weight loss could have a positive effect on readers. On the other hand, the writer who uses three thousand words to write an article called, "How to Explain Anything in Five Hundred Words or Less," will be lucky if he has any readers left at the end of the article.

Form, Meaning Format

> The format of your story
> is the arrangement, the layout
> And at a glance you can see
> that the format of a poem
> is the wrong form
>   for the content
>   Of this story.

However, you have seen many articles in which the writer made his format compatible with his content.

Here are some examples:

1. A profile of a famous playwright, written in three acts.
2. An article about the post office written in the form of a letter.
3. A story about a space mission written in the form of a countdown.

While these devices are obvious, and sometimes distracting, they do a lot of good work. They give the reader a sharper picture of the material. Don't try to do something like this every time you write, but with each story consider the possibility that there might be a format which would enhance the material.

Form, Meaning Slant

So far I have discussed the connection between form and content in ways that are obvious to your reader. She can see easily that your post office article is in the form of a letter, etc. But the less obvious merging of form and content is far more important. And form, meaning slant, is one of those less obvious connections.

There are hundreds of ways you can use slant to enhance your content (or misuse it, to the detriment of your content) but I will discuss just three to make the point.

1. A viewpoint slant.

Let's say that one day you get lucky and an editor from *Sports Illustrated* calls and offers you a couple of thousand bucks to write a piece on "A Day at the Kentucky Derby."

"Fly to Louisville," he says, "talk to the Churchill Downs management, talk to the Louisville town fathers, talk to the spectators, the jockeys, the trainers, the horse owners, and the people in the city."

But right after he hangs up, your hot water heater explodes, your husband runs off with a nurse, your dog Buster has puppies, and there's a strike at the airport. So, for various other reasons you don't get to Louisville until four hours before the race. By that time the managers are too busy to talk to you, the spectators are too rowdy, and the town fathers are all three sheets to the wind on mint juleps. In fact, the only sober people who will talk to you are the jockeys. So you whip out your tape recorder, interview six jockeys, catch the race, and fly home to feed the puppies.

Hmmm. The form you had planned was a broad view of the Kentucky Derby as a big Louisville event. But the actual content of the material you have is a bunch of interviews with jockeys. If you try to pass that off as a broad view of the Derby, your form and content will not be compatible. The reader will be annoyed because he has been promised one thing and given another. He will say to his wife, "Gee Marian, this is a lousy article. All this woman talks about is the jockeys."

You have to make the form, meaning slant, harmonious with the content of what you actually have, not with what you wish you had. What do you do?

Well, you could change the article from "A Day at the Derby" to "Jockeys of the Derby," but you'd get in trouble with your editor, who asked you to write an article about the Derby, not about jockeys. There is another solution. Find the best viewpoint. Find the imaginary place from which you have gotten the best view of the Derby. In this case the jockeys offer the best viewpoint. You didn't talk to everybody so don't write from everybody's point of view. You talked to the jockeys, so write about what they think on Derby Day. Their viewpoint is your content, so their viewpoint should be your form.

2. A metaphor slant.

An example should suffice here. In a *Boston Globe* article, Michael Blowen wrote about director Barry Levinson. For his slant, Blowen used a baseball metaphor — specifically, the progress from the minor leagues to the major leagues. Blowen's first paragraph:

> Barry Levinson, wearing a New York Knights baseball jacket, strides into the lobby of the fashionable Mayfair Hotel on Park Avenue. The writer-director, previously known for the $5 million movie, *Diner*, is publicizing his new film, *The Natural*, a $20 million all-star movie starring Robert Redford. Welcome to the big leagues.

Blowen does not take a hard swing at his baseball metaphor, but does from time to time put his words in baseball terminology. The metaphor works well and holds the piece together. The reason it works well is that much of Blowen's content concerns *The Natural*, a baseball movie. The baseball metaphor form is compatible with the baseball content, but Blowen went easy on the metaphor because baseball is only part of the content. If the film had no baseball content, the form would not have worked because the reader would be nagged by the question, "Why is he using a baseball metaphor for a movie director?" And if Blowen had used a football metaphor (Barry Levinson scores a touchdown with *The Natural*) the piece would have looked ridiculous.

3. A handicap slant.

Often, after you've gathered material, you will regard some aspect of a writing project as a handicap. It might be a short deadline or limited space or an editor who hates your guts. But often the handicap is the lack of certain information. It is content that you don't have, and we'll call it "negative content." If you ignore the negative content and proceed as if you had the information, you are going to end up with a hole in your story and angry readers will say things like, "Hey Marian, this writer is a real bozo; she's writing this article about the Kentucky Derby and she doesn't even say how much money was bet."

To eliminate the hole and make form compatible with negative content, you must neutralize the negative content or make it work for you. Putting it another way, you must make your handicap irrelevant or turn it into a strength.

To make your handicap irrelevant, find out what you don't have, then create a story that wouldn't include it even if you did have it. If you've gathered a lot of information about ice cream but you can't find out how it's made or who invented it, write a piece called, "Ten Odd Facts About Ice Cream" and there won't be any hole. If you've interviewed several people about religious views and abortion but didn't talk to any members of the clergy, write "Religion and Abortion: The Layperson's Perspective," and no one will fault you for leaving out ministers, priests, and rabbis.

Those are examples of form that makes the negative content irrelevant. Here's an example of form that makes negative content into a strength.

Denise Worrell wrote an article about Michael Jackson for *Time* magazine. Her handicap was one that many writers might regard as fatal: Jackson, living a reclusive life, wasn't giving interviews. If Worrell had ignored the fact that there was no Michael Jackson presence in her story, there would have been a hole. The reader would have felt defrauded and he would have said to his wife, "Gee, Marian, this woman is writing about Michael Jackson and she didn't even interview Jackson. Can you imagine?"

So Worrell made her form compatible with her negative content. She worked with the slant, "Michael Jackson is a recluse." In her article she writes about her visit to the Jackson house and her interview with Joe Jackson, Michael's father. She includes the information and anecdotes that a Michael Jackson fan would want to read. And through it all she creates a strong sense of Michael Jackson not being there. She doesn't have his presence so she turns his absence into information about him. When Worrell finally spoke to Michael, it was only long enough to say hello.

> We back out of the room and Joe shuts the door. We walk away and he says, "Michael has a friend over. He isn't about to give any interviews. You got pretty close, though."

And at the end of her piece, after she leaves the Jackson house, Worrell writes:

> This time the cab gets past the gates, which click closed behind us. On the street are two police cars and a group of teenage girls

hanging out, hoping for a glimpse of Michael.

It's the perfect ending for her slant. She has turned the weakness of her content into the strength of her form. Nobody would expect her to interview Michael Jackson for an article that says Michael Jackson doesn't give interviews. Perfect.

Form, Meaning Style

Style, you'll recall from Chapter 2, is not what you write, but how you write it. Style is sculpture, not clay. Of all the definitions of form in writing, style is the most important. Style can help you the most by being compatible with your content, and it can hurt you the most by being in conflict with your content. That is why I used an example of the wrong style to begin this chapter. Do you remember that first paragraph, the one that had the style of a vacation but the content of a classroom?

To use style in harmony with content, you must have a definite sense of who the reader is and why he is reading. If he has picked up your article on how to fix toasters, he is looking for information, nothing else. If he has come home from work and picked up your novel he might be looking for some poetic language that will lift him above the mundane world of the sneaker factory outlet where he works, so your style might be rich and musical.

Let us consider, as an example, the difference between a private detective novel and a category romance novel.

Content for the private detective novel reader is "what happens next, and then what happens." That is why most successful private detective novels are written in a style that is fast-paced and to the point. Something is almost always happening. Consider this opening from *Fletch's Fortune*, part of the highly successful Fletch series by Gregory McDonald:

> "C.I.A., Mr. Fletcher."
> "Um. Would you mind spelling that?"
> Coming into the cool dark of the living room, blinded by the sun on the beach, Fletch had smelled cigar smoke and slowed at the French doors.
> There were two forms, of men, sprawled on his living room furniture, one in the middle of the divan, the other on a chair.
> "The Central Intelligence Agency," one of the forms muttered.

Fletch's bare feet crossed the marble floor to the carpet.

The style is perfect for the content. Now, let's apply the same style to a category romance novel about a woman on vacation at Cape Cod.

> Carol woke up early. She got out of bed, went down to the window, knelt down. She didn't think about it. She just did it. A half hour later she stood up.

A romance reader would not read a romance written like that. The style is wrong because, while content for the private detective reader is mostly action, content for the romance reader is largely feelings. The romance reader wants to know what happens, but she also wants to know what it felt like.

So the form that Marian Chase used in *Share the Dream* is this:

> Carol woke up early. The breeze from the sea floated through her open window, filling the room with a delicious freshness. For reasons that were more instinctive than thought out, Carol slipped out of the comforting bed and, still in her nightgown, knelt by the window for half an hour. With her chin resting on her hands and her elbows planted on the windowsill, Carol stared out at the rising sun, listening to the cawing of morning seagulls and the soothing clap-clap-clap of the waves rolling onto the beach.

An understanding of the relationship between form and content comes with writing a lot. Even an experienced editor or writer can't always say why form and content are incompatible, but he knows the conflict when he sees it or hears it. He knows that feeling of being tugged in two directions at the same time. And he knows that the damage done to a story by disharmony can rarely be repaired simply by writing another draft. Usually the writer must start over. So think about form and content before you write. Consider your material and your reader. Make your decisions about story type, length, format, slant, and style first. And then just write.

Chapter Seventeen
Rewriting

All of the principles of good writing that we have talked about represent techniques you should apply to a manuscript by the time you write a final draft. You certainly don't have to accomplish all of this in the first draft. The first draft is just plain writing. It's in the rewriting, the second, and third, and fourth drafts, that you do the really good writing.

In fact, I encourage you not to try too hard to make the first draft good. Too many writers are so critical of themselves in the first draft that they never get to the second. They sit down to write, with a fussy little editor sitting on their shoulder, and after two or three paragraphs the little editor snickers. "Oh, that's awful," he says. Or, "What a stupid way of saying that. This is embarrassing." So the writer yanks the sheet of paper out of the typewriter, tosses it into a wastebasket, and starts over. Some writers never finish a story because of that little editor on their shoulder. Save your editor for the rewriting. Write the first draft without judgment. Take some risks. Put in the words that might seem ridiculous. Nobody but you has to see the first draft. It is better to rewrite bad writing than to be so inhibited in the first draft that you don't put in the good, imaginative writing you are capable of.

The way I look at it is that when you rewrite your story, article, chapter, essay, or whatever, you are sculpting the clay that you created. But when you write the first draft you are creating clay out of nothing. That, by itself, is a tough enough trick; don't burden yourself with the further requirement that it be any good. The first draft doesn't have to be good. It just has to be there.

However, after you write the first draft, it is time to rewrite. That's when you really go to work, incorporating all of the principles of good writing that we have discussed.

"Oh great, Gary," I can hear you saying, "all I've got to do is keep in mind about six hundred principles of good writing."

I know it seems that way. But here I am going to try to reduce your rewriting process to seven questions you should ponder as you rewrite.

1. Is It Tight?

Tight writing doesn't have to be short. Tight just means that every word is doing a job. Cut all unnecessary words, sentences, paragraphs, or scenes. When you rewrite, don't think about what you can put in. Think about what you can take out.

If you have written an article, for example, define your slant and cut words that don't relate to that slant. If you have written "Ten Tips for House Buyers," direct at least 90 percent of your words toward those ten tips, and devote relatively few words to such general material as the number of houses sold last year and the differences in interest rates as compared to a decade ago.

If you've written a story, make sure you have begun at the beginning. Many writers work their way into a story like burglars feeling their way into a dark house. In fact, it is not unusual for editors to cut the first three pages of a story without anybody noticing. Save them the work. Look at your first sentence. Is it doing any work? Is it really part of your story or is it just *about* your story, which you haven't begun yet? Cut the first sentence and see if you really lose anything. Cut every sentence until you come to one that must be there.

This also applies to nonfiction. The original opening of my article about apple picking was a typical unnecessary opening paragraph. It began, "I had decided to spend a day picking apples for a day's pay. I wanted to find out what it felt like." The paragraph goes on with a long explanation of why I had decided to spend a day picking apples. It was unnecessary. The article would eventually show all of that. In the rewriting I cut the paragraph out. Instead of beginning with a paragraph about my *decision* to do something, I began with the something.

> I reached the apple orchard at 9 on a brisk Wednesday morning.
> No form of logic had influenced my choice. I'd simply opened a

phone book and picked out an orchard in Harvard. I knew that all the orchards were looking for pickers.

2. Is It Clear?

When you write you should be direct. Look the reader straight in the eye and tell her what's on your mind, in the case of nonfiction, or, in the case of fiction, what exactly is going on.

In your rewriting watch for places where the reader might be confused. Pronouns are often the culprits. If you wrote, "Wilson and Strunk met at the Mustang Ranch in Las Vegas. He was working as a bouncer," the reader could become confused about which "he" was the bouncer. Don't be afraid to repeat a name if it will make things clearer. "Strunk was working as a bouncer."

Also, in dialogue, if you're not sure that you've made it clear who is speaking, write, "Luigi said," or "Schlaegel said," as often as you must.

In rewriting, keep in mind that writing gets its power from what you tell the reader, not from what you withhold. Avoid the pretentious use of a mysterious pronoun long before the noun has been introduced. Perhaps you've written something like this:

> He woke up in the hospital, bewildered and aching from the chest down. It was dark, and as he looked around, trying to adjust his sight to the darkness, he tried to remember how he had gotten here. From the corridor, where a dim light glowed, he could hear the sound of someone snoring in another room. And farther away, he heard the click, click of a woman's shoes.
> "Can anybody hear me?" Jeffrey called.

The problem with that is that the reader is wondering who the hell Jeffrey is until you make it clear that Jeffrey is the mysterious person you've been calling "he." In rewriting, call him Jeffrey in the first sentence and then refer to him as "he." The reader can see a "Jeffrey" much better than a "he."

Your writing is also robbed of clarity when you get lazy, tired, or distracted. In rewriting watch for those places where you drifted into vague, wishy-washy writing like this paragraph from the first draft of my apple article.

> Soon I was apple picking. Despite the normal problems, I found there was a certain joy and calmness about it, though of course

> there were some discomforting aspects of it, but nothing much
> to be really concerned about.

That's all very vague. What exactly is the narrator doing? What problems? What is he talking about? Cut the vague sentences. Clear it up. What are you trying to say? Here's what I wrote when I rewrote my apple-picking piece.

> I crawled in under the tree, found a place for my knees in the
> deep grass, and began quite merrily to pick apples. Now and then
> I'd grab an apple and from the quivering branch would come a
> cloud of tiny white bugs. They didn't buzz, sting, or deposit larvae
> on my shirt, so I didn't worry about them.

3. Is It Precise?

Precision and clarity are closely related. To be clear is to say what you mean. To be precise is to say exactly what you mean. Precision is also related to tight rewriting. A precise word often replaces a few words that are not so precise. A precise word etches a sharper picture on the reader's brain and eliminates the possibility of misunderstanding. We discussed this a bit in the style chapter when we talked about the style rule to "Be Specific."

When you rewrite make your writing more precise without making it more wordy. Make it more precise by whittling down all the possible word combinations to those few that say exactly what you want to say. Go through your manuscript and change the general word or phrase to the precise word or phrase. If the girl's team in the first draft of your novel for children "won by a large margin" change it to, "they won by forty-two points." If the first draft of your article says, "Various ethnic groups have settled in Newark," change it to "Greeks, Italians, and Puerto Ricans have settled in Newark."

You'll find that precision in writing increases believability. If I tell you that some people are out to get me, you're skeptical. If I tell you that three Jamaican policemen have threatened to garrote me, you begin to think maybe there's something to it.

The thesaurus is an important tool when you are rewriting. Use it to find the word that means precisely what you want to say.

In the following example from my apple-picking article, I rewrote to make a job, an age, an appearance, a machine, and a motion, all more precise. In some cases I saved a few words. In others I spent a few more. But in every case I improved the writing.

First draft:

> "I'm looking for work, picking apples," I called to the guy in charge. He was a large, balding older man, rough-hewn and no pleasure to look at. He looked down at me from his noisy machine, which he was driving around the apple trees.

Rewrite:

> "I'm looking for work, picking apples," I called to the foreman. He was a husky, balding man of about 60, every bit as weathered as the trees he tended. He had a fist for a face and it studied me from atop a yammering forklift which he jockeyed around the apple trees.

4. How Does It Sound?

Do you remember the Music chapter? Writing, we said, is not a visual art. It is more like composing music. When you rewrite well you create music that is pleasant to the ear. The music should flow, not leap. There should be no electric guitars shrieking amid the whispers of the flutes and violins. So part of your rewriting process should be to read your work out loud, and listen for the sour notes.

In that Music chapter we discussed the ways in which you could improve the music of your words. Apply those principles in your rewriting. Listen for the obscure word set down in an otherwise simple paragraph. Listen for the unintended humorous note in a somber story. The sour note you hear might be an accidental change in tense or person, or a sudden switch in viewpoint. It can even be in the way you punctuate. Generally, you create harmonious music in your writing by maintaining consistency in mood, reading level, and style.

Listen for that variety of sentence length and construction which we talked about, too. And finally, listen for the word that "just doesn't sound right," and even if you don't know why it doesn't sound right, get rid of it.

5. Is It About People?

If you discover that you have written about crop failures, rewrite so that you are writing about farmers in crisis. If you've written about romance, rewrite so that your story is about people in love.

Make sure you put people into everything you write.

If your article about the state's welfare crisis begins with statistics and dry background information on welfare legislation, then rewrite it so that you begin with an anecdote about one family that lives in a car because they cannot pay rent. If your novel describes a small town through its geography, then perhaps you can improve it in the rewriting by describing the town through the people who live there. Instead of describing the ocean, write about the fishermen.

Here's how I added some humanity to my apple-picking article. First draft:

> There are·a lot of spiritual reasons for spending a day picking apples and it is, as Bonnie said, "a way to get in touch with things." But the tough economic times and the high rate of unemployment accounted for the presence of most apple pickers.

Rewrite:

> I ate lunch in a clearing with Bonnie, Roy, and two black guys who had come up from Boston. The guys from Boston were unemployed. They had kids. They weren't picking apples for religious reasons. One of them, Sam, told me the $45 a day he was making would help to stretch his unemployment check. He ate lunch quickly so he could get back to picking and "put some bread on the table."

You'll remember that in the style chapter we talked about replacing passive writing with active writing. As you rewrite with the style tips in mind, you will find that passive writing is often writing without people in it, and when you make the writing active you will do it by inserting human beings. Don't write, "The glow from the fire could be seen against the night sky and the sound of sirens could be heard for miles. Smoke could be smelled from across the river and a tremor in the earth was felt every time another building toppled."

Who saw? Who heard? Who smelled? Who felt? Human beings, that's who. If you didn't put them in the first draft, get them in when you rewrite.

6. Is It Honest?

The easiest way to achieve honesty in your rewriting is just to be yourself. Take out any literary references that are only there so that you will appear learned. Cut those sentences that show you trying to bulldoze your way into a personal style. Take out the words you found in the thesaurus, but which you had never heard before. The thesaurus is a place for meeting friends, not picking up strangers.

In your nonfiction take out any damaging opinions that have no source. If you've written, "Governor Stackpole is widely regarded as incompetent" rewrite it to, "I think Governor Stackpole is incompetent," or "State Reps. Dinelli, Petrocelli, and Rigatoni all say that the governor is incompetent." But throw out punchless phrases like, "it is widely believed " or "most people think."

If you've put your opinion into a piece, fine, but in the rewriting make it clear that it is an opinion. If you've got a sixty-seven word unintelligible quote from the incompetent governor, then reduce it to eight or ten words that make sense, but make certain that you are true to the spirit of what was said, if not the form. Don't tamper with the truth.

However, honesty in writing cannot be measured by some outside yardstick. Ultimately, the only measuring tool of honesty that you have when you rewrite is your own conscience. Read each sentence and ask of it, "Is this me?" and "Is this true?" and finally, "Is this fair?"

My apple-picking piece might have been more positive, uplifting and idealistic if I had written, "There is nothing quite so perfect as a day in an apple tree, picking your way to heaven," and gone on to describe a wholly invigorating and untarnished apple-picking experience. But that would have been dishonest, and anybody who has spent much time in an apple orchard would spot it. So I wrote:

> I had picked 6,000 apples. My hands were as dry as blotters, my trapezius muscles had been stretched like taffy. My shoulders throbbed. The straps had been damn near grafted into my skin. My legs ached and my knees felt like a pair of bricks. I felt pretty good but it was time for me to split.

Keep in mind that it wouldn't matter whether I was writing an article about apple picking, or writing a short story about a guy who goes apple picking. Honesty is just as important in fiction as in nonfiction. Your characters must be true to their own natures, and what they experience must have about it the ring of truth, or your fiction will fail. In the chapter on description I talked about seeing your own beach, your own police officer, etc., not just grabbing stock description off the shelf. That also is honesty in writing. Avoiding clichés, word packages, stereotypes, and sentimental writing is also practicing honesty in writing.

I tell you to think about honesty when you rewrite, not because I want to improve your morals, but because I want to improve your writing. Dishonest writing just isn't good writing. It feels soft, weak, and unconvincing, and if you are dishonest it will usually take a good editor about twenty-three seconds to spot it. And if he doesn't, your readers certainly will.

7. Is It Poetic?

Writing should be, first of all, clear. A good word is not a good word if it clouds your meaning. And of course your writing should be tight, and easy on the ear, and honest, and all the other things we have talked about. In rewriting your stories and articles, your goal is to make sure you are communicating what you mean to communicate. Writing should be functional. Beautiful prose is not beautiful prose if it sabotages the job you are trying to do. Good writing entertains, informs, advises, illuminates. It cannot simply be. It must do.

Often after we have done the job of writing clearly, of telling our story, there is little room left for what is commonly called art, though writing simply and clearly is an art in itself.

But in much that you write there *is* the opportunity to do more than tell the reader what will happen or when or how or even why. There is the chance for you to lift him a few feet off the ground, to slip between him and the earth a layer of wonder and imagination. There is the chance for you to pull him beyond the content of your story and lead him with your words into a realm of thought that is alive with energy and inspiration. This is poetry and it can happen in a sentence or it can happen in a word. It can happen when you neither expect it, nor intend it. It can happen that you bring beauty into the reader's day.

Is there a figure of speech that will enhance your meaning, as well as etch across the reader's mind a vision that will endure beyond the last page? Write it. Can you choose words with such care and arrange them in such a way that reveals not just your point, but also a point about life? Do it. Can you tell an anecdote that will peel away one more layer of falseness and bring the reader an inch closer to the truth? Tell it. If you can turn an essay into a prayer, do it. If you can use words to crown a newspaper article with nobility, use them. And if you can bring your own deepest emotions to bear on a story in a way that is important not just to the story, but also to the reader, do that.

I attempted to put poetry into my apple-picking article by measuring the experience against a traditional fantasy of young men. Early in the article I planted the idea. I described the unfulfilled fantasy that my friend Cliffie and I had in 1962 when we got out of high school. I wrote:

> We wanted to cut cane in Louisiana, harvest lettuce in California, pick apples in New England. Move. Just like Tod Stiles and Buzz Murdock on *Route 66*, tooling down the highway, rubbing our way into people's lives between odd jobs.

In my final paragraph I didn't want to simply end with something like, "I left the apple orchard and went home." I wanted to lift the piece into the poetic realm if I could do so legitimately. I wanted to make it something more than just a piece about a day of apple picking. I wrote:

> My wife picked me up at the end of the day. Wisely, she parked the car across the highway from the orchard. She knows a thing or two about me and she gave me some time to walk, some space to think. For there is something about the feel of gravel underfoot and the taste of sweet air seeping out of the cool green orchard that lets a guy think for a moment that he is Tod Stiles. And if the world is gentle for a minute, he can be almost certain that Buzz is waiting in the Corvette around that next bend in the road.
>
> And that if the two of you can just peel off another 300 miles from the nearest highway, you will most certainly get in touch with things.

It made me feel good to write that. And it made the piece better. If you imbue your writing with humanity and poetry and love you will enrich both the reader and yourself.

Closing Words

If you have just finished reading this book and you're sitting there thinking, "Gee, Gary, there's more to this writing stuff than I thought," then I have done my job.

The techniques and principles we have been discussing are the things that make the difference between getting published and getting rejected. I hope that if you are getting published now, the things you have learned here will help you to get published more often and for larger paychecks. If you're not getting published, then I hope this book will help you to get published. But if it does, keep in mind that the difference between published and unpublished writers is one of degree, not of kind. Publication is not some magical turning point after which you suddenly know all there is to know about writing. It is more a measure of your progress along a path toward an imaginary point of writing perfection (which, of course, can never be reached).

For myself, I hope that this book has been a measure of my progress toward that imaginary point of perfect writing. And for you I hope it has been, and will continue to be, a lantern that illuminates that path and helps you move more quickly toward your own writing goals.

Index